Ethics and Race

Past and Present Intersections and Controversies

D1570632

Naomi Zack
Lehman College, CUNY

ROWMAN & LITTLEFIELD
Lanham • Boulder • New York • London

Acquisitions Editor: Natalie Mandziuk
Acquisitions Assistant: Sylvia Landis
Sales and Marketing Inquiries: textbooks@rowman.com

Credits and acknowledgments for material borrowed from other sources, and reproduced
with permission, appear on the appropriate pages within the text.

Published by Rowman & Littlefield
An imprint of The Rowman & Littlefield Publishing Group, Inc.
4501 Forbes Boulevard, Suite 200, Lanham, Maryland 20706
www.rowman.com

86-90 Paul Street, London EC2A 4NE

Copyright © 2023 by The Rowman & Littlefield Publishing Group, Inc.

British Library Cataloguing in Publication Information Available

Library of Congress Cataloging-in-Publication Data

ISBN: 978-1-5381-6671-0 (cloth)
ISBN: 978-1-5381-6672-7 (paperback)
ISBN: 978-1-5381-6673-4 (electronic)

♾™ The paper used in this publication meets the minimum requirements of American
National Standard for Information Sciences—Permanence of Paper for Printed Library
Materials, ANSI/NISO Z39.48-1992.

To my granddaughters, Cloe and Winnona.

Contents

Preface and Acknowledgments

Racial difference and racism are intense issues in the United States and throughout the world. These issues are both academic subjects and real-life conditions that affect people in practical ways. Within a society categorized by race and racial identities, no one is immune from the problems arising from race. People grapple with and contest most of these problems with ethical or moral fervor, although rarely with explicit ethical or moral labels or with the tools of ethical/moral reasoning. However, almost all the controversies, opinions, and analyses of and about race proceed from ethical or moral principles. Writers, thinkers, activists, and policymakers begin with what should be done toward justice or to correct injustice. Nevertheless, academic philosophers and scholars continue to address ethics and race as separate subjects or fields—there are courses, journals, books, and conferences about ethics, and there are courses, journals, books, and conferences about race. The subject of ethics/morality concerns human life, quality of life, and well-being in well-established ways, with roots in antiquity. Wide attention to race in academia only began during the late twentieth century, but it has taken off in the early twenty-first century because many think that more societal change is required for racial justice. This book aims to bring ethics and race together so that students on all levels can consider the ethical aspects of past and present intersections and controversies concerning race.

This book brings ethics and race together so that problems and controversies involving race are considered from ethical perspectives. The ethical problems concerning race are the result of past private and public decisions and resolving them will stem from present and future decisions. The basis for such decisions is made up of different moral systems and ideas about the common good for society.

Ethics and Race begins with an overview of moral reasoning and the history of race and racism. This background will anchor the main contemporary subjects and practical issues of race in the United States and *throughout the world*. From there, the main ethical focus will be on contemporary issues, such as George Floyd's killing, Black Lives Matter, the origins of the #MeToo movement, recent US Supreme Court rulings on voting rights, and so forth. Not every controversy involving race is an ethical issue. Some controversies involving nondiscrimination are already settled law and others are matters of free choice or taste. These and other important distinctions will be pointed out in the chapters. The overall aim is to present issues clearly.

The chapters follow a common structure. First, the introductory discussion frames the broad subject of the chapter and the sections that follow, zeroing in on specific issues. Keywords in bold are defined as used and also appear in a glossary at the end of the book. At the end of each chapter, the student is presented with five questions for thinking, discussion, and writing. Sources appear next, followed by several video suggestions to enliven all the chapter material. Sources are listed in their order of reference within each chapter.

Instructors are encouraged to use all or part of the book's contents. If the whole book is used, the twenty-four chapters, at two chapters per week, would fill an average semester. There are six parts to the book that could be treated as independent modules: Part I, Ideas and History of Race; Part II, Law and Policy; Part III, Social Institutions; Part IV, Social Disruptions; Part V, Identity and Representation; Part VI, The Natural and International World. At the beginning of each part, there is a brief orientation for the chapters therein. However, chapters also have cross-references to discussions of their subjects in other chapters, and instructors should feel free to mix and match chapter combinations.

I thank Natalie Mandziuk for overseeing the publication of this book with Rowman & Littlefield. I am also grateful to Sylvia Landis for organizing the external review process and to Elaine McGarraugh for production editing. The critiques of individual chapters by eight reviewers resulted in revisions that have contributed to a clearer and more informative textbook for students. I am also grateful to Simon Rackham for proofreading the penultimate manuscript.

Overall, the goal is to empower students to think ethically about issues of race, especially students for whom either or both ethics and race are new subjects. I have used the research for this book in a course to be called "Ethics and Race," at Lehman College, CUNY. Instructors and students should feel free to email me with feedback, suggestions, and questions.

Naomi Zack, Professor of Philosophy
Lehman College, CUNY
Naomi.Zack@Lehman.CUNY.edu

I

IDEAS AND HISTORY OF RACE

The present idea of race has a history that began in the seventeenth century and understanding this history allows us to understand the racism of race.

Chapter 1 introduces the connection between ethics and race, beginning with the words of Martin Luther King Jr. The discussion of individual character leads to the question of how moral neutrality is possible concerning race. In chapter 2, democratic ideals of equality are related to race relations in society. Racial divisions as a common social problem require a vision of the commons or what we all share, as well as the common good. Chapter 3 traces dominant ideas of racial divisions as explicit ideologies of white supremacy that led to policies of eugenics in the twentieth century. However, although the human biological sciences first posited strong hierarchical divisions among human races, chapter 4 explains how that science has corrected itself, first toward separating culture from inherited race, and second discarding the idea of biological human races after failing to find any biological foundation for a system of human races. Insofar as people continue to hold outdated, hierarchical ideas of human races, moral questions arise about how these views should be regarded.

1

What Are Ethics and Race?

Washington, USA, July 8, 2011: The reflection of demonstrators on a window shop. Woman carrying a sign with the image of Dr. King and the slogan "We Too Have a Dream" in reference to women and Latinx rights. Getty Images: Montes-Bradley.

Martin Luther King Jr. (MLK) (1929–1968) has worldwide fame for his leadership in the US civil rights movement during the 1960s. His famous "I Have a Dream" speech was an ethical or moral call for just treatment of African Americans. King not only thought it was ethically right that justice be realized but that an important part of justice was race relations based on moral judgment. Thus, he said, "I have a dream that my four little children will one day live in a nation where they will not be judged by the color of their skin but by the content of their character." King wanted his children to be judged based on *their* morality. So, he was morally calling for moral judgment in race relations, a double moral request. In effect, he was telling his white audience not only that they should behave ethically to African Americans, but that part of this ethical behavior entailed that they should judge them in ethical terms—that is, judge "the content of their character." To fully understand this, we need to understand the nature of ethics and morality, the nature of race, and how the two have been and continue to be related. We also need to understand the meaning of racial equality. After considering these subjects, we will return to King's dream about white judgment based on the content of the character of African Americans, in light of the ideal of racial equality.

WHAT IS ETHICS?

There is something distinctly human or at least special about ethics or morality. First, it is not merely a matter of intellectual judgment but is tied up with very strong feelings and emotions. Ethics is important, and most people take ethical issues very seriously. Still, ethical issues are not legal issues—moral law is not government law. There can be ethically bad laws or there may not yet be ethically good laws that enforce morally right judgments and feelings—that is, ethical reasoning may be ahead of or more **progressive** than legal reality.

Ethics or morality has two sides—right and wrong. Most people want to do the right thing and be morally or ethically good. With this comes praise of others who do the right thing and are morally good. The other side of praise for what is right or good is judgment and blame of those who do the wrong things and are morally or ethically bad. Of course, life is often complicated so doing the right thing may also involve doing the wrong thing, and doing the wrong thing may be unintentional or stem from good intentions. Nevertheless, right and wrong and good and bad are the fundamentals of ethical or moral thought and action.

Is there a difference between ethics and morality? Philosophers use the two terms interchangeably. But others may associate morality with personal behavior and ethics with workplace or professional action. The result is that a person's morality may be thought to pertain to behavior and opinions, whereas ethics is more formal and official. For example, choices in the consumption of nonfood substances and partners for intimacy may be a question of morality or "morals," whereas behaving fairly to employees and subordinates involves ethics. In this book, we will stick with the idea of ethics, and what may be considered morals will simply be flagged as ethically neutral or neither good nor bad but a matter of taste. Related to matters of taste, but more important, are private personal choices, which may have moral importance for the person choosing, but should not be judged by others. And finally, some moral issues related to race are arguable—two or more sides have equally plausible reasons for their positions so that moral conclusions cannot be determined.

Ethics is a general human thought process and standard for action for which philosophers have identified at least three specific systems: virtue ethics, deontology, and utilitarianism or consequentialism. But one major question arises before delving into these ethical systems: What is the source of ethics? The source of ethics has been religion, social norms or cultural traditions, and individual intuition. The ancient Greek philosopher Plato (428/427 or 424/423–348/347 BC) in his dialogue *Euthyphro* introduced a dilemma for claims that ethics comes from the gods or God: Is something morally good or right only because it comes from God or does God approve of something based on another standard? If coming from God assures moral goodness or rightness, then what if different religions posit different Godly wishes? (And why should God be the ultimate ethical decider?) But if God decides what is good based on some other standard, then we do not need God but can refer directly to that other standard. Plato's dilemma logically separated ethics or morality from religion, although based on intuition and cultural tradition, many people continue to connect ethics or morality to their religious beliefs.

At any rate, most agree that we should be good and do the right things. Differences arise in what specific traits and actions are considered good and right. Now is a good time to introduce the three main ethical systems identified by philosophers and from there we can answer the questions of what makes something a moral matter and who the subjects of morality are. **Virtue ethics** was introduced by Plato's student Aristotle (384–322 BC) in his *Politics* and *Nicomachean Ethics*. Aristotle believed that individual virtues could be developed by adults as part of living in a community. The virtues were neither inherited nor precluded by human nature but required two stages, first education in the virtues during childhood and second the practice of specific virtues. This practice required *phronesis* or **practical wisdom**: A person needs to identify the virtue called for in a given situation and act to the right degree based on their knowledge of that virtue. In time, such action would result in a settled trait of character and a *disposition* to act from that trait. For example, a person with the virtue of courage will identify a situation calling for courage and, drawing on their experience, act courageously after deliberation. The deliberation will allow them to avoid both extremes of cowardice and temerity (foolhardiness). Also, isolated good actions do not establish a virtue. For instance, if a lazy and selfish person saves a family from fire, that alone doesn't make them courageous.

The second great philosophical moral system is **deontology** or **duty ethics**, as developed by Immanuel Kant (1724–1804) in his *Groundwork of the Metaphysics of Morals* and other writings. Kant claimed that rational humans live in a "kingdom of ends" in which every member has intrinsic value because they have subjectivity and dignity. Morality was thereby absolute, stemming from goodwill in a person capable of rational deliberation. This deliberation consisted of two formulations of Kant's *categorical imperative*. A **categorical imperative** is a directive to action that is neither undertaken for the sake of something else or for its consequences.

The categorical imperative directs us to do something for the right reason and that intention and motivation is good-in-itself. Period. The first formulation is: Act in such a way so that you can will that everyone acts this way. The test of this formulation is to ask what would happen if everybody acted this way? For example, you may want to tell a lie to protect someone but if everyone lied for that reason, it would undermine trust in truth-telling. The second formulation of the categorical imperative is: Act in such a way as to treat others and yourself as ends in themselves, never as means to some other end. That is, don't use people. Kant recognized that we often use others in bargains or business interactions, but he was not talking about that. Rather, Kant's idea was not to use someone in a way that injures their dignity, for example, befriending a person or allowing oneself to be befriended because of their personal contacts.

Finally, we come to the most enduring and practical of all moral systems that began as **utilitarianism** by Jeremy Bentham (1748–1832) and John Stuart Mill (1806–1873) and is now known as **consequentialism** or that actions are to be judged by their consequences. The main idea is that human happiness and well-being are the only moral goods and that we should act to maximize them, thereby aiming for the greatest good for the greatest number. Bentham thought that all pleasures were equally valuable, whereas Mill distinguished between short-term bodily pleasures and long-term happiness accompanying the enjoyment of friendship, art, and literature. More modern thinkers have also distinguished between act and rule utilitarianism. Act utilitarianism consists of doing the act that will result in the greatest good for the greatest number, whereas rule utilitarianism consists of following the rule that will result in the greatest good for the greatest number. For example, a doctor with five ill patients and one healthy one could kill the healthy one to harvest and distribute vital organs that would save the ill ones. While this would immediately result in the greatest good for the greatest number, it would undermine trust in that doctor and the medical system. Therefore, it would be better to consistently follow the rule attendant with the Hippocratic oath, "Do no harm."

Religious ethical systems have intersected with virtue ethics, deontology, and utilitarianism, and endured on their own. All three philosophical systems have each been criticized as centered on white males and exclusive. Thus, African American scholars have proposed *insurrectionist ethics*, or moral principles based on resistance to racist oppression and feminists have explored *care ethics*, or moral principles that derive from natural caring roles, such as motherhood. Each of these moral systems is based on the perspective of groups who are oppressed or disadvantaged in society. Furthermore, as Jean-Paul Sartre (1905–1980) pointed out, because people are free, they have to choose an ethical system that will result in distinctive answers to a moral problem and that approach based on choosing a moral system constitutes *existentialist ethics*.

In applying any ethical system, two more important questions arise. Who are the subjects of ethics? What makes something an ethical matter? The language of ethics and morality is assumed to be universal, applying to all people. But historically, the different systems have focused on groups who are already dominant and privileged in society. Aristotle thought that women and slaves, as well as children and the poor, could not be virtuous. Religious ethics has often limited salvation as a reward for good behavior to practitioners of specific religions. Kantian deontology requires the use of abstract reasoning to test the categorical imperative and not all people have that ability. And although utilitarianism specifies that everyone is to count as one and no one more than once, the idea of higher and lower pleasures evokes privilege and the sacrifice of individuals or minority groups for the greater good is not generally excluded in reality. For example, oil pipelines have been built through Native Americans' ancestral lands, overriding their protests, because it is believed that more will benefit from jobs and energy than suffer from such destruction. This has been a utilitarian course of action, which seems to override both virtues (such as caring for the environment and respecting different cultures) and individual and group rights (that is, the rights of indigenous people to continue their sacred traditions).

What makes something an **ethical matter**? The answer is that human well-being or life is at stake. (Some have justified also counting the well-being and life of animals and other natural life-forms.) Who counts as human, the subjects of ethics, should include people of all races—this is the current egalitarian view and it is the first point at which ethics and race connect. Indeed, progressives who study race approach the subject in terms of what is morally or ethically right and good. Given a long history of disadvantages associated with nonwhite racial identities, to assess such past and ongoing disadvantages as unethical, nonwhites as well as whites must be recognized as the subjects of ethics. We, therefore, need to understand what race is and is not.

WHAT IS RACE?

At this outset, we need a somewhat general and superficial understanding of race and racial differences—greater depth and detail will be provided as the book progresses. In the United States, the word "race," as used in contexts calling for "honest conversation about race," does not literally mean race but **racism** or attitudes and behavior from whites that disadvantage, harm, or unjustly punish or limit the life opportunities of nonwhites. Almost everyone approaches issues of racism in moral or ethical terms, often emotionally. Thus, progressives believe that equality across racial differences is morally good and almost everyone believes that racism is morally bad. Disagreements about what racism is are very common. Many people also understand that **"race"** refers to human group differences, and there is a broad belief that racial differences rest on natural or biological differences. As we shall see in chapter 4, contemporary scientific studies of racial differences do not support that belief, but as a well-entrenched belief since the early modern period, it has shaped relations between racial groups in society.

The idea of human races is now supported by the US census, which in 2020 recognized the following taxonomy according to standards outlined in 1997 by the Office of Management and Budget:

White—A person having origins in any of the original peoples of Europe, the Middle East, or North Africa.

Black or African American—A person having origins in any of the black racial
   groups of Africa.
American Indian or Alaska Native—A person having origins in any of the original
   peoples of North and South America (including Central America) and who
   maintains tribal affiliation or community attachment.
Asian—A person having origins in any of the original peoples of the Far East,
   Southeast Asia, or the Indian subcontinent including, for example, Cambodia,
   China, India, Japan, Korea, Malaysia, Pakistan, the Philippine Islands, Thai-
   land, and Vietnam.
Native Hawaiian or Other Pacific Islander—A person having origins in any of the
   original peoples of Hawaii, Guam, Samoa, or other Pacific Islands.

More than one race can be reported. Hispanic/Latino is a further **ethnic** category
that respondents are required to affirm or deny. Also, respondents are expected to
self-identify.

Scholars and activists have criticized this system of categorization. For instance,
groups experiencing what resembles racial discrimination, such as Islamic, Southeast Asian Indians, who are all now characterized as white, have at times requested
redesignation as nonwhite. Indeed, the census itself has changed its racial categories continually since it began in 1790. The census presents what could be merely
varieties of human groups or physical types, but it is more than that. Racial identification marks both privilege and deprivation and being able to claim protection
because of oppression. Race is not only more than mere variety now, but since
the racial system of human categorization arose in the modern period, it never
has been mere variety.

To the extent that disadvantaged racial identities have been ascribed to members
of groups without their consent, the system of races in society is unethical. But to the
extent that members of disadvantaged racial groups have struggled to achieve justice
and better their lives as members of their assigned racial groups, the unethical system of races has served as a springboard for the development of individual virtues of
courage and loyalty, as well as the expansion of human dignity and ethical inclusion.
In other words, racial categories and unjust behavior based on them are ethically or
morally wrong, but correction of such injustice is morally good.

"JUDGED BY THE CONTENT OF THEIR CHARACTER"

Let's return to MLK's "I have a dream that my four little children will one day live in
a nation where they will not be judged by the color of their skin but by the content
of their character." Suppose there is basic human equality, in both ethical and moral
terms, and following that, by law. This means that all humans are entitled to or owed
the same treatment in a general sense. Some harms may not be done to human beings

without justification, and they are entitled to respect because they are human. These prohibitions and obligations should govern all humans, regardless of their race. It follows that the content of anyone's character is irrelevant to their being treated the same as anyone else. Yes, everyone should be judged based on "the content of their character" when necessary, but this judgment comes after general equality is realized. Morally, such general equality requires that people should receive the same praise/reward or blame/punishment, regardless of race. For instance, heroism should be recognized regardless of race, and bad people of any race do not lose their human equality to good people. They may be punished, but punishment itself should be equal, regardless of race. Therefore, not only should African American adults not be judged by the color of their skin or their race, but they need to be accepted as moral equals to those with white skin, before the "contents of their character" are judged.

In the spirit of MLK's "I Have a Dream" speech, the American child psychiatrist Robert Coles (1929–) provided an account of six-year-old Ruby Bridges, who remained steadfast and cheerful in the face of adult hatred directed toward her in 1960, when she was the first African American to attend the all-white William Frantz Elementary School in New Orleans, Louisiana. Coles and others have praised Ruby Bridges for "the content of her character" and celebrated her heroism. This assessment is just, but linked as it is to race, by picking out an exception to negative stereotypes, it omits the fact that had Ruby Bridges been less courageous, she would still have deserved to attend that school. White children who attended that school did not need to display any extraordinary traits of character, and it is not fair to base racial equality on examples of nonwhite heroism.

QUESTIONS FOR THINKING, DISCUSSION, AND WRITING

1. What is ethics in your view?
2. Explain Plato's dilemma for basing ethics on the word of God.
3. What is the main difference between the categorical imperative and utilitarianism?
4. Keeping the census categories in mind, what do you think race is?
5. What is left out in terms of human equality if we go directly to judging those of a different race "by the contents of their character"?

SOURCES
(listed in order referred to in the chapter)

Aristotle. *Politics and Nicomachean Ethics.* See also, *The Project Gutenberg eBook of the Nicomachean Ethics of Aristotle, by Aristotle,* https://www.gutenberg.org/files/8438/8438-h/8438-h.htm; *Politics: A Treatise on Government* by Aristotle.

Kant, Immanuel. *Practical Philosophy*. Translated by Mary Gregor. 1996. Includes: "An An-
swer to the Question: What Is Enlightenment?" *Groundwork of the Metaphysics of Morals,
Critique of Practical Reason*, and *The Metaphysics of Morals* or *Fundamental Principles of the
Metaphysic of Morals by Immanuel Kant*, https://www.gutenberg.org/ebooks/5682.

Native Knowledge 360°. "Treaties Still Matter: The Dakota Access Pipeline." https://american
indian.si.edu/nk360/plains-treaties/dapl.

Plato. *Euthyphro*. https://philosophyintrocourse.files.wordpress.com/2016/04/plato-euthyphro
.pdf.

Song, Miri. "Rethinking minority status and 'visibility.'" *Comparative Migration Studies* 8, no.
5 (2020). https://doi.org/10.1186/s40878-019-0162-2.

Troyer, John, ed. *The Classical Utilitarians: Bentham and Mill*. Hackett Classics, 2003.

US Census Bureau. "race." https://www.census.gov/topics/population/race/about.html.

Videos

Coles, Robert. *The Story of Ruby Bridges*. Mrs. Kim Reads. https://www.youtube.com/
watch?v=MRfy2xs8Xpg.

Dr. Martin Luther King. I Have a Dream Full Speech, Entiversal. https://www.youtube.com/
watch?v=bNBGvaSHWbY.

Martin Luther King Jr. "I Have a Dream" Speech, In Its Entirety. npr.org.

Moral Emotions/Ethics Defined, Texas McCombs School of Business. https://www.youtube
.com/watch?v=w87uqQdfKHg.

2

Democracy and Social Ethics

Multiethnic couple in love standing and holding hands. Getty Images: Ridofranz.

Modern democracies usually include respect for individual privacy and **autonomy** or self-rule in life and lifestyle choices. Individuals have rights as sole individuals. However, human beings are social animals. Although we are not as well organized into lifelong groups as ants or elephants, we are highly dependent on one another for survival, success, and personal happiness. The social animals seem to begin life by accepting their places in existing groups, without having to make choices about where they fit in. But human choices are less determined. Such free choices in behavior, as well as attitudes toward the behavior of others, have effects on the common good of the whole of society. In this chapter, we will see how that works with race-related choices of friends and marriage partners. Possibly unintended consequences on the whole of society by such choices and attitudes of others concerning them lead to the broader topic known as "the tragedy of the commons." Next, the ideas of Jean-Jacques

Rousseau and Jane Addams will help clarify different approaches to the common good or what is good for society in general. Finally, it is important to note the twentieth-century philosopher John Rawls's theory of justice as fairness, as a civic virtue.

RACE, FRIENDSHIP, AND MARRIAGE

Humans form the earliest relationships within their families, neighborhoods, and close communities. In societies where people marry within their same race and ethnicity and live among each other like families, friendships with those of different races and ethnicities are unlikely. Friendships are important for human sociality because they are personal bridges away from the family. Unlike relatives, friends are chosen, and they can broaden our social worlds and help us develop. As Aristotle (384–322 BC) put it, close friends, chosen based on shared virtues of character, can be "other selves."

Consider a 2016 national survey of cross-racial friendships in the United States. There were 1,055 respondents, 55 percent of whom were white, 32 percent black, and 74 percent female. Ages ranged from eighteen to sixty-five. Asians, Hispanics, and multiracial respondents were more likely to have cross-racial friends than white and black respondents. Females were less likely than males to have eight or more cross-racial friends, although they had deeper cross-racial friendships. Older respondents reported less depth. However, even in deeper interracial friendships, there was a reluctance to discuss racially charged events such as police shootings of unarmed black men. Other studies have reported that cross-racial friendship increases when people have neighbors and coworkers from races and ethnicities different from their own.

Researchers in behavioral neuropsychology have connected racial aversion and avoidance to emotional centers in the brain that are activated by perceptions of racial difference. We can conclude from such studies that the likelihood of not having cross-racial friends is deeply rooted in **emotional aversion** that is "hard-wired" in the brain. The presence of race-related aversion triggers in the brain is not surprising because much of our noncognitive behavior proceeds from such almost-automatic emotional patterns of response so that conscious awareness of what is causing us to respond is not necessary to respond. This means that a person who does not have many cross-racial friends doesn't even have to think about not forming a friendship with a person of a different race. However, people can rethink their immediate emotional responses—they can retrain their brains.

Should people who do not have any or many cross-racial friends retrain themselves? Is having cross-racial friends a moral obligation or is it morally neutral? On an individual level, this seems to be a morally neutral choice because democratic rights include freedom to associate with whomever one chooses. However, on a social level, full racial integration that enables deep cross-racial friendships is desirable and perhaps morally obligatory.

Friendship is private, whereas the cultural commons is public. But the existence of friendships across race affects the cultural commons. So does interracial marriage.

Online dating sites typically specify the race of the partner sought and people posting often specify their own race. The choice of a marriage partner is quintessentially personal and private in modern democratic nations. But after people are married, their official status as married brings them into the commons, and they get higher social recognition, higher status, and access to more resources through social connections that they would not have if single.

In 1967, all remaining state laws against interracial marriage were struck down by the US Supreme Court in *Loving v. Virginia*. According to the Pew Research Center, from 1967 to 2015, interracial marriage steadily increased in the United States. The percentage of newly married blacks with a spouse of a different race or ethnicity increased from 5 to 18 percent; among whites it rose from 4 to 11 percent. Among Asians and Hispanics, interracial or interethnic marriage did not increase. But Asians and Hispanics remained more likely than whites or blacks to marry someone of a different race or ethnicity—29 percent among Asians and 27 percent among Hispanics.

Approval of intermarriage as good for society is highest in urban areas at 45 percent of adults, compared to 38 percent in suburban areas and less than 24 percent in rural areas. Slightly more than half of Americans live in suburbs, about 31 percent in urban areas, and 14 percent in rural areas. Overall, according to the Pew studies, approval of intermarriage was 39 percent about fifty years after *Loving v. Virginia*. In terms of statistics and attitudes, the racial norm for marriage in the United States does not seem to favor intermarriage and the vast majority of marriages are not interracial. However, a majority do believe that interracial marriage is neither good nor bad for society—63 percent of those in rural areas, 49 percent in urban areas, and 51 percent in suburban areas.

It is important to note that according to Gallup polls conducted in July 2013, 86 percent of Americans favored marriage between blacks and whites, a huge shift from 4 percent in 1958. Black approval was 97 percent, whereas white approval was 84 percent. These numbers were from Gallup's Minority Rights and Relations poll of 4,373 Americans, including 1,010 non-Hispanic blacks, who participated in telephone interviews. It may be that the discrepancy between the data reported by the Pew Research Center and Gallup is the result of how the question was framed: Pew research sought opinions on what was good for society, whereas Gallup simply asked for individuals' approval or disapproval.

Regardless of the statistics, the moral nature of interracial friendships and interracial marriage in the United States gives rise to the same questions about disapproval of them: What would happen if everyone disapproved? The answer is that there would be diminished social goods for interracial friends and interracial married couples. From a utilitarian or consequentialist moral perspective, human happiness would be less than it would be if more people approved of interracial friendship and interracial marriage. A further question is whether it is a virtue to approve of interracial friendship and marriage.

These examples of interracial friendship and marriage are important to consider in moral terms because they offer an opportunity to consider how what is private and personal may affect what is social. But don't people have a moral right to disapprove of such personal choices made by others? The answer to that question depends on how sharp the line is between what is private and what is public. The fact that people care about what other people do in their private lives based on their free choices and think they have a right to judge them for them in itself blurs the private-public distinction. Theoretically, this effect of private choices on public goods is backed up by general social and political theories of the importance of the common good, also known as the greater good, or the good of the whole.

THE TRAGEDY OF THE COMMONS

As a social good, cross-racial friendship strengthens values and practices that are part of the commons. Interracial marriage is an even more private choice than interracial friendships but disapproval of it also affects the commons. Often, people do not connect their individual choices to the common good. The idea of the common good in society is based on our human interdependence. Some things and activities are private, but there is much we need to share impersonally for its own sake and to support our private lives—public spaces and amenities, roads and highways, commerce, and the natural environment. The contemporary idea of **the commons** refers to the cultural, humanmade, and natural resources that are available to all members of a society.

American ecologist Garrett Hardin (1915–2003) published a now-iconic essay in 1994 called "The Tragedy of the Commons." Garrett argued that certain problems, such as population explosion and over-grazing, did not have technical solutions but required moral or ethical approaches. If individual families benefit by having one more child or farmers benefit from one more grazing animal, assuming general freedom, there is no way to solve the issue of collective damage that results for everyone. As Garrett put it, such problems do not have technical solutions but require moral solutions. (The same can be true of individual cases of littering.) As discussed in chapter 1, Immanuel Kant's categorical imperative requires that we ask of an action, "What would happen if everyone did it?" This test applies to the commons and supports Hardin's call for moral solutions to the tragedy of the commons that results from individual choices that benefit individuals but harm the collective when they add up.

Racial equality requires that the commons not be legally restricted against certain racial groups. A 2008 study found that 58 percent of African Americans cannot swim. This is not due to inherent personal or group idiosyncrasy. In urban areas with large black populations, municipal pools were first segregated by race and then closed or paved over when racial integration in public facilities became the law in the 1960s. These pool closures were directed by dominant whites in communities. The effect of closing pools to avoid racial integration destroyed an important recreational commons, particularly during hot summers in the South, where the practice was prevalent.

Returning to the previous section, the commons can also become racially restricted as a result of many individual choices and individual racial aversion, extended to the race of a person's friends. If people have few friends of different races, then the cultural and social resources of racially dominant and subordinate groups—that is, in most cases, whites and nonwhites—are not as easily shared. If interracial married couples face disapproval and rejection as couples, that discourages their participation in the commons that is otherwise open to same-race married couples. These effects limit both what and who are included in the social commons and who has access to it. We will see in further chapters that such limitations on who participates in and benefits from the commons extends to other aspects of life, such as immigration, criminal justice, employment, wealth, education, health, media, and resilience in disasters, including the COVID-19 pandemic. Race-related exclusion or nonparticipation is not only bad in itself, but results in an overall loss to society as a whole.

THE COMMON GOOD

The idea of the common good is both abstract and concrete. As an abstraction, people have to think about the consequences of their individual actions for a whole greater than its parts or, at least, greater than their own circumstances. What is good for the whole will in turn benefit them and others, as individuals. The philosopher and novelist Jean-Jacques Rousseau (1712–1778) had an innovative approach to the role of government in promoting the common good. Rousseau was the first celebrity intellectual in the modern world. Devoted readers of his novels tried to imitate his main characters. Many intellectuals supported him after he was thrown out of Switzerland on account of his political ideas. Rousseau did not write about race, but after his death, his political thought made him an icon of the French Revolution, which began with a doctrine of human equality and the rejection of slavery.

In 1750, Rousseau won an essay competition from the Academy of Dijon. The topic was whether the arts and sciences had elevated or debased public morals. Rousseau argued in his *Discourse on the Sciences and Arts* (First Discourse) that the cause of human unhappiness and suffering was human relations in society and that science and art corrupted both individual and civic morality. He claimed that as beings in nature, outside of society, humans had **amour de soi**, or direct self-love. But as social beings living in society, they became obsessed with their reputations through **amour propre**, or self-love based on the views of others. As a result, people in society were afflicted with mutual dependence and manipulation. Rousseau proposed a top-down solution to this problem, through democratic government. A legislature of a select group of citizens would directly pass just laws and elect the executive. Both the laws and their application (by the executive) would express the general will, a collective desire for the good of everyone. Legal equality would eventually remove the differences supporting the corruption of amour propre because the laws would apply to all citizens in the same way. There was to be a state religion and strict censorship. In other words, Rousseau proposed strong government action to enforce human equality and, in the process, correct human social corruption.

Rousseau's approach to equality in society has not been accepted by all progressives. Others, including grassroots activists, have advocated social reform through changes in human relationships. Jane Addams (1860–1935), who was the second woman to win the Nobel Prize in 1931, put ideas of social equality into practice through her work in Hull House. Hull House was a settlement house in Chicago with the following mission: To provide a center for a higher civic and social life, to institute and maintain educational and philanthropic enterprises, and to investigate and improve the conditions in the industrial districts of Chicago.

Inspired by social reform work at Toynbee Hall, in London's East End, Addams and her friend Ellen Starr lived among poor immigrant working families. A year after Hull House was founded in 1889, services were provided for two thousand people. Available were: kindergarten classes and club meetings for children, night school for adults, an art gallery, public kitchen, coffeehouse, gymnasium, swimming pool, girls' boarding facilities, a bookbindery, an art studio, a music school, a drama group, a circulating library, an employment bureau, and a labor museum. Addams explained her theory of social uplift and reform for the poor and deprived in *Democracy and Social Ethics*: helping people required sharing and understanding their actual living conditions and physically living among them. Although Addams's subjects were poor white European immigrants, especially women, she was also a founding member of the National Association for the Advancement of Colored People (NAACP). She intended her concept of *sympathetic knowledge* to capture both empathy and caring for others through practical moral action.

To sum up, Rousseau's thought is representative of a moral role for government, while Addams's life and thought represent progressive activism. Progressives have taken each and both paths, the one of social reform through government and the other of social reform on the level of actual lives. Both Rousseau and Addams were privileged in comparison to those they believed, for moral reasons, needed reform. In some of the chapters that follow, we will consider morally motivated social reform from the standpoint of those who have suffered from racism, rather than such external approaches.

Rawls's Idea of Justice as Fairness

John Rawls (1921–2002) claimed that justice was the primary virtue of social institutions in societies, although he acknowledged that different societies had different *conceptions* of justice. Rawls developed an idea of justice as fairness. Rawls proposed justice as fairness as an ideal for a society that was already law-abiding and "well-ordered." This ideal meant that citizens of society would all be free, have equal basic rights, and cooperate economically. Opportunities for public office would be open to all citizens. According to Rawls, justice as fairness did not entail that everyone would have the same or equal amounts of wealth and other social goods. That is, some would be worse off than others. However, it was important that any policy changes not leave those already worse off, more worse off. We will return to these key insights of Rawls in the discussion of **equity** in chapter 7.

QUESTIONS FOR THINKING, DISCUSSION, AND WRITING

1. Do you have friends of different races and are those friendships deep? Do you think this is a moral issue? Why or why not? If people, without thinking, emotionally react against cross-racial friendships, is this a moral issue?
2. The attitudes of people of different races toward interracial marriages were mentioned in this chapter. Not mentioned was whether it is morally neutral, good, or bad to choose a marriage partner of the same race and exclude others from consideration. How do you assess what one ought to do concerning race in choosing one's marriage partner? Is it morally neutral, good, or bad?
3. Explain in your own words what the tragedy of the commons is. Give further examples of individual choices unintentionally affecting a greater whole.
4. How do you think that Rousseau's idea of amour propre is relevant to issues of race and racism?
5. Would the idea of settlement houses in poor nonwhite communities, which were run by white people, be considered condescending today?

SOURCES

Addams, Jane. *Democracy and Social Ethics.* Project Gutenberg e-book, https://iuristebi.files.wordpress.com/2011/07/democracy-and-social-ethics.pdf.

Hardin, Garrett. "The Tragedy of the Commons." *Science, New Series* 162, no. 3859 (December 13, 1968): 1243–48. https://www.hendrix.edu/uploadedFiles/Admission/GarrettHardin Article.pdf.

History.com Editors. "Loving v. Virginia." History.com, January 25, 2021, https://www.history.com/topics/civil-rights-movement/loving-v-virginia.

Livingston, Gretchen, and Anna Brown. "Trends and Patterns in Intermarriage." Pew Research Center, https://www.pewresearch.org/social-trends/2017/05/18/1-trends-and-patterns-in-intermarriage/ and https://www.pewresearch.org/social-trends/2017/05/18/2-public-views-on-intermarriage/.

Parker, Kim, Juliana Menasce Horowitz, Anna Brown, Richard Fry, D'Vera Cohn, and Ruth Igielnik. "What Unites and Divides Urban, Suburban and Rural Communities." Pew Research Center, May 18, 2018, https://www.pewresearch.org/social-trends/2018/05/22/demographic-and-economic-trends-in-urban-suburban-and-rural-communities/.

Phelps, E., K. O'Connor, W. Cunningham, E. Funayama, J. Gatenby, J. Gore, and M. Banaji. "Performance on Indirect Measures of Race Evaluation Predicts Amygdala Activation."

Journal of Cognitive Neuroscience (2000): 729–738. [PubMed] [Google Scholar] https://dash.harvard.edu/bitstream/handle/1/3512208/Banaji_PerformanceIndirect.pdf.

Plummer, D. L., R. T. Stone, L. Powell, and J. Allison. "Patterns of Adult Cross-Racial Friendships: A Context for Understanding Contemporary Race Relations." *Cultural Diversity and Ethnic Minority Psychology* 22, no. 4 (2016): 479–94. APA PsycNet, American Psychological Association, https://content.apa.org/record/2016-18408-001 https://doi.org/10.1037/cdp0000079.

Newport, Frank. "In U.S., 87% Approve of Black-White Marriage, vs. 4% in 1958 Ninety-Six Percent of Blacks, 84% of Whites Approve." Gallup, July 25, 2013, https://news.gallup.com/poll/163697/approve-marriage-blacks-whites.aspx

NPR. "Racial History of American Swimming Pools." May 6, 2008, https://www.npr.org/templates/story/story.php?storyId=90213675.

Rawls, John. *A Theory of Justice.* Cambridge, MA: Harvard University Press, 1971/1999. Chapter 1, "Justice as Fairness," pp. 3–46, https://giuseppecapograssi.files.wordpress.com/2014/08/rawls99.pdf.

Rousseau, Jean-Jacques. *The Social Contract and the First and Second Discourses.* Susan Dunn, ed. New Haven, CT: Yale University Press, 2002.

Videos

Audiopedia. "What Is General Will? What Does General Will Mean?" April 21, 2017. https://www.youtube.com/watch?v=EJsJUH-OWZs.

Masombuka, Thobekile. "It's Time to Have That Awkward Conversation with Your Friend Who's a Different Race to You." News24.com, November 5, 2018, https://www.news24.com/w24/selfcare/wellness/mind/its-time-to-have-that-awkward-conversation-with-your-friend-whos-a-different-race-to-you-20181105.

National Geographic, Resource Library. "Couples Share the Happiness and Heartache of Interracial Marriage." https://www.nationalgeographic.org/video/couples-share-happiness-and-heartache-interracial-marriage/.

Waterbuggi. "The Life and Work of Jane Addams." September 10, 2011. https://www.youtube.com/watch?v=Tw4GZeABlNI.

3

The History of Ideas of Race and Racism

Silhouette of heads. Getty Images: Leontura.

The connection of personal individual actions and attitudes concerning race to the common good of society was discussed in chapter 2. In that discussion, the existence of a general moral attitude of racial equality in a modern democratic society was assumed. However, the history of ideas of race held by dominant groups in Western society has coincided with the history of often brutal oppression of groups designated nonwhite and non-European. Religion has also played a role. The paganism of captured Africans during the early English slave trade was used to counter Queen Elizabeth I's initial warning that "if any African should be carried away without their free consent, it would be detestable, and call down the vengeance of Heaven upon the undertaking." Of course, the notion that those captured for slavery could consent seems self-contradictory, and Elizabeth overcame her moral objections to slave trading, for profit, in competition with Spain.

Ideas and theories of racial difference have very rarely been posits of mere variety among human beings but were commonly rankings of human racial groups to the advantage of white Westerners. This history has had repercussions, even after active oppression has stopped. When attempts are now made to treat people equally, regardless of race, the history of disadvantage due to racism has effects in the present that may make mere equality unequal. For example, lower levels of education in

African American families is a legacy of slavery when literacy was legally prohibited for slaves and also the result of unequal segregated schools. The ongoing result is that many cannot take the same advantage whites can of equal opportunities for the attainment of higher education.

The purpose of this chapter is to consider the moral aspects of the historical connection between *ideologies* of race and what we now consider racism. Racism consists of unjust treatment or unwarranted judgment based on race, namely **discrimination** and **prejudice**. An **ideology** is a false view of reality that justifies behavior and practices that would otherwise be morally unacceptable. The chapter begins with an analysis of ideology in terms of race as it pertained to the genocide of indigenous groups and the Nazi murder of six million Jews during World War II. The historical account follows: Ideas of human difference in the ancient world are considered in connection with slavery without racial categories. Slavery began to be associated with race during the Age of Discovery and the colonial period, and modern ideas of race were connected with the burgeoning science of biology. The science of anthropology soon followed, resulting in a general science of race that has since been discarded by scientists, as we will see in chapter 4. The now-discredited seventeenth- to nineteenth-century science of race culminated in eugenic practices in the early twentieth century.

From a moral point of view, much of this history can be condemned as very bad or evil. But the task here is to attempt to understand the relationship of racist ideas about race or racist ideology to actions justified by it. We are now morally obligated to ensure that history does not repeat itself and figure out how to curtail and obstruct current repetitions. This is a tremendous amount to understand over a few pages, so it will be sufficient to come away with major insights that could lead to further moral understanding of the role of race on the big stage of human history.

In studying historical practices that are now morally unacceptable, some are tempted to take a **morally relative view** that culture is all-powerful and determines what is good and right. This could avoid moral judgment by making allowances for different circumstances and blind confidence on the part of those now considered bad actors that they were doing the right thing. But when morally bad practices were opposed in their own time, notably abolitionist moral arguments against slavery, those objections show that relativism isn't plausible—if some could judge then, then we can judge now. The chapter begins with racism as ideology, followed by the history of ideas of race, and concluding with white supremacy and eugenics.

RACISM AS IDEOLOGY

If groups oppressed on the grounds of race deserved their oppression because of their actions or traits, the oppression would not need the kind of justification that has accompanied historical race-based oppression. Or, if oppressed racial groups were inferior forms of humanity or simply animals, then justification would not be necessary. For instance, regarding factory farming today, it is widely assumed that humans need the products and have a natural right to produce them. There is scant justification. But when settlers wanted to seize the land of indigenous groups in America and Australia, primarily because they just wanted their land, they first pretended that the land was unoccupied. According to the doctrine of **terra nullius**, unowned land could simply be seized. On both continents, culturally different forms of nomadic occupation, such as "walk-about" possession in Australia and seasonal agriculture in the United States, were conveniently ignored. When indigenous groups sought to retain their land, they were driven from it with claims that they were "vermin" in Australia and "savages" in America. In America, the ideological doctrine of **manifest destiny** justified settler expansion of the United States "from sea to shining sea," by driving Native Americans onto reservations and, after the US victory in the Mexican-American War, annexing large segments of the Southwest that had belonged to Mexico. Scholars differ in estimates of declines in indigenous populations in the Western hemisphere. Many were killed directly, others died from diseases novel to their populations, and all suffered from the destruction of their traditional natural environments and culture. A careful estimate might be that throughout the colonized world, by 1900, original populations had decreased by at least three-quarters.

The use of racist anti-Semitic ideology by the Third Reich in Germany was a more complicated form of dispossession with **genocide** or the aim to wipe out an entire people. Not only did the Nazis seek to seize the wealth of Jewish citizens but they made Jews a scapegoat for economic national ills, eulogized white Germans (Aryans) in contrast to them, and galvanized the German population for military campaigns toward world domination. In 1939, on the eve of World War II, just before Germany invaded Poland, the American writer and literary theorist Kenneth Burke (1887–1993) published a review of Hitler's *Mein Kampf* in light of his rise to power.

Hitler's title meant "my battle" and Burke's review was titled, "The Rhetoric of Hitler's Battle." Burke showed how Hitler's rhetoric constructed an ideology that was a new, motivational worldview for the German people. They needed relief from economic losses that had resulted from their humiliating defeat in World War I and the harsh terms for peace that had followed. Hitler's racist ideology was presented as their salvation and vindication, and it was backed up by violent enforcement as democratic political structures were demolished. Hitler's charisma and great popularity united a descent into madness by an entire modern nation. The Nazis used every manner of slander against Jews, reviving centuries-old anti-Semitic conspiracy theories. Such theories still linger, as evident in the white supremacist and white nationalist rally in Charlottesville, Virginia, in August 2017. Marchers shouted, "You will not replace us," referring to the conspiracy theory that Jews were enabling nonwhite immigration to take away employment for whites. (See chapter 16.)

THE HISTORY OF IDEAS OF RACE

The history of ideas of race is intertwined with the history of slavery, although slavery and race did not come together until modernity. Slavery was practiced in many human societies before there were ideas of biological race. Slave-owning societies have been defined as societies in which slave labor contributes at least 10 percent of the value of production and there have been five over history: ancient Greece, ancient Rome, the Caribbean, Brazil, and the United States South. In ancient Greece, slaves were called *andropoda* or man-footed beasts, compared to *tetrapoda* or four-footed beasts and that signaled their less than human status. Although, in contrast to later designations of slaves as racially distinct, in Greece and Rome slave status was less based on identities the slaves had, and more a social position in a society that was already hierarchical. Still, Aristotle described slaves as lacking decision-making reason, and the Roman Code of Justinian, in the section "Concerning the rights of persons," stated, "The chief division in the rights of persons is this: men are all either free or slaves." Throughout the ancient world, there were different rules for freeing slaves. Many slaves, who began their enslavement as captives in war, practiced what we would recognize as professions and had the liberty to earn wages in skilled crafts, as well as accounting, teaching, doctoring, and soldiering; they could also save their wages to buy freedom. In Rome, the grandchildren of freed slaves were able to enter the free population without stigma.

The association of modern biological race with slaves, especially enslaved Africans, required the idea of human races. François Bernier (1625–1688) provided that framework in his "New Division of the Earth" by proposing that humankind was divided into races based on the physical traits of skin color, hair texture, and bodily shape. The "first race," with the greatest difference from the others, was made up of Europeans, North Africans, Middle Easterners, and inhabitants of parts of Southeast Asia and the Americas. The other races included Africans, East and Northeast Asians, and the Lapps. These divisions were continually redrawn by subsequent theorists, but Bernier's major contributions endured: The whole of humanity could be divided into races regardless of the histories of peoples and Europeans were the "first" race. Racial **taxonomy** or classification in biological terms became the paradigm for the new system of human division that spread among leading intellectuals, as fast as European colonial empires grew. During the same time, Bernier's physical or biological racial classifications were augmented by moral, mental, temperamental, and aesthetic traits that were believed to be hereditary, along with the physical traits.

Every field in the humanities, human sciences, and arts and letters became permeated with ideas about human rankings from racist science. David Hume (1711–1776), the otherwise esteemed empiricist philosopher widely known for his mild temperament, wrote the following in a footnote to the 1754 edition of his *Essays*:

I am apt to suspect the negroes and in general all the other species of men (for there are four or five different kinds) to be naturally inferior to the whites. There never was a civilized nation of any other complexion than white, not even any individual eminent either in action or speculation.

The Scottish philosopher James Beattie (1735–1803) objected vociferously to Hume, claiming that he did not know enough about Negro civilizations to generalize in that way. But other influential philosophers followed Hume in white supremacy and the vilification of nonwhites. Canonical ethicist and epistemologist Immanuel Kant (1724–1804) quoted Hume as an authority on the self-evident existence of human races and wrote, "The white race possesses all motivating forces and talents in itself." Kant had a difficult career for decades and made a living teaching courses on anthropology and geography. Anthropology was the study of human history, geography, and natural history, which for Kant included his speculations about nonwhite races. The greatest systematic abstract theorist in the history of philosophy, Georg Wilhelm Friedrich Hegel (1770–1831), described Africa as outside of history, "the land of gold, forever pressing in upon itself, and the land of childhood, removed from the light of self-conscious history and wrapped in the dark mantle of night."

WHITE SUPREMACY AND EUGENICS

John Stuart Mill is usually associated with modern liberalism and equality. Friedrich Nietzsche is usually praised for expressing individual freedom. However, both were **white supremacists** who believed that the white race was superior to all others. It was a short step from such ideas of white superiority to advocacy for selective white racial breeding and nonwhite exclusion.

John Stuart Mill (1806–1873), who was well praised for his writings on women's rights, representative government, and utilitarianism, in his preface to *On Liberty* cautioned that his arguments against censorship were "meant to apply only to human beings in the maturity of their faculties," and not to "those backward states of society in which the race itself may be considered in its nonage." And he went on, "Despotism is a legitimate mode of government in dealing with barbarians." Mill was an empiricist, analytic philosopher, but Friedrich Nietzsche (1844–1900), who was more poetic, went furthest of all the philosophers as a racial **eugenicist** in favor of breading a pure, blonde, European race. He claimed that "it is not in the least possible that a human being might not have the qualities and preferences of his parents and ancestors in his body." In other words, Nietzsche summed up the notion that race, as hereditary, carried physical, cultural, and moral traits.

Nietzsche's ideas were made more specific and echoed in the early twentieth-century **eugenics movement**. Francis Galton (1822–1911), cousin of Charles Darwin, founded that movement in England, where it was not successful. But it took off in the United States. Charles Davenport (1866–1944) directed the Eugenics Record Office, which influenced restrictions on immigration and maintained extensive research on heredity and family traits at the Station for Experimental Evolution (SEE) in Cold Spring Harbor, New York. The general idea was that a "better" race could be bred to ward off threats from those deemed genetically "unfit": immigrants from Southern and Eastern Europe, Jews, those disabled, and the "morally delinquent." This movement, enthusiastically backed by millions of Americans, resulted in forced sterilizations and new restrictive laws in twenty-seven states. Families competed for measurements of their "genetic fitness" at state fairs. Hitler claimed to have been inspired by the movement. Even progressives such as W. E. B. Du Bois (1868–1963), founder of the NAACP and leading black public intellectual of his day, got on board in encouraging African Americans to "breed for better brains, for efficiency, for beauty." Thus, although the eugenics movement was a white supremacist movement, authoritarian approaches to private human relationships could also be taken up within nonwhite groups. Such uptake and the movement as a whole were based on the premises that genes and heredity controlled human worth, and human excellence could be molded by the leaders of society.

The history of racist oppression as justified by intellectual authorities meant that there could be no concept of a common good that included the lives and well-being of nonwhites, especially Africans. Let's return now to the subject of interracial friendship discussed in chapter 2. Consider Mark Twain's (Samuel Langhorne Clemens, 1835–1910) eponymous character in his 1895 *The Adventures of Huckleberry Finn*. Huck lied about the presence of his friend Jim, an escaping slave, to a group from his community who were hunting for him. Huck then concluded that he had rejected morality because, for him, morality was the views held by his slave-owning elders. This did not bother Huck because he easily decided that morality was just not for him, but it raises the question of how people should behave when, for good reasons, they cannot abide by what they accept as their moral code.

QUESTIONS FOR THINKING, DISCUSSION, AND WRITING

1. Are you willing to make moral judgments about bad actions in the past? Why or why not?
2. How was the ideology behind the Charlottesville rally of 2017 the same and different from Hitler's rhetoric?
3. What was the difference between slavery before and after the idea of biological race was introduced?
4. How do you assess the contribution of influential philosophers to the racist science of race? Should they be held to a stricter standard than others?
5. Would it have been possible for Huck Finn to reason differently after he had protected Jim, and if yes, what would that reasoning have been?

SOURCES

Beattie, James. "A Response to Hume." From "An Essay on the Nature and Immutability of Truth, in Opposition to Sophistry and Skepticism," in Emmanuel Chukwudi Eze, ed., *Race and the Enlightenment: A Reader*. Cambridge, MA: Blackwell Publishers, 1997, pp. 34–37.

Bernasconi, Robert. "Nietzsche as a Philosopher of Racialized Breeding." Naomi Zack, ed., *Oxford Handbook of Philosophy and Race*. New York: Oxford University Press, 2017.

Blake, John. "When Americans Tried to Breed a Better Race: How a Genetic Fitness 'Crusade' Marches On." CNN, October 18, 2018, https://www.cnn.com/2018/10/16/us/eugenics -craze-america-pbs/index.html.

Burke, Kenneth. "The Rhetoric of Hitler's Battle." *Southern Review* 5 (1939): 1–21.

Eze, Emmanuel Chukwudi, ed. *Race and the Enlightenment*. Cambridge, MA: Blackwell, 1997.

Finley, M. I. *Ancient Slavery and Modern Ideology*. New York: Penguin, 1983.

Griswold del Castillo, Richard. "Manifest Destiny: The Mexican-American War and the Treaty of Guadalupe Hidalgo." *Southwestern Journal of Law and Trade in the Americas* 5 (1998): 85–98.

Hume, David. "Of National Characters." *The Philosophical Works*, ed. Thomas Hill Green and Thomas Hodge Grose. Darmstadt, West Germany: Scientia Verlag Aalen 1964, 4 vols., 3 (quotation, p. 262, n.1).

Jackson, L. P. "Elizabethan Seamen and the African Slave Trade." *Journal of Negro History*, 1924. https://www.journals.uchicago.edu/doi/pdf/10.2307/2713432.

Justinian. *Digest of Justinian*. Translated by Charles Henry Monro. Cambridge, MA: Cambridge University Press, Book I, V. 3. p. 24.

Kant, Immanuel. "Grounding for the Metaphysics of Morals." In James W. Ellington, trans. *Kant's Ethical Philosophy*. Indianapolis, IN: Hackett, 1994 (quotation p. 117).

McCarthy, Thomas. *Race, Empire, and the Idea of Human Development*. Cambridge, MA: Cambridge University Press, 2009, p. 168.

Miller, Robert J. "American Indians, the Doctrine of Discovery, and Manifest Destiny." *Wyoming Law Review* 11, no. 2 (2011): 329–49. https://scholarship.law.uwyo.edu/wlr/vol11/iss2/2.

Peters, Michael A., and Tina Besley. "White Supremacism: The Tragedy of Charlottesville." *Educational Philosophy and Theory* 49, no. 14 (2017): 1309–12. https://www.researchgate .net/publication/320053853_White_supremacism_The_tragedy_of_Charlottesville.

Smith, David Michael. "Counting the Dead: Estimating the Loss of Life in the Indigenous Holocaust, 1492–Present." Native American Symposium; 12th, 2017, Representations and Realities. University of Saskatchewan. https://iportal.usask.ca/index.php?sid=533529724& id=67397&t=details.

Stuurman, Siep. "François Bernier and the Invention of Racial Classification." *History Workshop Journal*, no. 50 (Autumn 2000): 1–21. https://www.jstor.org/stable/4289688?seq= 1#metadata_info_tab_contents.

Tatz, Colin. "Australia: The 'Good' Genocide Perpetrator?" *Health and History* 18, no. 2 (2016). Accessed August 15, 2021, https://www.jstor.org/stable/10.5401/healthhist .18.2.0085.

Videos

College Students. "The History of Jim Crow Laws, Disc 2." 2011, YouTube, https://www .youtube.com/watch?v=W7Hn-n9v5SU.

GPB Education. "Cherokee Nation and the Trail of Tears." December 20, 2019, YouTube, https://www.youtube.com/watch?v=PZEUPlsJ4ek.

Riefenstahl, Leni. "1935: Triumph of the Will—The Power of Propaganda." 100 Years of Cinema (abridged), https://www.youtube.com/watch?v=p7hJVaTW45M.

Southern Poverty Law Center (SPLC). "White Nationalists Chant in Charlottesville Again: 'You Will Not Replace Us.'" https://www.splcenter.org/file/15770.

Thought and Word. "Huckleberry Finn: Why Jim Is Mark Twain's Most Meaningful Character." September 28, 2020, YouTube, https://www.youtube.com/watch?v=09JbdHbLDy4.

US Holocaust Memorial Museum. "A History of Eugenics." YouTube, August 26, 2020, https://www.youtube.com/watch?v=jeSM9vz6ylg.

4

Science and Race

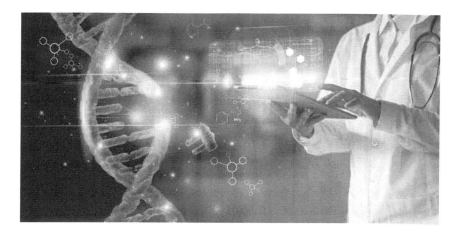

Analyzing DNA structure with the latest technologies. Getty Images: ipopba.

The history of modern race began with modern biology, but many of its methods would not be considered scientific today. Nineteenth-century studies of race included comparative measurements and sensational displays. For instance, "Sarah Baartman" was the name given to at least two South African Khoikhoi women known as the "Hottentot Venus," who were exhibited to learned audiences throughout Europe. After her death, the last one was dissected, with an intense focus on her sexual traits. Although science is usually considered beneficial to humankind and either benevolent or value neutral, until the twentieth century, the science of race was generally unethically biased against nonwhite groups. The bias was unethical because it did not have a factual foundation, and it was used to justify oppressive actions against those groups. However, race science no longer exists in that sense! There may be projects to resurrect it, but neither the social nor biological sciences in the mainstream approach race in the historically racist way.

Modern science in all fields constantly revises itself in the face of new data, and the new data concerning race has both a social science and a physical-biological side. The social sciences of anthropology and sociology have shown that the racial hierarchies and rankings previously constructed within society have no factual basis. The physical-biological sciences have shown that there is no independent biological evidence for the existence of distinct races among humankind. Acceptance of contemporary physical-biological and social science consensus can bring us to morally good attitudes and practices concerning race, which are based on reliable research.

In this chapter, we will first discuss the kind of moral reasoning relevant to issues of race, followed by contemporary social science findings of human racial differences, including the issue of nonwhite intellectual inferiority. Next, the absence of the physical-biological scientific foundation for human races supports up-to-date social science findings. The chapter concludes with a consideration of the moral virtues of racial loyalty and self-affirmation, which may rely on outdated scientific ideas of biological race, in contrast to the intellectual virtue of respect for truth. The truth is that science does not support the idea of race in either the physical or social sciences. But people may have positive moral investments in racial identities that are tied to now-false ideas of race and the chapter ends on this note.

MORAL REASONING AND RACE

Not all reactions to racial difference and race relations are moral in ways based on reasoning. Some are purely emotional. For instance, without consciously thinking about it, some people hate others of races different from their own, and others generously welcome racial differences. And of course, there are different gradations and nuances of hate and love, as well as different levels of acknowledgment of the nature of a person's own emotions concerning racial difference. The method here is conscious, intellectual thought about race that requires understanding what philosophers consider to be **moral arguments**. There are two kinds: **epistemic arguments** or arguments about what is true or what a person should believe, and **practical arguments** or arguments about what is right and what a person should do, so that the action itself concludes the argument.

Both epistemic and practical arguments can have the form of **syllogisms**, a classic form of argument. To call such patterns of reasoning **arguments** does not mean that those who use them are angry or contentious. Rather, as philosophical argument, a syllogism is a set of statements called premises and a conclusion that logically follows from those premises. It is logically impossible for the premises to be true and the logical conclusion to be false. If the premises are true and no logical mistake is made in getting to the conclusion, the argument is a **sound argument**. But if the premises are false and the conclusion logically follows from them, the argument is still **valid**. Consider the following sound examples.

Epistemic Moral Syllogism about Race (concerning beliefs)
Premise A. All human groups have the same cultural potential.
Premise B. African Americans and European Americans are human groups.
Conclusion C. Therefore, African Americans and European Americans have the same cultural potential.

Practical Moral Syllogism about Race (ending in action)
Premise A. Those who provide opportunities should treat members of all racial groups equally.
Premise B. As an employer, I can provide opportunities to qualified members of different racial groups.
Premise C. As an employer, I am obligated to hire the most highly qualified applicant.
Premise D. Candidate X is the most qualified applicant and X is a member of a minority racial group.
Conclusion E. I hire candidate X. THIS IS AN ACTION.

Syllogistic reasoning is not the whole of philosophical argument. True premises in syllogisms lead to conclusions that are logically certain. This is **deductive reasoning**. There are also inductive argument forms. **Inductive arguments** are based on the probability of premises. The premises are probably true, and the conclusion that logically follows from them is also probably true. The probability of the conclusion may be expressed as a generalization. Many scientific conclusions are probabilistic in this way. Probabilities state the frequency of something in a representative sample of a larger group and then draw a conclusion about the larger group. For example, "All observed swans have been white, therefore, all swans are probably white."

Most members of democratic societies believe that what we think and do concerning racial difference is a moral matter if it involves human life and well-being. Many or most scientific generalizations are probably true, given the evidence of data for them. But their truth is not certain, as in deductive arguments. Inductive or deductive, the goal of truth or high probability based on an argument form requires a commitment. This is a commitment to believing the best information or doing what is morally right. In the context of moral arguments, the commitment is a moral commitment. We will consider this further in the section on intellectual or epistemic virtue.

RACE IN SOCIETY AND SOCIAL SCIENCE

On May 17, 1998, the American Anthropological Association published a "Statement on Race" that represented the views of the majority of its members. After discussion of the historical connection of ideas of race with oppression, the statement provided clarification about the psychological and cultural aspects of different racial identities, as follows:

> "Race" thus evolved as a worldview, a body of prejudgments that distorts our ideas about human differences and group behavior. Racial beliefs constitute myths about the diversity in the human species and about the abilities and behavior of people homogenized into "racial" categories. The myths fused behavior and physical features together in the public mind, impeding our comprehension of both biological variations and cultural behavior, implying that both are genetically determined. Racial myths bear no relationship to the reality of human capabilities or behavior. Scientists today find that reliance on such folk beliefs about human differences in research has led to countless errors.
>
> At the end of the 20th century, we now understand that human cultural behavior is learned, conditioned into infants beginning at birth, and always subject to modification. No human is born with a built-in culture or language. Our temperaments, dispositions, and personalities, regardless of genetic propensities, are developed within sets of meanings and values that we call "culture." Studies of infant and early childhood learning and behavior attest to the reality of our cultures in forming who we are.
>
> It is a basic tenet of anthropological knowledge that all normal human beings have the capacity to learn any cultural behavior. The American experience with immigrants from hundreds of different language and cultural backgrounds who have acquired some version of American culture traits and behavior is the clearest evidence of this fact. Moreover, people of all physical variations have learned different cultural behaviors and continue to do so as modern transportation moves millions of immigrants around the world.
>
> How people have been accepted and treated within the context of a given society or culture has a direct impact on how they perform in that society. The "racial" worldview was invented to assign some groups to perpetual low status, while others were permitted access to privilege, power, and wealth. The tragedy in the United States has been that the policies and practices stemming from this worldview succeeded all too well in constructing unequal populations among Europeans, Native Americans, and peoples of African descent. Given what we know about the capacity of normal humans to achieve and function within any culture, we conclude that present-day inequalities between so-called "racial" groups are not consequences of their biological inheritance but products of historical and contemporary social, economic, educational, and political circumstances.

This section of the 1998 AAA Statement of Race is important because it draws a line in the sand between physical racial inheritance and cultural traits and human aptitude.

The Issue of Intellectual Inferiority

The history of racist science and racism posited nonwhite intellectual inferiority. In the nineteenth century, craniometric measurements were recorded to prove that whites had larger brains than blacks. In his 1996 book, *The Mismeasure of Man*,

Stephen Jay Gould (1941–2002) shows how Samuel George Morton (1799–1851) cherry-picked and falsified his data in favor of larger skulls for whites and even used different materials for measurement. During the second half of the twentieth century, best-selling books linking intelligence and achievement to racial identity came out regularly. In the twenty-first century, the issue of intellectual inferiority has come to a point in debates about the causes of lower scores on IQ and standardized aptitude tests by African Americans, Latinos, women, and poor people, compared to middle-class white male respondents. Mark Alfano, Latasha Holden, and Andrew Conway have discussed this discrepancy in terms of what the tests measure and how test-takers' attitudes can influence their scores. A person's scores on varied tests are highly correlated. The tests measure reasoning skills and knowledge. The racial gaps support the thesis that the tests all measure skills and knowledge widely prevalent in dominant racial groups, but not as prevalent among nonwhites due to different cultural experiences.

Alfano et al. focus on **stereotype threat** or the negative performance effect on test-takers of prior reminders that members of the group to which they belong do not perform as well as others on such tests. They suggest that test-takers need to be reeducated about the nature of intelligence itself, away from beliefs that intelligence is an essential thing or trait associated with race, and toward a view of intelligence as acquired and capable of improvement through growth and self-affirmation by considering what one values. Research supports the effectiveness of self-affirmation interventions for raising test scores. Given that human culture is not hereditary and human aptitudes are evenly distributed across racial groups, the socially constructed racial test gaps are unfair, constituting a social injustice that can and should be corrected.

THE LACK OF PHYSICAL-BIOLOGICAL RACE IN SCIENCE

Race is a matter of physical difference that most people can recognize in skin color, hair texture, facial features, and bone proportions. These physical traits are inherited and heredity can be studied scientifically, ultimately in genetics. So, isn't that enough to say that biological science provides a foundation for race or has proved that human races exist? The answer to this question is No. Some theorists have proposed a new way of approaching the scientific foundation that retains traits associated with races in society but that would require ignoring what the relevant scientists report. Required for a scientific foundation for race is independent scientific findings that human beings are physically divided into races. That is, for a scientific racial taxonomy or system of classification, humankind needs to be studied for evidence of biological divisions that would qualify as races, without beginning with racial divisions in society.

For race to be real in science, there would need to be races—plural, because one race would just be the whole of humanity—with something about each race that is distinct to its members and not shared by members of other races. Because the number of human races posited in society has ranged between three and sixty, there would need to be independent scientific confirmation of a certain number of human races. One of the historical posits of racist science and racism was that each race had its own distinct essence. No **racial essence** or general trait causing specific physical or cultural traits associated with any group considered a race in society has ever been discovered in science.

All of the candidates for scientific racial distinctions have failed: blood types, phenotypes, geographical origin, and genes. While blood types, like essences, have mythically been associated with races, for instance in expressions such as "black blood," there are hundreds of different human blood types besides the four identified for transfusion purposes and no blood types exclusively coincide with social races. **Phenotypic variation** or traits in individuals such as skin color are **clines** in nature, traits that vary gradually due to environmental conditions. Social races are the result of breeding norms imposed on groups brought into contact with other groups, such as black Africans and white plantation owners in the US South during slavery. Both the skin color contrast and enforcement of white breeding to exclude nonwhite ancestors made it seem as though racial differences were natural and substantial. Most variation of all hereditary traits occurs within social races or groups considered racial groups within society and not between them. That is, there is a greater variation of traits within social races than between them.

Geography is not a valid foundation for scientific ideas of race, because all human groups are believed to have originated in Africa, with mixing following migrations. The human **genome** or all human genes were mapped in 2000 by Celera Genomics and the National Institutes of Health and US Public Genome Project. There were no genetic findings about racial distinctness in ways that generally identified racial membership. J. Craig Venter, head of Celera Genomics and chief private scientist in the project, claimed that "'race' is not a scientifically valid construct." He added, "We all evolved in the last 100,000 years from the same small number of tribes that migrated out of Africa and colonized the world."

For a while in the mid-twentieth century, some researchers sought to substitute the idea of **populations** or groups in the same geographic area who breed within themselves, for the idea of race. However, between fifty and hundreds of thousands of human populations have been identified. To reduce that number to a single digit of races would require beginning with social ideas of race, which undermines the independence of the human biological sciences.

INTELLECTUAL VIRTUE, SCIENCE, AND RACE

Intellectual virtues are mental dispositions or virtues, such as honesty, courage, skepticism, and critical thinking. Indeed, there is a free charter middle school in Long Beach, California, that emphasizes critical thinking, the Intellectual Virtues

Academy (IVA). Philosophers have identified the subfield devoted to the study of intellectual virtues as virtue epistemology. **Epistemology** is the study of knowledge, how it is justified and what knowledge is. Thus, "virtue epistemology" means a morally good approach to the operations of the mind. The moral aspects of beliefs about social racial differences and the right actions concerning race are straightforward. We should believe true things about racial differences and do the right things in situations involving racial differences.

However, the intellectual virtues concerning race come into play regarding scientific findings of the reality of physical races. This is a more abstract issue that may have only subtle or as yet unknown moral effects. We do not know what would happen if the current scientific consensus about the scientific nonexistence of race were widely taught and understood. Some people might become less racist if they understood that there is no scientific foundation for what they experience as racial differences, because the differences may come to seem not as great as they were believed to be. But others may become more racist after they understand race to be purely a **social construction**—that is, a system created in society; they may feel free to believe whatever they choose—especially if they already distrust science. Also, many people of color might feel betrayed if their group's racial identities were developed to resist racism and now scientists and their advocates seem to be undermining those identities.

Philosophers have taken different positions on the lack of a foundation for biological race according to science. **Racial eliminativists** have advocated the removal of ideas of biological race throughout society, particularly in education. But progressive **racial conservationists** have argued that ideas of race should be retained so that nonwhites can continue to resist racism, based on their own racial identities, and for their own self-affirmation, generally. Also, regressive racial conservationists may want to retain the idea of race to preserve beliefs about white superiority.

The first intellectual virtue that applies here is respect for truth. Race is believed to be biological but biologists can't find it in human beings. They may find it in the future but there is no evidence that they will. Scientists cannot prove that human races do not exist, because it is impossible to empirically prove a negative. But they have inductively eliminated all candidates for a scientific foundation for biological human races. Also, the greater variety of racial traits within rather than between social races seems to preclude finding a foundation for race that lines up with social race. Biological science is our ultimate authority for physical-biological reality. Therefore, respect for truth in this case requires accepting the scientific consensus that there is no known biological foundation for human races. However, other moral virtues that are not completely intellectual virtues, come into play.

In 1897 W. E. B. Du Bois (1868–1963) gave an address to the American Negro Academy called "The Conservation of Races." He argued that the social races had their own unique historical destinies and that African Americans should retain their racial identities to fulfill their racial potential. This nineteenth-century idea of historical destiny would not appeal to many today. But loyalty to one's group racial identity and racial self-affirmation are relevant contemporary moral virtues. However, both of these virtues may be strongly associated with the now-false idea that race is biologically real.

There is also an intellectual virtue of respect for truth. The beliefs in racial destiny, loyalty, and self-affirmation might not be held as strongly if the lack of scientific foundation for physical-biological race were recognized. To sum up, older, racist ideas about human races have been discarded in both the physical-biological and social sciences. And yet, some people of color may have aspirational and affirmative ideas about their racial identities that are still attached to discarded scientific ideas. This creates a space for opinion, discussion, and further moral reasoning.

QUESTIONS FOR THINKING, DISCUSSION, AND WRITING

1. Create specific epistemic and practical syllogisms for something you believe and can do concerning race. (Two arguments in the form specified in the first section in this chapter.)
2. Explain how the American Anthropological Association's 1998 Statement of Race separated physical race from psychological and cultural capacities.
3. Spell out why the race-associated difference in IQ and aptitude scores are a moral matter and the moral obligations that arise from them.
4. How would you explain how "race" has no basis in science to a twelve-year-old?
5. How do you balance the virtue of respect for truth regarding the lack of human races in contemporary biological science with other moral virtues pertaining to race?

SOURCES

Alfano, Mark, Latasha Holden, and Andrew Conway. "Intelligence, Race, and Psychological Testing." In Naomi Zack (ed.), *The Oxford Handbook of Philosophy and Race*. Oxford: Oxford University Press, 2017, pp. 474–86. https://philarchive.org/archive/ALFIRAv2.

American Anthropological Association (AAA). "Statement of Race." May 17, 1998, https://www.americananthro.org/ConnectWithAAA/Content.aspx?ItemNumber=2583.

Angier, Natalie. "Do Races Differ? Not Really, Genes Show." *New York Times*, August 22, 2000, https://www.nytimes.com/2000/08/22/science/do-races-differ-not-really-genes-show.html.

Appiah, Kwame Anthony. "The Conservation of 'Race.'" *Black American Literature Forum* 23, no. 1 (Spring 1989): 37–60, https://www.jstor.org/stable/2903987?seq=1#metadata_info_tab_contents.

Du Bois, W. E. B. *The Conservation of Races*. The American Negro Academy Occasional Papers, No. 2. Washington, DC: Published by the Academy, 1897. Project Gutenberg, www.gutenberg.org/etext/31254.

Frith, Susan. "Searching for Sara Baartman." *Johns Hopkins Magazine* 61, no. 3 (June 2009). https://pages.jh.edu/jhumag/0609web/sara.html.

Gould, Stephen Jay. *The Mismeasure of Man*. New York: Norton, 1996.

Hardimon, Michael O. "The Ordinary Concept of Race." *Journal of Philosophy* 100, no. 9 (2003): 437–455. www.jstor.org/stable/3655723.

Intellectual Virtues Academy (IVA). https://www.ivalongbeach.org/.

McCann-Mortimer, P., M. Augoustinos, and A. Lecouteur. "'Race' and the Human Genome Project: Constructions of Scientific Legitimacy." *Discourse and Society* 15, no. 4 (2004): 409–32. doi:10.1177/0957926504043707.

Relethford, John H. "Biological Anthropology, Population Genetics, and Race." In Naomi Zack, ed., *The Oxford Handbook of Philosophy and Race*. New York: Oxford University Press, 2017, pp. 160–69.

Relethford, John H. "Race and Global Patterns of Phenotypic Variation." *American Journal of Physical Anthropology* 139 (2009): 16–22. 10.1002/ajpa.20900.

Sharpley-Whiting, T. Denine. *Black Venus: Sexualized Savages, Primal Fears, and Primitive Narratives*. Durham, NC: Duke University Press, 1999.

Templeton, Alan R. "Human Races: A Genetic and Evolutionary Perspective." *American Anthropology* 100, no. 3 (September 1998): 632–50. https://doi.org/10.1525/aa.1998.100.3.632.

Turri, John, Mark Alfano, and John Greco. "Virtue Epistemology." *The Stanford Encyclopedia of Philosophy* (Fall 2019 Edition), Edward N. Zalta, ed., https://plato.stanford.edu/archives/fall2019/entries/epistemology-virtue/.

Videos

Bradford, Alina. "Deductive Reasoning vs. Inductive Reasoning." Live Science, https://www.livescience.com/21569-deduction-vs-induction.html.

California NewsReel, "Race-The Power of an Illusion." YouTube, https://www.youtube.com/watch?v=Y8MS6zubIaQ&t=121s.

Jablonski, Nina. "Skin color Is an Illusion." TED, 2009, https://www.ted.com/talks/nina_jablonski_skin_color_is_an_illusion?language=en.

Nobis, Nathan. "Moral Arguments: Syllogisms." YouTube, August 13, 2013, https://www.youtube.com/watch?v=xw8DJQRYWXg.

II

LAW AND POLICY

Law is what's written down and enforced by government, and **policy** refers to social rules and practices that may apply law or create egalitarian progress that is not prohibited by law.

Civil rights both safeguard freedoms in societies and allow for citizens in a democracy to participate in government. Chapter 5 explains this social and political distinction within civil rights and the difference between the negative right not to have one's civil liberties interfered with and the positive right to basic goods of life, such as education, health care, poverty relief, and other basic social goods. In chapter 6, the Anglo-dominant aspects of US immigration law before 1965 are first discussed, followed by consideration of new waves of immigration from Latin America and Asia that have required immigration reform that is still in progress. DACA or the policy of deferred action for childhood arrival has had uneven success due to partisan politics. The chapter ends with a dialogue concerning the rights of DACA recipients who were brought into the United States as children by their undocumented parents. Affirmative action was a policy that focused on supporting minority student and employee applicants. Chapter 7 shows how affirmative action was supplanted by ideals of diversity that consider racial integration for all members of an institution. In chapter 8, the policies of compensation, reparation, rectification, and reconciliation are analyzed and contrasted. While all these policies have sometimes led to programs seeking to redress harm to innocent victims, they have different degrees of moral blame ranging from compensation that does not come with blame to rectification that may have an element of punishment. Reparations require acknowledgment of wrongdoing by perpetrators, in addition to compensation, and reconciliation is an effort to publicly air both grievances and wrongdoing and to move on.

5

Civil Rights and Political Rights

President Lyndon Baines Johnson (LBJ) signing the Civil Rights Act, July 2, 1964, with Rev. Dr. Martin Luther King Jr. looking on. Alamy Stock Photo: Photo 12 / Ann Ronan Picture Library.

Voter turnout rose during the 2020 US presidential election and was the highest since at least 1980. Almost two-thirds of eligible voters cast 158.4 million ballots, which was 7 percentage points higher than the 2016 election. Among registered voters, 83 percent said that the contest between incumbent Republican President Donald Trump and Democratic challenger Joe Biden "really mattered." COVID-19 pandemic-related early voting and mail-in ballots were believed to enable the increase. However, even with these figures, voter turnout in the United States ranks twenty-fourth out of thirty-five members of the Organization for Economic Cooperation and Development.

In the 2020 US presidential election, voting by whites without college degrees increased from 65 to 71 percent, and among all racial and ethnic groups, white turnout was highest. There was a 10 percent increase among Asian American voters and 6 percent among Latino and Hispanic voters. Black voter turnout at 63 percent was highest among nonwhite groups, but not as high as it was for the two elections that Barack Obama won in 2008 and 2012. These numbers show that when eligible voters think that an election really matters, nonwhite voters are more likely to vote. But the question is why 2020 presidential voter turnout was not higher among nonwhite voters, especially African Americans, in the wake of George Floyd's killing and protests in response. In the United States, as in other democratic nations, voting is a political right, but it is not a civic obligation—should it be?

While making voting obligatory, perhaps with fines for noncompliance, might increase voter turnout, it would not guarantee informed voting. Informed voting may be the underlying issue for voter turnout because if people do not understand what they would be voting for, they are probably less likely to vote. This means that motivating voter turnout begins not with any election campaign, but in civic education, before the electorate reaches voting age. The idea of an educated and informed electorate has a long history in political philosophy, going back to Plato and Aristotle, who rejected democracy because they thought it would entail rule by the uninformed masses.

In the United States, the term "civil rights" is closely associated with the mid-twentieth-century African American civil rights movement and minority voting access continues to be a pressing and contentious issue. More exactly, **civil rights** are the rights of citizens in societies under government to participate in public life. Civil rights now include the **political rights** of citizens to participate in government, particularly the right to vote. Not everyone, for instance, prisoners and children, or recent immigrants, have full citizenship rights that include political rights. Universal suffrage is a relatively new right. Women did not have political rights until they gained suffrage in 1918 in England and the United States in 1920. Earlier in US history only property owners could vote in.

It is now assumed in modern democracies that nondominant or nonwhite racial identities will not preclude people from having civil rights that include political rights. Civil rights are legal rights under government, and government is supposed to use force, if necessary, to protect them. However, people may have full civil rights and government may fail to protect them or enforce laws against their violations. While civil rights are explicitly protected by law, welfare rights have tended to be matters of policy. Policy is not required by law but may be instituted to apply law, within a jurisdiction or by an institution. Both laws and policies may be morally assessed, and moral principles may be used to advocate legal reforms and innovations. Another way of viewing this structure is that law has a practical reality and citizens are obligated to be law-abiding. Policy is also practical, but compliance has a strong voluntary component. For instance, a policy requiring vaccination may be a condition for employment or participation in an institution, but there is no direct penalty for not getting vaccinated. Morality is a system of values and judgment that can be used to evaluate both laws and policies, but unlike law, it is not enforced, and unlike policy, it is not regulated.

At this time, progressive moral advocacy for greater political equality is most likely to succeed if the history of these ideas and movements is understood. The idea of civil rights has expanded both historically and over recent decades in two parts: securing basic political civil rights and specifically providing for the welfare or wellbeing of minority citizens and residents. If minorities already have the right to vote, then protection of that right or freedom from suppression of it is a **negative right**. Welfare and well-being rights are **positive rights**. This chapter begins with a historical discussion of US minority civil rights, followed by the Voting Rights Act and its reversals, and ending with a consideration of welfare rights as positive rights.

MINORITY CIVIL RIGHTS IN THE UNITED STATES

The US Civil Rights Movement

The African American US civil rights movement is popularly dated from 1948 to 1968, although its history goes back to the initial drafting of the US Constitution, the Emancipation Proclamation constitutional amendments following the Civil War, and a legacy of both rights gained and the incompleteness of racial equality. Also, although African American civil equality was the subject of the civil rights movement, Native Americans and people with disabilities launched concurrent movements in the United States, and the US civil rights movement itself caught on globally. Here is an abridged version of the US civil rights timeline provided by History.com.

July 26, 1948 President Harry Truman issued Executive Order 9981 that made segregation in the armed services illegal.

May 17, 1954 The US Supreme Court decided *Brown v. Board of Education,* to end racial segregation in public schools.

August 28, 1955 Fourteen-year-old Emmett Till from Chicago was brutally murdered in Mississippi for allegedly flirting with a white woman. *Jet* magazine published a photo of his beaten body in an open-casket funeral. Those accused of his murder were acquitted.

December 1, 1955 Rosa Parks refused to give up her seat to a white man on a Montgomery, Alabama, bus. Her arrest prompted a year-long Montgomery bus boycott.

January 10–11, 1957 Sixty black pastors and civil rights leaders from several southern states—including Martin Luther King Jr.—met in Atlanta, Georgia, to coordinate non-violent protests against racial discrimination and segregation.

September 4, 1957 Black students known as the "Little Rock Nine" were blocked from integrating into Little Rock Central High School in Little Rock, Arkansas. President Dwight D. Eisenhower sent federal troops to escort them but harassment continued.

September 9, 1957 President Eisenhower signed the Civil Rights Act of 1957 to protect voter rights, by allowing federal prosecution of those who suppress others' right to vote.

February 1, 1960 Four African American college students in Greensboro, North Carolina, refused to leave a Woolworth's "whites-only" lunch counter without being served. The Greensboro Sit-In inspired further "sit-ins" throughout the city and in other states.

November 14, 1960 Six-year-old Ruby Bridges was escorted by four armed federal marshals as the first black student to integrate William Frantz Elementary School in New Orleans.

1961 Throughout 1961, Black and white activists, known as Freedom Riders, took bus trips through the American South to protest segregated bus terminals and attempted to use "whites-only" restrooms and lunch counters. The Freedom Riders were met with violence from white protestors, but they drew international attention to their cause.

June 11, 1963 Governor George C. Wallace stood in a doorway at the University of Alabama to block two black students from registering. President John F. Kennedy sent the National Guard to the campus.

August 28, 1963 About 250,000 people took part in the March on Washington for Jobs and Freedom. Martin Luther King Jr. gave his "I Have a Dream" speech.

September 15, 1963 A bomb at the 16th Street Baptist Church in Birmingham, Alabama, killed four young girls and injured several others before Sunday services.

July 2, 1964 President Lyndon B. Johnson signed the Civil Rights Act of 1964 into law, preventing employment discrimination due to race, color, sex, religion, or national origin. Title VII of the act established the US Equal Employment Opportunity Commission (EEOC) to help prevent workplace discrimination.

February 21, 1965 Black religious leader Malcolm X was assassinated by members of the Nation of Islam.

March 7, 1965 Bloody Sunday. In the Selma to Montgomery March, around 600 civil rights marchers walked from Selma, Alabama, to Montgomery to protest black voter suppression. Local police blocked and attacked them. After court battles for their right to march, Martin Luther King Jr. and other civil rights leaders led two more marches and finally reached Montgomery on March 25.

August 6, 1965 President Johnson signed the Voting Rights Act of 1965, which outlawed literacy tests as a voting requirement and allowed federal examiners to review voter qualifications and federal observers to monitor polling places.

April 4, 1968 Martin Luther King Jr. was assassinated in Memphis, Tennessee. James Earl Ray was convicted of the murder in 1969.

April 11, 1968 President Johnson signed the Civil Rights Act of 1968, also known as the Fair Housing Act, providing equal housing opportunity regardless of race, religion, or national origin.

There were several historical motivations for the civil rights movement: The US Constitution had stipulated that slaves were to count as three-fifths of a person for political representation. After the Civil War there were three constitutional amendments toward racial equality for freed slaves: The Thirteenth Amendment abolished slavery; the Fourteen Amendment provided for equal protection under the law, regardless of "race or color"; the Fifteenth Amendment gave black men the right to vote, stating that this right could not be "diluted or abridged" based on "race or color." However, racially discriminatory **Jim Crow** policies set in after Reconstruction, when Union forces had occupied the defeated South and African Americans achieved a measure of civil equality. In southern states, the right to vote was suppressed by literacy tests, all-white electoral primaries, and violent deterrents for blacks who voted. Segregation prevailed in public facilities. In education, racial segregation was upheld under the fiction that schools were "separate but equal," although schools for African Americans were never equal to the resources or teacher qualifications in schools for whites. Public bathrooms, restaurants, and water fountains were also segregated, as was housing, but voter suppression and segregated education had direct effects on blocking future nonwhite leadership in society.

As documented, the US civil rights movement was a struggle that consisted of presidential orders, protests, violent reactions, federal executive laws, and court decisions. The main civil issues were racial integration in public facilities and voting rights. The battles involved were moral matters for those who pushed for change but also struggles for access to resources and power in society. To a large extent, the Civil War amendments had set legal, constitutional precedent for the movement's demand for protected civil rights. This shows that even morality and law together may not be enough to create progressive change, and it raises further moral questions about what can be done, at this time. We will discuss employment, education, and housing, where racial inequalities persist, in the chapters of part III. Here, it is important to note how racial voter suppression has become indirect compared to outright Jim Crow racial voter suppression.

THE VOTING RIGHTS ACT AND ITS REVERSALS

The 1965 Voting Rights Act (VRA) reduced state legal control over voting, moving much of it to the federal government. Voting qualifications and procedures that had "denied or abridged" minority voting were banned. The "coverage formula" of the VRA was applied to jurisdictions that used a literacy test for registration or had less than half of eligible voters registered or voter turnout of less than half. Federal examiners were appointed to prepare and maintain voting rolls, and federal approval was necessary to change state election rules. In 2006, the VRA was reauthorized to block *voter dilution* where at-large county board voting had been substituted for election by districts, of which some were majority black—the votes from majority black districts had thereby been outnumbered or diluted.

In the 2013 US Supreme Court ruling in *Shelby County v. Holder*, the coverage formula was struck down. The Court claimed that there had been improvement in black registration and voting throughout the South and referred to a legal principle that "all states enjoy equal sovereignty." In other words, the Court was more concerned that all states be treated equally than that all citizens have equal voting rights or not concerned that supporting states' rights might undermine the rights of eligible black voters.

In addition to legal principles such as states' rights that are connected to voter dilution, there are indirect effects of party politics, which have included *gerrymandering* or redrawing electoral districts so that a favored party has a majority in districts that formerly may have gone to the other party or been contentious. It has been claimed that Republicans throughout the United States have since 2000 masterminded gerrymandering in their favor, with the indirect result that bias against Democratic victories reduces the impact of minority voters who vote Democratic. This is a difficult problem to correct. After the Supreme Court had ruled that states should create districts with a majority of minorities, and some states did that, it was claimed that this redistricting had the effect and therefore the intention to reduce Democratic voters in districts adjacent to the new districts with racial-minority majorities.

Party politics has also made it more difficult for minorities to cast ballots in states where Republican legislatures have introduced new voter restrictions out of unfounded stated concern about voter fraud and other irregularities. After the civil rights legislation, President Nixon and other Republicans had appealed to white voters with implied alignment with their antiblack racism and white grievance, through the so-called Southern Strategy. Such implicit appeals may have been behind recent Republican state laws that Democrats have viewed as forms of minority voter suppression. After Joe Biden's Democratic win in the 2020 presidential election voter suppression was spurred on by former President Trump's unfounded but politically popular claim that this election was stolen from him. Two new laws in Arizona were challenged, the first banning collection of absentee ballots by anyone other than a relative or caregiver, and the second allowing ballots cast in the wrong precinct to be discarded. On July 1, 2021, the US Supreme Court ruled in favor of these Arizona laws, dismissing their effect on minorities as minor, referring to similar laws in other states, and dismissing the lack of evidence for fraud because states have a right to pass preemptive laws to prevent it. To sum up, although racial minorities have legal voter protection, the law itself in both states and the US Supreme Court has been used to weaken that protection. What's left are moral claims that may motivate fresh legal action to protect voting rights for minorities.

WELFARE AS POSITIVE RIGHTS

Aspirations of minorities often include enforcement of their rights and sometimes new rights are claimed by them and their advocates. As noted, there are two kinds of rights at issue here: **negative rights** or freedoms from certain harms as legally specified and **positive rights** or claims for greater well-being. The US Bill of Rights is the first ten amendments of the Constitution. Notice the language of Amendments I, II, III, IV, and V as italicized herein.

Amendment I
Congress shall make no law respecting an establishment of religion, or prohibiting the free exercise thereof; or abridging the freedom of speech, or of the press; or the right of the people peaceably to assemble, and to petition the government for a redress of grievances.

Amendment II
A well-regulated militia, being necessary to the security of a free state, the right of the people to keep and bear arms, *shall not be infringed.*

Amendment III
No soldier shall, in time of peace be quartered in any house, without the consent of the owner, nor in time of war, but in a manner to be prescribed by law.

Amendment IV
The right of the people to be secure in their persons, houses, papers, and effects, *against unreasonable searches and seizures,* shall not be violated, and *no warrants shall issue,* but upon probable cause, supported by oath or affirmation, and particularly describing the place to be searched, and the persons or things to be seized.

Amendment V
No person shall be held to answer for a capital, or otherwise infamous crime, unless on a presentment or indictment of a grand jury, except in cases arising in the land or naval forces, or in the militia, when in actual service in time of war or public danger; *nor shall any person be* subject for the same offense to be twice put in jeopardy of life or limb; nor shall be compelled in any criminal case to be a witness against himself, *nor be deprived* of life, liberty, or property, without due process of law; nor shall private property be taken for public use, without just compensation.

These amendments, such as establishing religion and freedom of speech (I), keeping arms (II), being secure in their persons and possessions, fair legal procedures (III and IV), and a trial according to law (V) refer to preexisting rights and the emphasis is on what government is not allowed to do to citizens regarding these rights. What government is not allowed to do is the sphere of **negative rights** or, here, freedoms from harms that would violate natural rights. **Natural rights** are the rights human beings are supposed to have, either before the existence of government or morally, independently of government.

Racial and ethnic minorities in the United States and throughout the world have fought hard for recognition of their negative rights. However, many progressives also believe that all people, and especially racial and ethnic minorities who are disadvantaged compared to dominant groups, have positive rights. **Positive rights** are freedoms to certain necessary goods of life, such as education, health care, unemployment compensation, and government assistance in special emergency or disaster circumstances. In many democratic countries, they now include permanent safety-net programs and can be generally called "welfare" or "entitlements." Many now believe that the existence of and justification for positive rights is self-evident. All three moral systems of virtue ethics, deontology, and utilitarianism can be used to justify positive rights: Altruism or concern for the welfare of others is a virtue. Those well off are obligated to help those worse off. If those worse off become better off, the sum-total of well-being in society will increase. However, in the United States, such positive rights have been contentious and subject to political victories or defeats. We will continue the discussion of positive rights regarding racial minorities in future chapters. But we should note here that legislation and policy to protect negative rights, such as the political civil right to vote, which is already legally granted, have been easier to secure than positive rights, although not without backlash. The political opposition to positive rights for minorities presents a further obstacle for progressives that is borne out historically.

QUESTIONS FOR THINKING, DISCUSSION, AND WRITING

1. Why do you think black voter turnout was higher for Barack Obama's election than for the 2020 election? Should eligible voters who fail to vote be fined? (Give reasons pro or con.)
2. What do you think the main moral issues were in the US civil rights movement?
3. Explain how voter suppression has become entangled with both states' rights doctrine and party politics. Does each of these make voter suppression less or more of a moral issue?
4. Is freedom from voter suppression a negative right or a positive right? Explain.
5. Explain how welfare rights are positive rights compared to negative rights. Do you think positive or negative rights are more important morally? Why? (Hint: This could be reasoned out by considering the difference between not being allowed to harm someone and being obligated to help them.)

SOURCES

Aistrup, Joseph A. *Southern Strategy Revisited: Republican Top-Down Advancement in the South.* Lexington: University Press of Kentucky, 1996.

Baldwin, Bridgette. "Backsliding: The United States Supreme Court, Shelby County v. Holder and the Dismantling of Voting Rights Act of 1965." *Berkeley Journal of African-American Law and Policy* 251(2014), HeinOnline, https://heinonline.org/HOL/LandingPage?handle=hein.journals/afamlpol16&div=35&id=&page=.

DeSilver, Drew. "Turnout Soared in 2020 as Nearly Two-Thirds of Eligible U.S. Voters Cast Ballots for President." Pew Research Center, January 28, 2021, https://www.pewresearch.org/fact-tank/2021/01/28/turnout-soared-in-2020-as-nearly-two-thirds-of-eligible-u-s-voters-cast-ballots-for-president/.

Foldvary, F. E. "Positive Rights." In D. K. Chatterjee (ed.), *Encyclopedia of Global Justice.* Springer, Dordrecht, 2011, https://doi.org/10.1007/978-1-4020-9160-5_359/.

Frey, William H. "Turnout in 2020 Election Spiked among Both Democratic and Republican Voting Groups, New Census Data Shows." Brookings, May 5, 2021, https://www.brookings.edu/research/turnout-in-2020-spiked-among-both-democratic-and-republican-voting-groups-new-census-data-shows/.

Soffen, Kim. "How Racial Gerrymandering Deprives Black People of Political Power." HeinOnline, Sup. Ct. Preview 438 (2016–2017), https://heinonline.org/HOL/LandingPage?handle=hein.journals/suemrtpre24&div=94&id=&page=.

Totenberg, Nina. "The Supreme Court Deals a New Blow to Voting Rights, Upholding Arizona Restrictions." NPR, July 1, 2021, https://www.npr.org/2021/07/01/998758022/the-supreme-court-upheld-upholds-arizona-measures-that-restrict-voting. See also, *Brnovich, Attorney General of Arizona, et al. v. Democratic National Committee et al.*, https://www.supremecourt.gov/opinions/20pdf/19-1257_g204.pdf.

Videos

History.com, Editors. "9 Civil Rights Leaders You Need to Know." https://www.history.com/topics/civil-rights-movement/9-civil-rights-leaders-you-need-to-know-video.

History.com, Editors. "Civil Rights Movement Timeline." History, December 4, 2017/January 19, 2021, https://www.history.com/topics/civil-rights-movement/civil-rights-movement-timeline.

History.com, Editors. "How the Montgomery Bus Boycott Accelerated the Civil Rights Movement." https://www.history.com/topics/black-history/montgomery-bus-boycott-video.

6

Immigration

Cleveland, Ohio, USA, July 18, 2016: Young Hispanics support the Dream Act at the "Stop Trump" march on the first day of the Republican National Convention. The DACA (Deferred Action for Childhood Arrivals) program defers immigration enforcement action against young people brought to the United States illegally as children.
Getty Images: vichinterlang.

Since pre-recorded times, human beings have been on the move. The recognition of nation-states from the seventeenth century onward resulted in two often vague moral principles about who may cross national borders to join a nation. The first is that nations have a right to protect their interests by excluding some from joining them and regulating lawful immigration. The second principle is that nations should be hospitable to refugees or those fleeing oppression. There is a third factor of self-interest—nations adopt policies of immigration that serve their internal interests, such as needs for workers in expanding economies or needs for specialists in technical and professional fields.

There have also been norms for how immigrants are treated after they arrive. In a society such as the United States that is dominated by members of specific racial and ethnic groups, regardless of how hospitable and welcoming members of dominant groups describe themselves, immigrants need to begin their new lives where they fit into existing racial and ethnic hierarchies. Some black immigrants to the United States have been surprised to encounter antiblack racism, while others express apprehension about their transition in status from societies in which they were members of racial majorities to a society in which they will be a minority. For instance, Robert, a college student from Trinidad and Tobago, said, "Being around everybody that's white, predominantly, and you're the only person of some type of color in there . . . I've never really done it, so that's one thing I'll be kinda nervous about."

Black immigrants from Africa and the Caribbean usually arrive with fluency in English but may still require help with language skills, in addition to facing distinct vulnerabilities and disadvantages. Racially biased attention from police can result in criminal deportation. They are least likely to become homeowners among all immigrant groups. And although since 1970, black immigrants have increased to make up 10 percent of the African American population, their problems as immigrants are likely to be overlooked because immigration is more often associated with differences in non-black ethnicity or national origin, rather than black race.

All immigrant groups have faced obstacles to civil and social equality in the United States. During the colonial period, Scots and Germans were at a disadvantage compared to the English who were culturally dominant. Over the nineteenth century, through the early twentieth, different waves of immigrants from Europe, for instance from Germany, experienced lower status compared to earlier arrivals from their countries of origin. Immigrants from Ireland and southern and eastern Europe faced distinct aversions and hostilities. However, all the disfavored European groups eventually assimilated into the American mainstream, when what was first considered racial difference came to be seen as ethnic difference—all the European ethnic distinctions morphed into a generic white American identity.

For a while, immigration from Asia was virtually banned and Asians were not among the groups who became generically white. Immigrants who arrived after the 1960s no longer had mainly European origins but came from South and Central America, Africa, and Asia, as well as the Middle East. These groups have neither fully assimilated nor been welcomed as Americans by dominant European groups. This chapter aims to highlight key aspects of these diverse movements. The first section presents an overview of European American immigration before 1965, followed by a very different immigration pattern after 1965. The second section contains a dialogue about the moral issues raised by the predicament of "Dreamers" or Deferred Action for Childhood Arrival (DACA) groups. The last section provides an overview of the main tensions embedded in US immigration, from colonial times to the present.

US IMMIGRATION BEFORE AND AFTER 1965

Immigration before 1965

The United States is often called "a nation of immigrants," and the famous inscription on the Statue of Liberty by Emma Lazarus proclaims their welcome: "Give me your tired, your poor, Your huddled masses yearning to breathe free, The wretched refuse of your teeming shore." However, except for original English settlers and planters, no immigrant group has received a whole-hearted welcome upon arrival. During the colonial period, the English showed contempt for the Scots, and Benjamin Franklin was concerned that those of German "complexion" would taint British culture. Over the nineteenth and through the early twentieth century, different groups, such as Poles, Italians, Jews, and Irish, who would later assimilate with great success as whites, were not considered racially white. Indeed, Madison Grant's (1865–1937) hugely popular 1916 book, *The Passing of the Great Race: Or, The Racial Basis of European History* provided a ranked taxonomy among groups now considered white.

Franz Boas (1858–1942), acclaimed German Jewish-American anthropologist, who had helped separate ideas of inherited biological race from culture, warned his colleagues about the habits and cultures of "types different from our own." In "Problems of Race in America," his 1908 address to the American Association for the Advancement of Science, Boas expressed concerns about differences in culture brought by a new wave of immigrants from eastern and southern Europe. He said:

> With the economic development of Germany, German immigration has dwindled down; while at the same time Italians, the various Slavic people of Austria, Russia, and the Balkan Peninsula, Hungarians, Roumanians, east European Hebrews, not to mention the numerous other nationalities, have arrived in ever-increasing numbers. There is no doubt that these people of eastern and southern Europe represent a physical type distinct from the physical type [from] northwestern Europe; and it is clear, even to the most casual observer, that their present social standards differ fundamentally from our own. Since the number of new arrivals may be counted in normal years by hundreds of thousands, the question may well be asked, What will be result of this influx of types distinct from our own, if it is to continue for a considerable length time?

The immigrants Boas referred to were nonetheless welcome as workers in the factories in American cities, during a time of great industrial expansion. Over the same period, immigrants from Scandinavia contributed to the expansion of the US west. All groups took advantage of economic opportunities. European groups eventually moved out of their ethnic enclaves in cities to create American suburbia following World War II. Immigration law grudgingly accommodated them, over time.

However, a well-entrenched tradition of blaming immigrants for economic problems persisted. After agitation from white landowners, the Chinese Exclusion Act of 1882 banned Chinese laborers from coming to the United States. In 1892, Ellis

Island in New York Harbor was designated a federal immigration station—by 1954, twelve million were to pass through. The peak year was 1907 during which 1.3 million arrived. In 1917, immigrants over age sixteen were required to pass a literacy test. The Immigration Act of 1924 established a quota system restricting entry to 2 percent of the number of people from each country who were already in the United States. Those in the majority, such as northern Europeans, had better prospects for entry and further population growth in the United States and which was the general intention.

Immigration after 1965

The Immigration and Naturalization Act of 1965/Hart-Celler Act was in spirit part of the civil rights movement in decreasing official and public racial and ethnic discrimination. The traditional quota system based on national origin alone was replaced by policies to reunite families and encourage skilled workers to immigrate. As a result, instead of coming predominantly from Europe, immigrants increasingly came from Asia, Africa, and Latin America. And along with the geographical shift, there was a racial and ethnic shift, away from white, non-Hispanic/Latinx immigrants. By the end of the twentieth century, over nineteen million legal immigrants entered the United States, and this was triple the number between 1935 and 1965. Of these, 4.3 million came from Mexico and 1.4 million from the Philippines, while 700,000 to 800,000 came from each of Korea, the Dominican Republic, India, Cuba, and Vietnam.

The 1990 Immigration Act further increased immigrant diversity by allowing for increased admission from "underrepresented countries." The immigration flow continued in the 2000s except for a decrease during the 2008–2009 Great Recession and the COVID-19 pandemic. New problems concerning undocumented immigrants captured public concern, with periodic laws and policies to offer amnesty, which were then withdrawn. Some have voiced concern about greater competition for low-skilled jobs and the loss of cultural homogeneity (or overall sameness). The ease of air travel and practice of remittance or sending money home to relatives have made it easier for some post–1965 US immigrants to retain identities based on their birth nations. However, current research suggests that immigrants after 1965 have been more successful as time goes on, with progress in education, earnings, language skills, and occupational mobility. Although members of native-born groups continue to be more successful, women in the new immigrant groups have also made greater progress than women in traditional waves of European immigration—perhaps because of the success of the feminist and womanist movements after 1970.

Immigration following the 1965 act changed the racial and ethnic demographics of the United States. According to 2020 census data, between 2016 and 2019, the white population in the United States declined by half a million to make up 61 percent of the total population. Between 2010 and 2020, the 6.3 percent growth in the national population was entirely due to increases in racially and ethnically diverse groups: Latino or Hispanic, Asian American, and black populations grew by rates of 20 percent, 29 percent, and 8.5 percent, respectively. Numbers such as this are said to make many white Americans feel anxious, insecure, and fearful. Such white apprehension, stoked by populist politicians, is based on several assumptions. The first is that democracy is governed by numerical majorities. We know this isn't always true. For instance, some of the most repressive southern states had black majorities as did South Africa under apartheid. Second, respect for individual rights is an important component of democracy, regardless of the nature or wishes of any majority. And third, insofar as the United States is already a racially hierarchical society, there is little reason to believe that a shift in demographic numbers alone could change that.

Finally, the apprehension of losing position because one's racial group is no longer in the numerical majority bypasses recognition of the value of belonging to a cosmopolitan whole. **Cosmopolitanism** is an ideal that locates individuals into a diverse totality of humanity. As an aspiration going back to ancient Greece and Rome, with followers among philosophers and the Roman statesman Cicero (106–43 BC), cosmopolitans have posited human equality, while also allowing for stronger ties of individuals to family, group, and nation. The idea of a nation of immigrants could be a cosmopolitan ideal because the experiences of diverse racial, ethnic, and national groups could be shared as parts of a unifying identity.

THE MORAL ISSUE OF DACA

The Dream Act was first proposed in the US Senate as Development, Relief, and Education for Alien Minors Act (D-R-E-A-M) in 2001. It would have given lawful residence for six years to those illegally brought to the United States before age sixteen, who passed criminal background checks, and who had high school or GED degrees. Those qualified would then be eligible for permanent status or a "green card." The Dream Act was proposed to Congress at least ten times but has not yet passed. A recent version cleared the House of Representatives as "The American Dream and Promise Act of 2021," but awaits Senate passage. This act specifies three stages: first, "conditional permanent residence" that grants work authorization and protection from deportation; second, a green card; and third, after five years of holding a green card, Dreamers could apply for **naturalized citizenship** or citizenship granted to those whose parents were not citizens when they were born.

Pending passage of a Dream Act, in 2012, President Obama created DACA, which is a renewable, two-year work permit. The future of DACA as well as the Dream Act has become entangled in party politics, with Democrats in support and Republicans opposed. However, there are moral questions behind this political tension. As of March 2021, there have been 616,030 DACA recipients with total eligibility of 1,331,000. California and Texas have the highest DACA numbers. Mexico leads as the country of origin, followed by El Salvador, Honduras, and Guatemala. Additional origin countries include Korea, Brazil, Ecuador, and Columbia. The Hispanic/Latinx majority of DACA applicants signals that this immigrant population is part of the growing US racial/ethnic minority population.

People are not generally held responsible for the actions of their parents. DACA immigrants may be deported simply because of their unofficial US resident status or if they are convicted of crimes for which other immigrants who are in the United States legally would not be deported. Both deportation based on the undocumented status of one's parents and deportation triggered by actions applying only to members of one's immigrant group are not fair. But are such official actions morally wrong and if they are, why? Let's consider a pro and con dialogue.

Against deportations: These deportations are morally wrong because deportation is viewed as a form of punishment, akin to banishment, and those deported are innocent of behavior for which they can be justly banished.

Pro deportations: Members of the DACA group are not being punished but simply prevented from continuing to benefit from something that their parents illegally obtained for them. If a parent steals an expensive toy for their child, the child is not entitled to keep the toy simply because they are a child. And by the same token, all children experience advantages or disadvantages based on their parents' resources. The children of parents without the resources of legal residence face the disadvantage of deportation. This is no worse than the disadvantage of not getting a college education simply because one's parents cannot afford to pay for one.

Against deportation: If the removal of the toy would traumatize the child, that is a new harm to the child. If young adults are sent to their places of original national origin, when in many cases they do not know anyone there or speak the language, then a new harm is being inflicted on them. Also, just as "possession is nine-tenths of the law," having a lifestyle should not be disrupted, because a person has a natural right to their lifestyle and deportation takes that away. Thus, the longer the period in which the child of undocumented immigrants resides in the United States, the stronger their right to continue to reside there.

Pro deportation: This argument is like claiming that if someone repeatedly commits a crime without having been caught and punished, then they should never be caught and punished. Rather, the longer the period in which the child of undocumented immigrants resides in the United States, the greater their offense and the stronger the right of the government to deport them.

Against deportation: But the child did not commit the crime, the parent did. Also, when children are placed in disadvantaged circumstances by their parents, they are usually helped, for instance, financial aid to college students from poor families. DACA children or young adults should be helped.

Pro deportation: When their undocumented parents brought them to the United States, they thought they were helping them by giving them a better life. And DACA children and young adults have experienced a better life. To say that they should be helped because of disadvantage is to overlook the fact that their only disadvantage is deportation and to say that they should be helped because of that is to beg the question or assume what has to be proved.

Against deportation: A final consideration is whether the deportation of DACA recipients is discriminatory, given the US history of different immigration policies for non-European immigrants and the fact that the majority of DACA immigrants are Hispanic/Latino. We could ask whether the opposition to the Dream Act is based on the race or ethnicity of its applicants and whether this opposition would be as strong were the DACA applicants from traditional European immigrant groups. We might also wonder whether some of the political opposition is meant to play on fears among parts of the white electorate that the United States will soon no longer be a white non-Hispanic-majority nation, demographically.

TENSIONS EMBEDDED IN US IMMIGRATION

It is correct to call the United States "a nation of immigrants," but only if the focus is on newcomers who have been recognized as white upon their arrival or over generations become accepted as white. Immigration implies voluntary arrival. Enslaved Africans who were forcibly brought to US shores were not immigrants and neither were Native Americans living on the continent before European settlers arrived. Also, recent years have seen widespread refusal to recognize Asian Americans and Islamic Americans as immigrants, attaching a permanent status as "foreigners" to them. This last shows that many in the United States still have a strong sense of "them versus us." A good part of what makes a group "them" is visible nonwhite minority identities.

Interwoven with issues that have connected US nationality with racial whiteness are the issues of how and when there are economic benefits from immigration and the issue of an international obligation to provide entry and welcome to refugees. To an extent, preference for racially white immigrants obscures the issue of international obligation. But as climate change progresses and civil unrest breaks out in poor, nonwhite parts of the world, this issue is likely to become more intense. Americans have had plenty of discussions about the appeal of a free country to political refugees. Indeed, the often-quoted Emma Lazutus poem focuses on political freedom. However, an international moral obligation to open borders to those seeking entry for material reasons, including an ability to survive, has not received as much attention. What should US policy be toward those seeking entry who may not at the outset provide needed work or skills, but present desperate needs? That is a moral issue, calling for religious and secular virtue ethics, duty ethics, and utilitarianism, if the whole world is included as a subject for the greater good.

QUESTIONS FOR THINKING, DISCUSSION, AND WRITING

1. Granted that newly encountered racial discrimination among black immigrants is unfair, how do you think these immigrants might respond?
2. How can pride in the United States as a "nation of immigrants" be reconciled with restrictions on immigration?
3. Contrast the US history of European immigrants with the majority of immigrants after 1965. Do you think that natural citizens have a moral obligation to immigrants and do immigrants have moral obligations to natural citizens? If yes, what are they in each case?
4. What does white fear of a demographic shift toward whites becoming a minority assume? How do you evaluate those assumptions, and do you think anything is left out in the account of them in this chapter? If so, what?
5. Should DACA children and young adults be deported, or do they have a moral right to remain in the United States? State your reasons either way and refer to the dialogue in this chapter.

SOURCES

American Bar Association. "Helping Dreamers Realize Their Dreams: The Nuts and Bolts of DACA." Webinar program, Commission on Hispanic Legal Rights and Responsibilities, https://www.americanbar.org/groups/diversity/commission_on_hispanic_legal_rights_responsibilities/Webinars/daca-helping-dreamers-webinar/.

Chishti, Muzaffar, Faye Hipsman, and Isabel Ball. "Fifty Years On, the 1965 Immigration and Nationality Act Continues to Reshape the United States." Migration Policy Institute, October 15, 2015, https://www.migrationpolicy.org/article/fifty-years-1965-immigration-and-nationality-act-continues-reshape-united-states.

Frey, William H. "The Nation Is Diversifying Even Faster Than Predicted, According to New Census Data." Brookings, July 1, 2020, https://www.brookings.edu/research/new-census-data-shows-the-nation-is-diversifying-even-faster-than-predicted/.

Glick, Leonard B. "Types Distinct from Our Own: Franz Boas on Jewish Identity and Assimilation." *American Anthropologist* 84, no. 3 (September 1982): 545–65. Published by Wiley on behalf of the American Anthropological Association Stable URL, https://www.jstor.org/stable/677332.

History.com Editors. "U.S. Immigration before 1965." History, April 20, 2021, https://www.history.com/topics/immigration/u-s-immigration-before-1965.

History.com Editors. "U.S. Immigration since 1965." History, June 7, 2019, https://www.history.com/topics/immigration/us-immigration-since-1965.

Immigrant Learning Center. "What Does It Mean to Be a Black Immigrant in the United States?" June 19, 2020, https://www.ilctr.org/what-does-it-mean-to-be-black-immigrant-united-states/.

Kleingeld, Pauline, and Eric Brown. "Cosmopolitanism." *The Stanford Encyclopedia of Philosophy* (Winter 2019 Edition), Edward N. Zalta, ed., https://plato.stanford.edu/archives/win2019/entries/cosmopolitanism/.

Migration Policy.org. "Deferred Action for Childhood Arrivals (DACA) Data." Tools, https://www.migrationpolicy.org/programs/data-hub/deferred-action-childhood-arrivals-daca-profiles?gclid=CjwKCAjw4KyJBhAbEiwAaAQbE4LHnQEXXpmV2M-sHe_LwCOfR0u-OGb4Fqg92f86oeprYJxuAlG7PhoCi40QAvD_BwE.

Morse, David. "Fears of a Non-White Majority." New American Dimensions, https://www.newamericandimensions.com/how-to-mitigate-fears-of-a-non white-majority/.

Petts, Jonathan. "All about the DREAM Act 2021," Immigrationhelp.org, April 30, 2021, https://www.immigrationhelp.org/learning-center/all-about-the-dream-act-2021.

Sears, David O., Mingying Fu, P. J. Henry, and Kerra Bui. "The Origins and Persistence of Ethnic Identity among the 'New Immigrant' Groups." *Social Psychology Quarterly* 66, no. 4 (December 2003), https://www.jstor.org/stable/1519838?seq=1#metadata_info_tab_contents.

Thernstrom, Stephan, Ann Orlov, and Oscar Handlin. *Harvard Encyclopedia of American Ethnic Groups.* Cambridge, MA: Belknap Press, 1980.

Videos

ARCGIS.com. "Ethnic Landscapes: A Story Map." TEDx, https://www.arcgis.com/apps/MapJournal/index.html?appid=5312ef7ade7e4b5ba71ff194a52d8718.

Immigrant Legal Center (ILC). "We Are Dreamers." YouTube, February 8, 2018, https://www.youtube.com/watch?v=jOdLqct0rmo.

Muscato, Christopher. "Ethnic Enclaves in America." Study.com, https://study.com/academy/lesson/what-is-an-ethnic-enclave-definition-examples-types.html.

7

Affirmative Action and Diversity

College friends walking on campus and talking. Getty Images: Prostock-Studio.

Basic or core human abilities and aptitudes, as well as innate skills, do not vary according to race (see chapter 3). But that is not always evident in society. Since the 1960s civil rights movement, racial equality has been a widely shared legal norm that is also believed to be morally right. But how to reach equality and the very meaning of equality in a racially unequal society have been contentious and controversial subjects. Should people be treated unequally based on race to reach racial equality? Does equality require not only equal opportunities but equal outcomes based on the racial proportions of those in the larger population who take advantage of them? If outcomes are not equal, does that mean there were not equal opportunities to begin with, and do we need to consider equality in access to opportunities? These questions are especially important regarding higher education because a college degree can open doors to greater socioeconomic mobility and well-being in general.

These are the census statistics for 2019 among ages twenty-five and higher, who had a bachelor's degree: 40.1 percent of non-Hispanic whites, 26.1 percent of blacks, 58.1 percent of Asians, and 18.8 percent of Hispanics. About 41 percent of the US population attends college, and people of color are less likely to achieve college degrees than whites. But the US undergraduate student body has become more diverse over time. In 2015–2016, approximately 45 percent of all undergraduate students identified as nonwhite, compared with 29.6 percent in 1995–1996. Much of this increase in diversity is due to higher Hispanic/Latino enrollment, which went from 10.3 to 19.8 percent from 2015–2016 to 2019. Over the same time, black enrollment increased from 12.3 to 15.2 percent. While these figures are close to the proportions of Hispanic/Latinos and blacks in the overall population, they are not evenly distributed over the entire system of US higher education. In states with small numbers of minority populations, specific schools may have far fewer minority students than is representative of their percentage of the whole population. Also, elite colleges and universities may have lower than proportional minority enrollment. As a result, some schools may have an urgent mission to recruit more minority students.

The opportunities for college admission are open to all applicants, regardless of race. Still, consider an African American high school student who has not been well prepared for college entrance exams or received counseling on how to apply to college. Consider, by contrast, a white applicant who has had attentive counseling and whose parents have paid for a private preparation course for college entrance exams. Comparing any two individuals in this way may not be generally informative, but it is well known that white middle-class high school students, as a group, are better prepared to successfully apply to college than their peers who are students of color—even if they live in the same city.

New York City has a few specialized high schools that prepare their students for attendance at top colleges and universities. Since 1970, a standardized test for admission to these high schools has been available to all middle school students. Black and Hispanic students have scored lower on this test than white and Asian students and, as a result, their enrollment in the specialized high schools has decreased by about two-thirds. There is an effective preparation course for the test that costs about $1,000 for eight sessions, although very few of the parents of the black and Hispanic students can afford it or even know that it is necessary. Notice that being unable to take a prep course for a standardized test can be a barrier to the opportunity presented by the test. Also, if a black or Hispanic student does take the test, they may not be as well prepared academically as white or Asian students, depending on the quality of the schools they have attended thus far. And they may experience stereotype threats (see chapter 3) in embarking on the test. There may not be support for higher education in their families, based on generational experience. These racial and ethnic differences in opportunities for higher education raise the question of whether intervention is required to increase equality of access. And there is a related question about the effect of intervention on white students.

After college or high school, comes employment. Recent studies indicate that those whose names signal nonwhite identities are less likely to get job interviews. In response to this data, some nonwhite applicants have begun to "whiten" their resumés. Throughout major institutions in US society, top leadership positions such as CEOs and presidents are not proportionately occupied by minorities: 30 percent Asian, 19 percent Hispanic/Latino, and 5 percent black. The racial and ethnic proportions in the population in percent are: white, 63.7; black, 12.2; Hispanic, 18.7; and Asian, 4.7. So whites and Asians are over-represented at the top, blacks the most under-represented, and Hispanic/Latinos about proportionately represented.

About fifteen million Americans hold management positions, earning twice as much as average workers, but managerial employment is not equally distributed based on race/ethnicity in the larger population. Among the top three racial/ethnic groups, whites occupy 82 percent, African Americans 7.98 percent, and Asians 6.3 percent. However, many corporations and institutions, as well as colleges and universities, now include racial and ethnic diversity as an asset to strive for. This raises questions about what can be done legally and what should be done morally.

Altogether, the statistics for education and employment consistently show that African Americans are the most disadvantaged among the most populous racial/ethnic groups. It is therefore not surprising that discussions of affirmative action and diversity have focused on African Americans. The first part of this chapter is about the history of affirmative action and diversity and the second part is a comparison of affirmative action and diversity and discussion of their obstacles and benefits.

THE HISTORY OF AFFIRMATIVE ACTION AND DIVERSITY

The legal history of affirmative action begins with nondiscrimination legislation and ends with the development of its goals of diversity. Most Americans would agree that it is morally wrong, as well as illegal, to discriminate against people in admission to higher education or for employment based on their race or ethnicity. However, there have never been positive rights to nondiscrimination, only negative rights not to be discriminated against (see chapter 6). Title VII of the 1964 Civil Rights Act barred race, religion, national origin, and gender discrimination by employers and labor unions. The act also created an Equal Employment Opportunity Commission with the power to file lawsuits on behalf of aggrieved workers and it empowered the Office of Education, now Department of Education, to assist with school desegregation.

The phrase **affirmative action** first appeared in 1961, when President John F. Kennedy created the Committee on Equal Employment Opportunity and an African American lawyer wrote it in the margins of a draft of Kennedy's executive order. The idea was to encourage employers, specifically government contractors, to hire nonwhite applicants and women. In 1966, President Lyndon B. Johnson told contractors to "take affirmative action to ensure that applicants are employed, and that employees are treated during employment, without regard to their race, color, religion, sex, or national origin." In the late 1960s some colleges and universities, began considering nonwhite race as a positive factor for admissions. In 1969, President Richard Nixon signed an executive order "to promote the full realization of equal employment opportunity through a continuing affirmative program in each executive department and agency."

The idea and policy of affirmative action were innovative in asserting and acting on what could be done to correct inequality concerning race, instead of focusing on what could not be done, such as enforcing the antidiscrimination Civil Rights Act. The problem with the nondiscrimination law was that it took a long time to prove discrimination in the courts and defendants could claim that they failed to hire or admit someone of color for reasons other than race. Affirmative action policies shifted the emphasis from employer's motives to results or outcomes of successful applicants compared to their percentage in the population overall or the application population.

Affirmative action was never required by law, but neither was it prohibited by law. In 1969 many elite universities admitted twice the number of black students as in 1968. Reactions from white applicants included claims of **reverse discrimination** that they were being excluded because they were white. If higher education is a scarce resource, then new people of color in its ranks does mean fewer white people, but that in itself is not evidence of discrimination. It would only be discrimination if people of color were admitted with lower qualifications compared to whites, and US Supreme Court rulings have carefully eliminated that possibility. Still, the American public has perceived affirmative action as minority hires and admission with lower qualifications than those of white applicants. For instance, US Supreme Court Justice Clarence Thomas claimed that affirmative action had stigmatized him because white employers assumed that his admission to Yale University based on race meant that he had received "special treatment" and was not qualified.

In *Regents of the University of California v. Bakke*, the US Supreme Court ruled in 1978 that UC Davis's **quota system** or set admission of a specific number of black students was unconstitutional. Quotas for nonwhite students were said to violate the **Equal Protection Clause** of the Fourteenth Amendment, specifying that race could not be used as a factor for protection under the law. That is, the Court outlawed the use of black race alone for admission. But the Court did allow that race could be used for admission as one factor among others.

Two US Supreme Court cases in 2003 specified how race could and could not be a factor in college admissions. In *Grutter v. Bollinger*, the Court allowed the University of Michigan's law school admissions program in which applicants were considered individually, with race as one factor among others. The Court recognized a "compelling interest" in "an educational benefit that flows from student body diversity." But in *Gratz v. Bollinger*, the Court rejected the admissions program of the University of Michigan's College of Literature, Science and the Arts, which granted points based on race and ethnicity and did not provide for a holistic review of each applicant's entire file.

In 2020, Californians voted to retain Proposition 209, which was first passed in 1996 to ban affirmative action or the consideration of race for admission to public colleges and universities. According to exit polls, Hispanic/Latinos voted against jettisoning Proposition 209, even though according to the University of California Board of Regents, the number of black and Hispanic/Latino students in that system had "not kept pace with the diversity of students in California K–12 schools or with the overall California population."

Finally, in 2016, in *Fisher v. University of Texas*, the Court held that race could not be considered for admission. But the Court let stand the University of Texas policy to admit the top 10 percent of high school graduates. This policy increases the number of minority students admitted, and it also benefits poor white rural applicants who, like the nonwhite applicants have not attended high schools that are as academically strong as predominantly white middle-class suburban high schools.

AFFIRMATIVE ACTION AND DIVERSITY, COMPARISONS AND PROS AND CONS

In a 2016 Gallup poll, 60 percent of Americans said they supported affirmative action, generally, but 70 percent did not believe it should be a policy for college admission. This discrepancy may be due to a lack of understanding of what affirmative action is or it may amount to supporting diversity and not affirmative action. The difference between the two is important because they have different subjects. The **subject of affirmative action** is the person of color who benefits from it. The **subject of diversity** is the whole group that the person of color joins. From the decision in *Regents of the University of California v. Bakke* onward, the US Supreme Court has shown that while it values racial and ethnic diversity, it shares the American public's suspicion of affirmative action. This shift to diversity was implied in the Court's approval of the Michigan law school's admissions policy in *Grutter v. Bollinger*. Justice Sandra Day O'Connor wrote in the Court's opinion:

> Enrolling a "critical mass" of minority students simply to assure some specified percentage of a particular group merely because of its race or ethnic origin would be patently unconstitutional. But the Law School defines its critical mass concept by reference to the substantial, important, and laudable educational benefits that diversity is designed to produce, including cross-racial understanding and the breaking down of racial stereotypes. The Law School's claim is further bolstered by numerous expert studies and reports showing that such diversity promotes learning outcomes and better prepares students for an increasingly diverse work force, for society, and for the legal profession. Major American businesses have made clear that the skills needed in today's increasingly global marketplace can only be developed through exposure to widely diverse people, cultures, ideas, and viewpoints. High-ranking retired officers and civilian military leaders assert that a highly qualified, racially diverse officer corps is essential to national security. Moreover, because universities, and in particular, law schools, represent the training ground for a large number of the Nation's leaders, the path to leadership must be visibly open to talented and qualified individuals of every race and ethnicity. Thus, the Law School has a compelling interest in attaining a diverse student body.

The *Grutter v. Bollinger* US Supreme Court opinion also stressed what it hoped would be the temporary nature of considering race for higher education admission. In 2003, O'Connor thought that the job would be done by 2028, writing, "The Court expects that 25 years from now, the use of racial preferences will no longer be necessary to further the interest approved today." In other words, O'Connor assumed that after the leadership group in US society was **racially diverse** or inclusive of nonwhites, in one generation, minorities would be equal to whites throughout society. That in turn would be to assume that whites would welcome blacks in leadership positions and that this new leadership class would somehow—she did not say how—ensure racial equality on all levels.

The advantages of affirmative action include direct benefits and broadening of experience for those who do not need affirmative action. But some whites do seem to need and get affirmative action. White applicants whose parents have attended an elite institution are likely to benefit from admission as **legacies** or those who are admitted because their parents or grandparents were graduates. High-performing athletes or applicants with rare skills may also be "affirmed" in this way. And, as noted in the *Fisher* case, poor whites may not have fully competitive academic records or preparation for college admission.

However, claims of reverse discrimination, while perhaps incoherent in historical terms, have nevertheless proved very persuasive. Historically, minorities, particularly African Americans, find it more difficult to compete for college admission because of a history of antiblack racism. But neither the American public nor the Supreme Court has shown a willingness to take history into account as a justification for affirmative action. Greater minority access to higher education has garnered little support as compensation or even reparations for past discrimination. (Compensations and reparations is discussed in chapter 8.) Instead, the American public insists on fairness in the present, and the Court insists on fairness according to constitutional law. This idea of fairness is a core element of a belief in justice. As noted in chapter 1, philosopher John Rawls offered a theory of justice as fairness. We might say that justice as fairness is realized when opportunities for admission to higher education are open to all, no matter their race. However, it is well known that minorities are disproportionately under-admitted compared to white applicants.

During the 1970s, affirmative action was designed to facilitate fairness because it was believed that racial minorities could not avail themselves of equal opportunities. As we have seen, legal support for affirmative action shifted to diversity, a change that is more focused on the benefits of racial integration for whites and people of color, than on the success of people of color considered separately. Both affirmative action and diversity are instances of insuring fairness to include not only equal opportunities but equal access to those equal opportunities. This equality of access as part of the goal of fairness is often called equity. **Equity** pertains to policies that make it possible for racial minorities to take better advantage of equal opportunities.

Fairness now and according to law are clear values in a democracy, so much so that longer-term benefits from affirmative action are often unrecognized. In their 1996 book, *The Shape of the River: Long-Term Consequences of Considering Race in College and University Admissions*, William G. Bowen and Derek Bok, former presidents of Princeton and Harvard universities, presented the results of interviews and questionnaires submitted to eighty thousand black and white students who had attended twenty-eight elite schools from 1976 to 1989. These were their findings: Among black enrollees, 79 percent graduated compared to a national 32 percent rate of black graduation. Among those who were admitted because of affirmative action, there were 60 lawyers, 70 doctors, and 125 business executives. Overall, Bowen and Bok presented a case for the individual and community benefits of affirmative action policies at elite schools. Like O'Connor, they did not attend to relations and attitudes concerning race in parts of society outside of elite communities, that is, the major part of US society.

QUESTIONS FOR THINKING, DISCUSSION, AND WRITING

1. As a matter of virtue ethics, do you think it's right for applicants to "whiten" their employment résumés? What is the relevant virtue?
2. How do you assess the statistics on minority and white college degrees and enrollment and employment? Try to formulate what the numbers mean in terms of racial equality in general terms. Can any moral or ethical conclusion be drawn from the numbers themselves, including how they change over time?
3. Discuss several pros and cons of affirmative action. How do you assess white claims of reverse discrimination?
4. Explain in terms of its focus and intended benefits, how goals of racial and ethnic diversity differ from affirmative action goals. Which moral principles underly the different kinds of goals?
5. Explain how and why racial integration at elite levels of society does not result in racial equality throughout society. If racial integration is just, are the limits to it unjust?

SOURCES

American Council on Education (ACE). "Race and Ethnicity in Higher Education," https://www.equityinhighered.org/indicators/enrollment-in-undergraduate-education/enrollments-in-undergraduate-sectors/.

Bowen, William G., and Derek Bok. *The Shape of the River: Long-Term Consequences of Considering Race in College and University Admissions.* Cambridge, MA: Cambridge University Press, 1996.

Carlton, Genevieve. "A History of Affirmative Action in College Admissions." Best Colleges, August 10, 2020, https://www.bestcolleges.com/blog/history-affirmative-action-colleges/.

Fuchs, Erin. "How Clarence Thomas Grew to Hate Affirmative Action." October 15, 2013, https://www.businessinsider.com/how-clarence-thomas-grew-to-hate-affirmative-action-2013-10.

Jones, Nicholas, Rachel Marks, Roberto Ramirez, and Merarys Ríos-Vargas. "US Census, 2020 Census Illuminates Racial and Ethnic Composition of the Country." US Census, August 12, 2021, https://www.census.gov/library/stories/2021/08/improved-race-ethnicity-measures-reveal-united-states-population-much-more-multiracial.html.

Justia, US Supreme Court, *Grutter v. Bollinger*, 539 U.S. 306 (2003), Volume 539, https://supreme.justia.com/cases/federal/us/539/306/#tab-opinion-1961290.

Schwantes, Marcel. "Harvard Study Says Minority Job Candidates Are 'Whitening' Their Resumes When Looking for Jobs. Ever Changed Your Name on a Resume to Get More Job Interviews?" Inc.com, June 24, 1921, https://www.inc.com/marcel-schwantes/why -minority-job-applicants-mask-their-race-identities-when-applying-for-jobs-according-to -this-harvard-study.html.

Shapiro, Eliza, and K. K. Rebecca Lai. "How New York's Elite Public Schools Lost Their Black and Hispanic Students." *New York Times*, June 3, 2019, https://www.nytimes.com/interac tive/2019/06/03/nyregion/nyc-publicschools-black-hispanic-students.html.

Statista. "Share of Companies in the United States with Racial and Ethnic Diversity of CEOs from 2004 to 2018." 2021, https://www.statista.com/statistics/1097600/racial-and -ethnic-diversity-of-ceos-in-the-united-states/.

US Census. "U.S. Census Bureau Releases New Educational Attainment Data." March 30, 2020, Release Number CB20-TPS.09, https://www.census.gov/newsroom/press-releases/ 2020/educational-attainment.html.

US Equal Employment Opportunity Commission. Title VII of the Civil Rights Act of 1964, https://www.eeoc.gov/statutes/title-vii-civil-rights-act-1964

Zuckerman, Arthur. "37 Leadership Statistics: 2020/2021 Data, Trends & Predictions." Com- parecamp, May 29, 2020, https://comparecamp.com/leadership-statistics/.

Videos

Above the Noise. "Affirmative Action: Should Race Be a Factor in College Admissions?" PBS digital studios, YouTube, https://www.youtube.com/watch?v=ZhUOw0KidZg.

Franek, Rob. *The Princeton Review*, "Learn How You Can Score 1400+* on the SAT." https:// www.princetonreview.com/college/sat-test-prep.

Martin, Roland S. "What Role Should Affirmative Action and Legacy Play in College Admis- sions?" YouTube, October 17, 2017, https://www.youtube.com/watch?v=C0QSRNRwLJ0.

8

Compensation, Reparation, Rectification, and Reconciliation

PUBLIC SALE
OF SLAVES!!

FRANKLIN CIRCUIT COURT.

JAMES HARLAN'S Administrators, Plaintiffs,
vs.
JAMES HARLAN'S Heirs, Defendants,

In Equity.

The undersigned, as COMMISSIONER of said Court, will, on

Monday, November 16, 1863,

(County Court day,) sell at public auction, the following Slaves, viz:

THREE NEGRO MEN;
ONE NEGRO WOMAN AND A SMALL CHILD, ADOPTED;
ONE NEGRO WOMAN AND TWO CHILDREN.

TERMS—Six months credit, with interest from date, the purchasers giving bond with security, to have the force and effect of replevin bond.

OCTOBER 30, 1863.

GEORGE W. GWIN,
Master Commissioner.

A poster advertising a slave sale being held by a man named George W. Gwin who is listed as Master Commissioner. James Harlen was the previous owner, and the sale is taking place to settle an equity dispute between the administrator of his estate and his heirs. Three men, two women, and three children are listed for sale. Six-month credit terms with interest are being offered on the purchase of the slaves. Frankfort, Kentucky, 1863. From the New York Public Library. Alamy Stock Photo: Gado Images.

If your family's house is destroyed by a forest fire or hurricane, it is expected that on behalf of the entire community in a locality, state, or nation, you will be compensated with direct help or funds to rebuild or buy another home. Such **compensation** in natural disasters does not have an aspect of blame. The aim is simply to make the damage less severe toward a return to conditions before the destruction. If your family has never been able to afford a home and has less income than the national average, because of racial discrimination and segregation in past generations, **reparations** would provide official recognition of the past harm, an apology, and some monetary benefit. The punishment of wrongdoers, as after the Nuremberg trials of Nazi war criminals, was important **rectification** to put things right. If you live in a place where there has been injustice against some racial groups and there is a collective desire to move ahead into a more equal society, there may be official attempts at **reconciliation** or efforts of **restorative justice** so that offenders and victims can move on.

Where there are no programs or policies already in place for compensation, reparations, and reconciliation, or in support of such programs when they do exist, deep moral responses are often evoked. Overall, such moral response is **altruistic** or focused on improving the well-being of others, and sympathetic—most believe that those who have been harmed ought to be helped, and some feel that they themselves must help. Altruistic feelings motivate donations of time, money, and material goods to private and public charities and other nongovernment organizations (NGOs). Altruism is also motivating for those who support reparations, and altruistic ideals of the common good can motivate reconciliation. In addition, blame, punishment, and demands for responsibility are components of reparations motivated by the desire for justice. However, concern for the common good is not purely altruistic, because the common good includes everyone so that those who were not harmed nonetheless do benefit because the collective to which they belong is more just. Rectification that involves punishment is a matter of applying law, but it also speaks to moral desires to see that extreme wrongdoers suffer or die.

All four of these entitlements to address harm—compensation, reparation, rectification, and reconciliation—have occurred throughout the world, as public issues affecting large numbers of people. They may have private versions when individuals are harmed, which are handled through civil lawsuits or direct negotiations. The broad subject we are considering here is efforts to restore and "make whole" members of minority groups who have been disproportionately harmed by government policies and actions. Compensation has been the easiest to put into effect because it is not a racial issue, although how people are compensated may vary according to their race and their vulnerability may be related to their race as the result of substandard housing, for example. But even if victims of natural disasters have not adequately prepared or failed to evacuate devastated areas before extreme events, they are still regarded as innocent of the harms they have experienced, and generally, no one is held responsible or blameworthy for damage caused by natural events. Reparations, by contrast, require admission of moral wrongs committed in the past and apology for those wrongs by people living in the present. This admission, apology, and assumption of responsibility is a controversial subject, with strong political tensions. Reconciliation requires a willingness of injured groups to move on for the greater good, with some measure of forgiveness of wrongdoers, and it is controversial because it lacks rectification or the justice of punishment of those wrongdoers.

In this chapter, the focus will be on compensation, reparations, and reconciliation. The scope will be international because compensation, reparations, and reconciliation have been regarded and put into effect differently, throughout the world. (See also chapter 20 on memorials and chapter 22 on natural disasters.)

COMPENSATION

Natural disasters disproportionately affect poor white people and poor people of color. While there may be tension in how much or how they should be compensated, there is broad public agreement that they should be compensated. However, there may be bureaucratic or logistical problems in delivering compensation, which disproportionately affects people of color. For example, before Hurricane Ida struck New Orleans in September 2021, the Department of Homeland Security announced that it would no longer require deeds to their property from those who claimed homeowner assistance from the Federal Emergency Disaster Assistance (FEMA). Many African Americans in US southern states own homes as *heirs' property* that has been handed down to them without formal wills or recordings of deeds. Whereas FEMA had before simply rejected written applications for disaster assistance from heirs' property owners, a policy change was announced on September 2, 2021, whereby it would send inspectors to the properties and accept alternative forms of documentation.

Earlier, during Hurricane Katrina in 2005, relief and relocation efforts had been sharply criticized as racist. Katrina's impact was most devasting to the Lower Ninth Ward of New Orleans, which was mainly populated by working poor black residents. It took two days after the initial flooding for FEMA personnel to reach the area and President Bush first flew over it on the fifth day. About 250,000 people were evacuated after squalid temporary shelter in the New Orleans Convention Center. Infrastructure, including roads, hospitals, and schools, was difficult or impossible to rebuild and many evacuees were never able to return home.

Public outrage at the government response to Hurricane Katrina was loud and widespread, but it was and still is difficult to distinguish between inadequate preparation and emergency response, and outright racism. None who were ultimately blamed, such as the mayor of New Orleans and secretary of FEMA, were formally demoted or punished. Even early plans to rebuild were accompanied by speculative buying up of damaged properties and high-end development intended to change the demographics of the city by making it whiter and more affluent, overall. Something similar occurred in Sri Lanka after the 2004 tsunami when poor people were evacuated from the coast and barred from returning, while their land was sold to wealthy developers for luxury resorts. Nevertheless, government-funded evacuation undoubtedly saved lives in both New Orleans and Sri Lanka, and if responses were biased against victims, they were more opportunistic than deliberate, independent initiatives to harm those people.

REPARATION

After World War II, as West Germany reconstituted itself as a democratic country, reparations for Jewish Holocaust survivors and their relatives were an important part of its rehabilitation. In 1951, West German chancellor Konrad Adenauer resolved to pay "moral and material indemnity" for the "unspeakable crimes . . . committed in the name of the German people." Reparations agreements with Israel and other countries followed. Germany is estimated to have paid about $92 billion over twenty years, with some payments to individuals ongoing. In 1946 and 1978, the US government paid about $1.3 billion to Native American tribes for appropriating their lands. And in 1988, Japanese Americans received $1.6 billion for their forced internment during World War II. However, the project of reparations for black slavery and Jim Crow has not moved beyond proposal and debate.

The arguments for black reparations are moral demands for apology, compensation, and collective recognition of injustice imposed and supported by the US government. Arguments against black reparations highlight the complexity of history itself. The core of arguments for reparations is that slavery and Jim Crow were moral wrongs for which the nation has never collectively apologized and African Americans continue to be disadvantaged economically and socially for past racist oppression. The main objections are that many whites today did not have ancestors who owned slaves or practiced Jim Crow oppression, and people are not generally liable for the misdeeds of their ancestors. Also, immigrants after the civil rights movement had no white American ancestors. The force of counterargument is that all whites benefit from the collective wealth and racial status that is part of the legacy of past antiblack oppression.

In February 1965, two towering public intellectuals, African American writer James Baldwin (1924–1987) and white American founder of the conservative *National Review* William F. Buckley Jr. (1925–2008), debated this question: "The American Dream Is at the Expense of the American Negro." Their audience was the Cambridge Union Society of Cambridge University made up of future British politicians. Baldwin began:

> It would seem to me the proposition before the House . . . is the American Dream at the expense of the American Negro . . . one's response to that question—one's reaction to that question—has to depend on effect and, in effect, where you find yourself in the world, what your sense of reality is, what your system of reality is. That is, it depends on assumptions which we hold so deeply so as to be scarcely aware of them.

Baldwin went on to personalize his black identity perspective, proclaiming: "*I* picked the cotton, and *I* carried it to the market, and *I* built the railroads, under someone else's whip. For nothing. For nothing." That is, Baldwin believed that the question could be answered only from the standpoint of someone who had experienced life as an American Negro. Buckley rejected that standpoint, insisting: "The fact that you sit here, carrying the entire weight of the Negro ordeal on your shoulders, is irrelevant to the argument we are here to discuss." Subsequent scholarship on race would insist that the idea of objectivity Buckley put forth was in this context biased in favor of a white perspective that ignored Baldwin's claims.

Baldwin documented experiences of African Americans as exploited by and subordinated to whites. Buckley often resorted to personal insults against Baldwin and he finished by invoking faith in the goodness of the United States since its founding, and Allied efforts in World War II that in the end benefited defeated Germans as well as the victors:

> If it finally does come to a confrontation between giving up the best features of the American way of life and fighting for them, then we will fight the issue. We will fight the issue not only in the Cambridge Union, but we will fight as you were once asked to fight—on the beaches, in the hills, in the mountains. And just as you waged war to save civilization, you also waged war for the benefit of the Germans, your enemies. We, too, are convinced that if it should ever come to that kind of confrontation, then our determination will be to wage war not only for the whites but also for the Negroes.

Baldwin won the debate after the Union voted 544 to 164 in his favor.

The Baldwin-Buckley debate pinpoints the nature of demands for black reparations that remain relevant today: If whites benefited from black labor and mistreated and held blacks in contempt, then whites today owe blacks both compensation and an admission of guilt. The argument about reparations based on racial identities might easily be escalated by whites who reject both a debt and responsibility for past harm by their ancestors. Except as the kind of rhetorical defense put up by Buckley, faith in the goodness of American institutions is irrelevant to the question of reparations. We don't know if Buckley realized the irrelevance of his reference to the stated goodness of American institutions, but the force of his objection to Baldwin's moral claims points to the adamance of opposition to black reparations. Former President Barack Obama responded to this adamance in an interview by author Ta-Nehisi Coates in December 2016:

> I'm not so optimistic as to think that you would ever be able to garner a majority of an American Congress that would make those kinds of investments above and beyond the kinds of investments that could be made in a progressive program for lifting up all people. So to restate it: I have much more confidence in my ability, or any president or any leader's ability, to mobilize the American people around a multiyear, multibillion-dollar investment to help every child in poverty in this country than I am in being able to mobilize the country around providing a benefit specific to African Americans as a consequence of slavery and Jim Crow. Now, we can debate the justness of that. But I feel pretty confident in that assessment politically.

In other words, Obama did not think that reparations for African Americans were politically viable, although some of its goals might be accomplished by programs that benefited whites, as well as African Americans. This pragmatic approach might secure some of the material and cultural benefits of reparations, but recognition and apology would be left out. In other words, it would be compensation. All would benefit as a result of a racially neutral program to lessen childhood poverty—and African Americans might benefit more than whites—but the factors of recognition of past harm, taking responsibility for it, and apology, would be lost. Obama's compensation view of what is possible amounts to reparations stripped of their moral meaning. Nevertheless, the moral cause persists. In 1989, Congressman John Conyers Jr. (D-MI) sponsored a bill to study proposals for reparations, and as HR40, it was introduced into every session of Congress thereafter. In 2017 Sheila Jackson Lee (D-TX) took over as first sponsor of HR40 that is summarized on the US Congress website as follows:

> H.R. 40—A bill to address the fundamental injustice, cruelty, brutality, and inhumanity of slavery in the United States and the 13 American colonies between 1619 and 1865 and to establish a commission to study and consider a national apology and proposal for reparations for the institution of slavery, its subsequent de jure and de facto racial and economic discrimination against African-Americans, and the impact of these forces on living African-Americans, to make recommendations to the Congress on appropriate remedies, and for other purposes; to the Committee on the Judiciary in Conyers' bill, now called HR 40, the Commission to Study Reparation Proposals for African Americans Act.

For the theoretical reasons discussed earlier, and present political divisions—HR 40 is sponsored by Democrats—and with white adamance, a national black reparations policy does not seem viable at this time. However, very specific, contextualized reparations programs have sprung up throughout the United States, although not without controversy. For example, on October 29, 2019, the president of Georgetown University, announced a commitment to raise $400,000 a year for reparations to the descendants of 272 slaves that Georgetown sold before the Civil War. Some students objected to the form of this commitment because it resembled philanthropy or charitable giving, rather than real reparations. When a reparations plan to give sixteen black residents of Evanston, Illinois, $25,000 each for property costs was announced, it was criticized for not making direct cash payments.

RECONCILIATION

Unlike compensation and reparation, which involve action as well as speech, reconciliation is a matter of attitudes and conversation. Reconciliation has been called a form of **transitional justice** because it aims to make it possible for a society in which some groups have been treated unjustly by other groups to resolve both anger and guilt to move on with greater harmony. Telling the truth in public about what was perpetrated and suffered is an important part of reconciliation, which may also be thought to require both forgiveness and forgetting. Forgiveness is a longer process of individuals internally letting go of blame and governments abandoning plans for punishment. Forgetting may be a response to truths so terrible that memories of them simply cannot be borne. For example, in the late 1970s, the killing fields of the Khmer Rouge government of Cambodia resulted in the brutal deaths of up to two million people, or one-fifth of the population. Plans for truth commissions were met with ambivalence until a new generation found their elder's accounts unbelievable. In 1999, the prime minister granted amnesty from prosecution to the leaders of the atrocities and advised citizens "to dig a hole and bury the past."

During **apartheid** in South Africa, from 1948 to 1991, the majority African population was strictly segregated without civil rights, and their movements were controlled by the white minority. The South African Truth and Reconciliation Commission (TRC), led by Archbishop Desmond Tutu (1931–2013), was formed to offer amnesty from prosecution to former white officials on the condition that they fully and truthfully testify about their human rights abuses that were committed for political purposes. Some of the seventeen commissioners invoked the moral concept of **ubuntu** meaning "I am because we are," which affirmed the requirement of community recognition for personhood. At stake was both the acknowledgment of past suffering and the possible commitment of officials who had committed crimes to the principle that "This must never happen again." Approximately 21,000 victims testified, and there were 7,112 amnesty applications of which only 849 were granted. Dissatisfaction with the absence of justice in the form of deserved punishment was widely voiced.

Ongoing reparations projects for past atrocities against indigenous populations have been undertaken in Australia, New Zealand, and Canada. These projects are often viewed as restorative justice with goals of both just treatment in the present and future, together with recognition of past injustice. They have the important component of inclusivity through outreach to youth and families within indigenous communities. There have also been attempts to connect European ideas of reparations with traditional indigenous practices, as well as programs for criminal justice reform within the dominant society when members of indigenous groups have been disproportionately subject to harsh punishment and incarceration.

Reconciliation programs have been a softer approach compared to the Nuremberg trials of top Nazis after World War II. Those trials took place in an international court and convictions carried the death penalty. There was no reconciliation. But in terms of the rectification aspect of reparations, the Nuremberg trials were the beginning of a major top-down cultural shift in Germany that included Holocaust memorials. (See chapter 20 for discussion of memorials.)

QUESTIONS FOR THINKING, DISCUSSION, AND WRITING

1. Do you think that flawed and biased disaster compensation is a serious moral wrong that should be criminally punished under the law? Explain why or why not.

2. Distinguish between the different elements of reparations discussed in the Baldwin-Buckley 1965 debate.
3. Distinguish between theoretical and pragmatic objections to reparations. If the theoretical objections are correct, then reparations for black slavery and Jim Crow may be impossible. But if the pragmatic objections are correct, explain how they could be morally justified according to utilitarianism.
4. In purely deontological and virtue ethics terms and not pragmatic or utilitarian terms, do you think the United States should have a program of reparations for African Americans regarding US chattel slavery? Why or why not?
5. In terms of forgiveness and justice, how do you evaluate the Cambodian governments advice to forget about the atrocities of the Khmer Rouge?

SOURCES

Adams, Char. "Evanston Is the First U.S. City to Issue Slavery Reparations. Experts Say It's a Noble Start." NBC News, March 16, 2021, https://www.nbcnews.com/news/nbcblk/evanston-s-reparations-plan-noble-start-complicated-process-experts-say-n1262096.

Chandler, David. "Coming to Terms with the Terror and History of Pol Pot's Cambodia (1975–79)." In *Dilemmas of Reconciliation: Cases and Concepts*, C. A. L. Prager and T. Govier (eds.), Waterloo, Ontario: Wilfrid Laurier University Press, 2003, pp. 307–26, quote from page 310.

Cunneen, C. "Reviving Restorative Justice Traditions." In *The Handbook of Restorative Justice*, J. Johnstone and D. Van Ness, eds., Cullompton: Willan Publishing, 2007, pp. 113–31.

Department of Homeland Security. "DHS Announces Changes to Individual Assistance Policies to Advance Equity for Disaster Survivors." September 2, 2021, https://www.dhs.gov/news/2021/09/02/dhs-announces-changes-individual-assistance-policies-advance-equity-disaster.

Di Corpo, Ryan. "Georgetown Reparations Plan for Slaves Sold by University Draws Criticism from Students." *American Magazine*, November 4, 2019, https://www.americamagazine.org/politics-society/2019/11/04/georgetown-reparations-plan-slaves-sold-university-draws-criticism.

History. "Nazi War Criminals Sentenced at Nuremberg." This Day in History, October 1, 1946, https://www.history.com/this-day-in-history/nazi-war-criminals-sentenced-at-nuremberg.

"The American Dream and the American Negro" (1857–current file), March 7, 1965; ProQuest Historical Newspapers *The New York Times* (1851–2004), pg. SM32, https://www.nytimes.com/images/blogs/papercuts/baldwin-and-buckley.pdf.

Timsit, Annabelle. "How Germany Paid Reparations for the Holocaust: The Blueprint the US Can Follow to Finally Pay Reparations." Quartz, October 22, 2020, https://qz.com/1915185/how-germany-paid-reparations-for-the-holocaust/.

US Institute of Peace. "Truth Commission: South Africa," https://www.usip.org/publications/1995/12/truth-commission-south-africa.

Vincent, Subramaniam. "Reparations: The Missing Chapter in America's 'Pragmatic' Quest for Justice to African Americans." Markkula Center for Applied Ethics at Santa Clara University, https://www.scu.edu/ethics/all-about-ethics/reparations-the-missing-chapter-in-americas-pragmatic-quest-for-justice-to-african-americans/.

Zack, Naomi. *Ethics for Disaster*. Lanham, MD: Rowman & Littlefield, 2009, chap. 6, pp. 105–14.

Videos

AP Archive. "South Africa: Truth and Reconciliation Commission." November 25, 1997, YouTube, https://www.youtube.com/watch?v=424Ob5GY4ww.

Democracy Now! "Environmental Justice Professor Robert Bullard on How Race Affected the Federal Government's Response to Katrina." Democracynow.org, October 24, 2005, https://www.democracynow.org/2005/10/24/environmental_justice_professor_robert _bullard_on.

Riverbends Channel. "James Baldwin debates William F. Buckley, 1965," YouTube, https://www.youtube.com/watch?v=oFeoS41xe7w.

III

SOCIAL INSTITUTIONS

In the United States, rules and practices, as well as inertia against change in major institutions, have disadvantaging effects on racial and ethnic minorities. The criminal justice system, policing, the economic system, education, and the medical system, plus health practices are interlocking institutions in the big picture of institutional racism.

Chapter 9 presents the disproportionate minority presence in the US criminal justice system. The institution of the modern prison began with utilitarian ideals of reform, but at present, reform has focused on racial justice. Chapter 10 considers the structure of US police departments that first bring people into the criminal justice system. While high-profile police killings have evoked calls for reform, police reform is difficult to enact because 18,000 distinct police departments in the United States are all subject to local rule, police unions have political clout, and the US Supreme Court has supported police discretion in the use of violent force, over several cases.

Income and wealth are strongly connected to human dignity. In chapter 11, racial and ethnic minorities are compared to whites in income and accumulation of wealth through homeownership. Homeless people are also disproportionately people of color, which due to ongoing racism adds to the indignities of being unhoused. Chapter 12 considers the structure of K–12 and higher education in the United States and its relation to income and wealth in terms of racial and ethnic identity. Included are current controversies about educational content over the 1619 project and critical race theory. Chapter 13 focuses on health and disability, with attention to racial and ethnic disparities. The importance and availability of good nutrition, how disabled people are overlooked, and the lack of access to mental health care are addressed.

9

The US Criminal Justice System

Row of small prison cells with bars in front. Inside the cell is a bed and toilet.
Getty Imges: FrankvandenBergh.

An institution is a structure in society with rules and resources, and participation in it may be either voluntary or compulsory. A **literal institution**, in addition to set rules and behavior, has an actual location or physical center. The US criminal justice system is a literal institution. However, society has many forms of organization, and the word "institution" is used metaphorically to refer to any established pattern of behavior affecting large numbers of people. Marriage, for example, is an institution in this sense.

People often become **institutionalized**, which means that membership or participation in an institution deeply changes them so that they not only carry out the institution's rules and practices while within the institution but bring them with them when they leave. Because institutions are believed to be necessary for society as a whole and most are vastly more powerful than their individual participants, participants often feel helpless to change them. Actual reform may seem impossible, but the first step toward it is moral evaluation.

Imprisonment puts people into a literal institution. Incarceration is a form of punishment that removes people from normal life in society by confining them in specific places where their behavior is regulated for specified periods of time. The main ideas are that while imprisoned, criminals are both being punished for their crimes and prevented from committing new crimes. There may also be punishments for crimes or infractions committed in prison, such as solitary confinement, corporal punishment, and deprivation. **Capital punishment**, the death penalty, is a sentence of its own, as a course of punishment officially specified. Because prisons are usually located within the borders of society and have connections with both other institutions and free people, they are social institutions. Indeed, although imprisonment removes people from society, at the same time it draws them into more intense social relationships, with other inmates through crowding, with guards through discipline and surveillance, and with regulation of their bodies and activities, such as what they eat, when they can exercise, what they must wear, and so forth. Rehabilitation of prison inmates is an ideal, but many do advance their education and work to change themselves.

Institutional racism is a pattern of beliefs and behavior that disadvantage people of color, even though the leaders of different institutions may not explicitly intend to do that. An entire society, viewed as a web of both literal and metaphorical institutions, may be considered racist, which is the main meaning of **institutional racism**. Institutional racism as racism *in* a specific institution may shape that institution with rules and practices coming from outside of the institution or from inertia within the institution itself that simply carries on past explicit and deliberately racist practices. Those who understand how institutions are racist in both of these senses usually assess institutional racism as unjust and morally wrong. Such understanding and moral judgment often motivate projects of reform. Many of the ethical issues regarding a mammoth institution such as the US criminal justice system and institutional racism more generally are largely matters of thought, because most people do not have direct influence or the individual power to bring about change. However, in a democracy, activism through reform projects is possible and voters can be motivated by moral conclusions in evaluating the policies put forth by political candidates. To date in the United States, prison reform has been made up of many small, specific projects. Prison reform projects with a focus on increasing racial equality regarding entry into, life within, and life after incarceration for people of color have an even more narrow focus. The first section of this chapter is about the nature of punishment and reform, followed by the demographics of prisons in the United States. The third section is about reform projects that are important for the well-being of people of color in prison who disproportionately make up inmate populations.

PUNISHMENT AND REFORM

Prisons are both literal places of confinement and places where punishment is administered. For the ancient world, records exist of the Roman "Carcere Mamertino" a converted water cistern in use since 600 BC. Sentencing has a long history. French philosopher Paul-Michel Foucault (1926–1984) provided this gruesome report of a sentence for European punishment, before the modern prison, at the beginning of chapter 1 of his 1977 *Discipline and Punish: Birth of the Prison*: [**Trigger warning, violent description**]

> On 2 March 1757 Damiens the regicide was condemned "to make the *amende honorable* before the main door of the Church of Paris," where he was to be taken and conveyed in a cart, "wearing nothing but a shirt, holding a torch of burning wax weighing two pounds"; then, "in the said cart, to the Place de Grève, where, on a scaffold that will be erected there, the flesh will be torn from his breasts, arms, thighs and calves with red-hot pincers, his right hand, holding the knife with which he committed the said parricide, burnt with sulphur, and, on those places where the flesh will be torn away, poured molten lead, boiling oil, burning resin, wax and sulphur melted together and then his body drawn and quartered by four horses and his limbs and body consumed by fire, reduced to ashes and his ashes thrown to the winds."

Foucault is famous for his analysis of the new forms of cruelty and control of the bodies of prisoners in the institution of the modern prison, but the point here is that before the institution of the modern prison, punishment was far harsher and explicitly violent by modern standards. Indeed, the Eighth Amendment to the US Constitution reads: "Excessive bail shall not be required, nor excessive fines imposed, nor cruel and unusual punishments inflicted."

One hundred thirty years after the punishment reported by Foucault, English philosopher and social reformer Jeremy Bentham (1748–1832) published *Panopticon Letters* (1787). Bentham presented a design for a prison with spiraling architecture in which every inmate could be constantly observed. He aimed to make it possible to reform both the behavior and thoughts of prisoners. Bentham's guiding principle was his philosophy of utilitarianism—pleasure is good and pain bad and the moral goal is the greatest good for the greatest number. While Bentham's design was never implemented, surveillance and reform were combined with confinement in a specific place as the three major elements of the modern prison. Elizabeth Fry (1780–1845) also fought for English prison reforms, including the protection of female prisoners from rape and exploitation. In the United States in 1829, Eastern State Penitentiary in Philadelphia began to enforce solitary confinement as a tool for rehabilitation on the theory that interactions among prisoners furthered their criminality.

However, Bentham and Fry's ideas for prison reform have over time become realities requiring further reform. By 2005, the United States had over forty supermax prisons with constant twenty-three-hour periods of isolation, housing about eighty thousand by 2011. The use of supermax prisons was intended to reduce violence within even maximum-security prisons and they have been designed to control the most dangerous inmates, although they may also house death-row inmates.

Supermax prisons were a response to "tough on crime" attitudes in the 1980s. They are expensive to build and run and are reported to cause rage, mental illness, and suicidal depression in prisoners. These facilities are operated with closed-circuit television and the use of robots. Litigation concerning these conditions based on the Eighth Amendment has evoked both concern from the courts and a reluctance to evaluate non-physical punishment. Philosopher and political activist Angela Y. Davis (1944–) has claimed that black men are disproportionately incarcerated in supermax prisons. She relates what supermax inmates consider inhumane treatment to overall institutional antiblack racism in the history of US prison system and society overall. For instance:

> Albert Wright, Jr., is a fifty-year-old African American man who is serving a forty-year term in the Western Illinois Correctional Center. In this prison of 2,000 men, of whom some 66 percent are black, he wrote in an impassioned plea to readers of *Emerge*, a black monthly magazine: "[T]here is seldom a positive response to the cries for help in combating the inhuman treatment that we are subjected to daily. Few of you know what the treatment is like. What prison administrators tell you is not anything near the truth." Wright makes it very clear that he is not asking for financial support or material goods. "I am talking about genuine interest in what is happening to your people. We are still people. We just happen to be in prison."

From the extreme and instant bodily punishment described by Foucault to the **dehumanization**, or treatment as less than human, chronicled by Davis, we can see that the norms of criminal punishment have changed. The overall intention has been to make it less cruel. But the definition of cruelty depends on whether quality of life and not only physical harm is taken into account. There is also the issue of the death penalty.

In 1976, the US Supreme Court ruled that capital punishment or the death penalty remained constitutional. Between 1977 and 2019, almost 1,500 people were executed, mostly by lethal injection. Capital crimes are mainly murders but treason and espionage are also included. The death penalty has been controversial in modern times. Philosopher Immanuel Kant, the author of deontology (see chapter 1) advocated it on the grounds of *lex talionis* or the **law of retribution** that the punishment should fit the crime, "an eye for an eye, a tooth for a tooth." Modern advocates of the death penalty say it preserves law and order, deters crime, and costs less than life imprisonment. Opponents of the death penalty point to studies that show that the death penalty does not deter similar crimes. Also, it is wrong for governments to take human life, and people of color are disproportionately executed—as are all poor people who cannot afford effective legal representation; they also claim that life imprisonment is less harsh and less expensive because those sentenced to death spend years on death row, appealing their sentences.

Public defenders or attorneys provided by a court are a constitutional right. According to the Sixth Amendment of the US Constitution, an indigent person cannot be prosecuted unless the state provides them with an attorney. Some state public defense offices assign the same public defender throughout a defendant's criminal proceedings, that is "vertically," from beginning to end, while others assign specialists for different parts of it. In the specialized or "horizonal" assignment there may not be adequate communication between the different public defenders. Often, public defenders have large caseloads, which some handle better than others—defendants have no choice of who their public defenders will be. There are also different state standards for what counts as indigence. Many observers believe that the US public defender system is inadequate for effective defense of those charged with crimes, who are more likely than those with privately paid lawyers to be convicted or receive long sentences.

DEMOGRAPHICS

It is important to understand the demographics or numbers of people in prison, broken down into race, to understand the different needs of specific groups of people of color who are imprisoned. The term **mass incarceration** is an apt name for the fact that in the second decade of the twenty-first century, over two million people are held in prisons or jails at any given time in the United States. The enormity of this figure is evident if we note that the population of the United States is about 4 percent of the world population, while its prison population is over 20 percent of the world figure. In other words, the likelihood of a citizen or resident of the United States being imprisoned is five times that of the world average. Compared to the rest of the world, every US state has a higher prison population than nearly every other country. Even Massachusetts with the lowest rate of US incarceration has a higher rate than Iran, Colombia, and all the founding NATO nations. Rates of incarceration have increased since the 1970s, and the two million-plus people in prisons and jails amount to an increase of 500 percent.

According to leading criminologists, the reasons for this increase in the US prison population have been attributed to several factors. However, one major cause was not a change in criminal behavior. Rather, more sophisticated police strategies and technology resulted in more arrests, and more severe sentencing and post-release policies were mainly responsible. Average sentences increased under *determinate or mandatory sentencing* based on the category of crime and a convict's record, which replaced the discretion of judges. Truth-in-sentencing laws required that inmates serve at least 85 percent of their sentences before they were eligible for parole. There was also the "War on Drugs." While between 1984 and 2002, property offenses increased 30 percent and violent crimes 70 percent, drug offense imprisonment increased over 550 percent. Finally, stricter parole policies led to an increase in parole violations resulting in 40 percent of those admitted to prison being sent back.

The number of people incarcerated in the United States are disproportionately people of color according to the 2010 US census—black Americans are about five times more likely to be incarcerated than white Americans and almost twenty times more likely than Asian Americans. Several reasons have been given for this racial discrepancy: People of color are subject to greater police surveillance than whites and may be unjustly brought into the prison system through arrests (see chapter 10); people of color have fewer resources for legal defense once indicted.

REFORM PROJECTS IMPACTING PRISONERS OF COLOR

Insofar as people of color are disproportionately incarcerated, they benefit substantially from all prison reform projects. Ten of these projects and their anchor institutions are listed next with their websites. The student is invited to explore these efforts, evaluate them, and participate if inclined.

- The Innocence Project was founded in 1992 by Peter Neufeld and Barry Scheck at Cardozo School of Law. It aims to exonerate those wrongly convicted through DNA testing. They have also taken steps to correct eyewitness missidentification. https://innocenceproject.org/about/
- Families Against Mandatory Sentencing (FAMM). High rates of incarceration affect families and communities, not only inmates themselves, so activism against determinate sentencing involves more than individual inmates. https://famm.org/famm-allies-justice-now-action-center/
- Vera Institute of Justice works with government leaders on behalf of immigrants, youth, LGBT people, and those with disabilities who are incarcerated. https://www.vera.org/issues
- Prison Policy Initiative is a thinktank that uses research, advocacy, and organizing to curtail **over-criminalization**, or designating too many as criminals, when other social measures would be less disruptive. https://www.prisonpolicy.org
- The Marshall Project supports criminal justice journalism intending to report abuse and examine solutions for the problems in the US criminal justice system. The voices of prisoners themselves are made public. https://www.themarshall project.org/
- Penal Reform International (PRI) is a nongovernmental global organization seeking to promote criminal justice systems that uphold human rights for all. PRI runs practical human rights programs. https://www.penalreform.org/about-us/
- Dream Corp seeks to support diversity by overcoming political and racial divisions within society. https://www.thedreamcorps.org/about/
- Aid to Inmate Mothers (AIM) seeks to reunite mothers and children who have been separated by prison. Visitation programs bring families together and ongoing extended-family childcare and educational and cultural programs are developed. https://inmatemoms.org/programs/
- The National Coalition to Abolish the Death Penalty (NCADP) is an umbrella organization for more than one hundred local organizations that aim to abolish

the death penalty, in the United States and internationally. https://www.ncadp
.org/pages/about-us
• The Inside-Out Prison Exchange Program supports dialogue and education between prisoners and students in higher education. http://www.insideoutcenter
.org/

These prison reform projects and others like them seek to address and correct the
moral and legal injustices that people of color encounter in the US prison system.
They also correct the feelings of helplessness that many experience as inmates, family
members, or concerned observers. While they are not substitutes for legal reform of
the US prison system, they raise awareness of the need for legal reform.

QUESTIONS FOR THINKING, DISCUSSION, AND WRITING

1. Is it morally wrong that people feel helpless about institutions? What can
   be done about this on an individual level?
2. Which is worse, violent punishment as described by Foucault or
   dehumanization in modern supermax prisons?
3. What is your moral view on the death penalty, and why?
4. Based on contributing factors, is the disproportionate number of African
   Americans in prison a moral wrong?
5. Why might the separation of newborns born in prison from their mothers
   be immoral? (See Alysia Santo video.)

SOURCES

Bentham, Jeremy. *The Panopticon Writings*. Ed. Miran Božovič. London: Verso, 1995.
Butler, H. Daniel. "Supermax Prisons: Another Chapter in the Constitutionality of the Incarceration Conundrum." *Rutgers Journal of Law and Public Policy* 9, no. 1 (Spring 2012),
https://rutgerspolicyjournal.org/sites/jlpp/files/JLPP_9-1_Griffin_RTP.pdf.
Davis, Angela Y. "From the Convict Lease System to the Super-Max Prison." In *States of Con-
finement.* J. James, ed. New York: Palgrave Macmillan, 2000, https://doi.org/10.1007/978
-1-137-10929-3_6 (quotation from abstract).
Foucault, Michel. *Discipline and Punish: Birth of the Prison*. Trans. Alan Sheridan. New York:
Vintage Books, Random House, 1977, quotation p. 14.
Henderson Hurley, Martha L. "supermax-prison." Britannica.com, https://www.britannica
.com/topic/supermax-prison.
Raphael, S., and M. Stoll, "Why Are So Many Americans in Prison?" In *Do Prisons Make Us
Safer? The Benefits and Costs of the Prison Boom*, S. Raphael and M. Stoll, Eds. New York:
Russell Sage Foundation, 2009, pp. 27–72.
Portman, Janet. "The Public Defender in a Criminal Case." Nolo.com. (from *The Criminal
Law Handbook*, by Paul Bergman, J.D., and Sara J. Berman, J.D.), https://www.nolo.com/
legal-encyclopedia/the-public-defender.html.

Prison History. "Prison Timeline," http://www.prisonhistory.net/prison-history/prison-time
line/.
Prison Policy Initiative. "U.S. Incarceration Rates by Race and Ethnicity, 2010." https://www
.prisonpolicy.org/graphs/raceinc.html?gclid=Cj0KCQjw4eaJBhDMARIsANhrQACoRIvls
kYMQnW3FKQUqJ8GWuI5si2Hvj_eSsAdDQf0zgsr3dG5l3UaAqU7EALw_wcB.
ProCon.org. "Should the Death Penalty Be Allowed?" Dec, 30, 2019, https://deathpenalty
.procon.org/.
Sentencing Project. "Criminal Justice Facts," https://www.sentencingproject.org/criminal
-justice-facts/.
Widra, Emily, and Tiana Herring. "States of Incarceration: The Global Context 2021." Prison
Policy Initiative, September 2021, https://www.prisonpolicy.org/global/2021.html?gclid=C
j0KCQjw4eaJBhDMARIsANhrQAD-_sdcI-ajyiekPU8-KihLhjtxV3GVwajijHNXsCRM
wvWQGlksyPcaAsDTEALw_wcB.

Videos

Fresh Out. "What Happens to Inmates with Disabilities? Prison Talk 6.6." July 1, 2016,
https://www.youtube.com/watch?v=ExRtzCH2R3c.
Santo, Alysa. "For Most Women Who Give Birth in Prison, 'The Separation' Soon Follows." Frontline, PBS, May 6, 2020, https://www.pbs.org/wgbh/frontline/article/for-most
-women-who-give-birth-in-prison-the-separation-soon-follows/.
Vera Institute of Justice. "Angela J. Davis on Racial Disparities in the Criminal Justice System." Symposium on Justice, Race, and the Criminal Justice System, Harvard Law School,
November 21, 2014, https://www.youtube.com/watch?v=0FFMTQG8ODY.

10

Police Departments

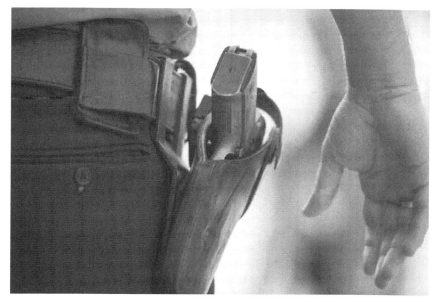

Close-up of a police officer's service firearm. Getty Images: wellphoto.

Police officers represent the criminal law in most US jurisdictions and the arrests they make help populate the prison system. However, there is no national police system on its own that matches the prison system. Rather, the 18,000 police departments or agencies in the United States provide defendants for the courts in the criminal justice system, and those who are convicted or plead guilty become inmates of the prison system. The police departments and agencies include county sheriff's offices, state police or highway patrol, and federal law enforcement agencies. The long and short of it is that police officers arrest people who often end up serving time in prison or jail.

As discussed in chapter 9, the US criminal justice system has a disproportionately large number of African American inmates. There is no evidence apart from their convictions and sentencing for crimes that African Americans are more likely to commit crimes than other racial and ethnic groups. Their over-population of US prisons and jails is viewed by most political progressives, people of color, and social scientists as a form of institutional racism. It is therefore not surprising that antiblack racial bias has been attributed to police officers. As with other forms of institutional racism, police racial bias need not be deliberate or explicit racism. Often, to call police action "racism" is to judge it by its effects. African Americans are disproportionately picked out for arrest based on factors unrelated to the race of individuals but tied to shared behaviors in African American communities that are distinct to those communities. Cocaine arrests are an important example of this.

Cocaine is a dangerous drug that has a debilitating effect on users and addicts and cocaine use and addiction are widespread in the United States. In white suburban and urban neighborhoods, cocaine is consumed in powder form, whereas in black urban areas, it has been more often consumed in "crack" form that is cheaper for intense single-use effects. The chemical compositions of cocaine powder and crack are the same. But the consumption of crack cocaine has been treated as a more serious crime, with harsher penalties. Crack has been portrayed as highly addictive and more likely to induce violence. Two federal sentencing laws in 1986 and 1988 carried a penalty for possession and dealing that amounted to 1 percent of the amounts of crack compared to amounts of cocaine powder. Crack-use postconviction sentences are eighteen times longer than those for cocaine powder. Therefore, police would generally be more highly motivated to make arrests for crack than cocaine powder use and dealing.

The institutional nature of the racism in the crack cocaine powder legal differences lies in the fact that police officers need not explicitly or deliberately consider race in making arrests for crack use and dealing, because its criminality alone makes it more serious than cocaine powder use and dealing. But the higher use of crack in black communities compared to white means that race is already embedded in such arrests. That is the institutional racism involved. However, the discrepancies between police attention to crack and powder cocaine are subtle compared to recent high-profile cases of police killings of unarmed black men. The first section of this chapter is about such killings, ending with the George Floyd case. This is followed by an account of the US Supreme Court rulings that have supported police legal immunity in all such cases. The third section of the chapter is about police reform and its difficulties.

POLICE ACTIONS IN HIGH-PROFILE KILLINGS

No one knows exactly how many unarmed African Americans are killed by police in the United States because police departments vary in reporting practices and central data collection is uneven. The *Washington Post* maintains a year-to-present database and as of September 10, 2021, the latest number was 933 for all police shootings and killings. Half of the fatalities are white but based on their percentages of the total US population, black Americans are killed at twice the rate of white Americans, followed closely by Hispanic/Latino Americans. Not all of the black deaths by white officers involve shootings and most do not make the national news, but a few remain seared in public memory, as follows.

- Eric Garner, age forty-three, died in New York City from a chokehold placed by an officer. He was recorded saying "I can't breathe" numerous times. A grand jury did not indict the officer.
- Michael Brown, age eighteen, was shot in August 2014 in Ferguson, Missouri, followed by weeks of often violent protests. The St. Louis County prosecuting attorney declined to charge the officer after a five-month review.
- Laquan McDonald, age seventeen, was shot sixteen times and killed while walking away from officers in October 2014. The officer was found guilty of second-degree murder and sentenced to seven years in prison.
- Tamir Rice, age twelve, was killed by a Cleveland police officer in November 2014. A grand jury declined to indict.
- Walter Scott, age fifty, was shot in the back after a traffic stop in South Carolina in 2015. The officer was sentenced to twenty years in prison.
- Freddie Gray, age twenty-five, died from a spinal injury while handcuffed and shackled in a Baltimore police van in July 2015. Three officers were acquitted.
- Philando Castile, age thirty-two, was shot five times by a Minnesota police officer during a 2016 traffic stop, after telling the officer he was armed. The officer who killed him was acquitted of manslaughter.
- Jordan Edwards, age fifteen, was killed in Texas after an officer fired at a car with teenagers driving away from a house party in April 2017. The officer was convicted of murder and sentenced to fifteen years in prison.
- Breonna Taylor, age twenty-six, was shot to death in her hallway after Louisville plainclothes narcotics officers raided her apartment in the middle of the night of March 13, 2020. A grand jury brought no charges.

And then there was George Floyd, age forty-six, who was suffocated by Officer Derek Chauvin in Minneapolis, Minnesota, in May 2020. Like Eric Gardner, Floyd repeatedly protested that he could not breathe. The full video recording of George Floyd's death from a knee on his neck for over nine minutes went viral worldwide. Over twenty-six million people participated in protests in the United States. For many, George Floyd's death was a wake-up call about police brutality against African Americans and the problems with US race relations, more generally. Officer Derek Chauvin was convicted of both murder and manslaughter a year later and sentenced to twenty-two and half years in prison in June 2021. Chauvin's arrest and conviction were seen by many as an important turning point for making police officers accountable.

US SUPREME COURT RULINGS AND POLICE IMPUNITY

Many observers, as well as those close to victims, have been sorely disappointed by the lack of police convictions in what appear to be cases of homicide or murder. Many high-profile police killings have been the result of "stop and frisk" practices gone bad. Each year, US police departments voluntarily report "justifiable police homicides" to the FBI, in what is considered an incomplete record. Out of 2,600 justifiable homicides reported from 2005 through 2011, forty-one officers were charged with murder or manslaughter. (Federal agencies have not updated this data since 2014.) The *Washington Post* has reported over five thousand police killings between 2015 and 2020. It is important to realize that grand juries and trial juries receive instructions about the legal definitions of these crimes that are ultimately based on US Supreme Court rulings. Three US Supreme Court decisions are highly relevant: the 1968 opinion in *Terry v. Ohio*, the 1989 opinion in *Graham v. Connor*, and the 2014 ruling in *Plumhoff et al. v. Rickard.*

The decision in *Graham v. Connor* specifies something other than constitutional rights as a standard for what police officers may not do to individuals. In this case, Graham, a diabetic, asked his friend Berry to drive him to a convenience store to purchase orange juice. Graham saw that the store was crowded and hurried out again. Officer O'Connor thought that Graham's movements were suspicious and asked him and Berry to wait while he checked the store. Backup officers arrived and handcuffed Graham, causing injuries. Graham sued, claiming that excessive force had been used in violation of his Fourteenth Amendment rights (to equal protection under the law). The Court held that all claims that enforcement officials have used excessive force must be analyzed under the "objective reasonableness" standard of the Fourth Amendment (freedom from unreasonable search and seizure), rather than a substantive due process standard requiring that "all government intrusions into fundamental rights and liberties be fair and reasonable and in furtherance of a legitimate government interest," according to the Fourteenth Amendment's equal protection clause. The Court framed the objective reasonableness standard in Graham on whether the officers' actions are "objectively reasonable" in light of the facts and circumstances confronting them, without regard to their underlying intent or motivation. The "reasonableness" of a particular use of force must be judged from the perspective of a reasonable officer on the scene, with an allowance made for the fact that police officers are often forced to make split-second decisions about the amount of force necessary in a particular situation. US police academies systematically teach "Graham Factors" for determining when lethal force may legitimately be used: How severe is the crime? Does the suspect pose an immediate threat to the safety of officers and others? Is the suspect resisting arrest or trying to flee?

The legal reliance on the instant judgment of police officers was strengthened in *Plumhoff et al. v. Rickard.* The US Supreme Court ruled in 2014 that individuals' Fourth Amendment rights violations must be balanced against an official's qualified immunity unless it can be shown that the official violated a statutory or constitutional right that was "clearly established" at the time of the challenged conduct. Both *Graham* and *Plumhoff* were a change from a focus on the constitutional rights of citizens against unreasonable (that is, unprovoked and unwarranted) search and seizure to what it seems "reasonable" for a police officer to do in the heat of the moment.

Many Americans still believe that police officers are constrained to behave in ways that make the use of deadly force "a last resort." They may think that the legal world is still governed by the 1985 US Supreme Court ruling in *Tennessee v. Garner*, where the Court wrote, "The use of deadly force to prevent the escape of all felony suspects, whatever the circumstances, is constitutionally unreasonable." But, after *Graham* and *Plumhoff*, if "suspicious" people try to flee, it can be construed as "reasonable" that police officers kill them, because once labeled "suspicious," police officers can reason that the suspect poses a danger to them or other members of the community. Moreover, if police officers fear for their lives—or later report that they feared for their lives—then their use of deadly force can be legal, because according to the Court, their "underlying intent and motivation" are irrelevant to that standard. For example, if officers are biased against black people and believe they are dangerous, in general, they may be quicker to use deadly force against black suspects than those who are not biased in this way.

The context of **stop and frisk**, or stopping people and searching them over their clothing, is often the factor enabling the current uses of deadly force that so many consider unjust. To understand the legality of that situation, we need to go back to Chief Justice Earl Warren's 1968 opinion in *Terry v. Ohio*. Warren first distinguished between "stops" and "arrests" and between "frisks" and "searches": "stops" are brief police interrogations based on suspicion, and "arrests" are taking suspects into custody based on criminal evidence; "frisks" are determinations of whether the suspect has a weapon, restricted to superficial searches or "pat downs" of the surface of the body, undertaken for the officer's immediate safety, whereas "searches" are more invasive investigations that can be performed only after arrests. Mindful of the **exclusionary rule** requiring that criminal evidence be obtained lawfully, before an arrest, the Court narrowed its attention to "whether it is always unreasonable for a policeman to seize a person and subject him to a limited search for weapons unless there is probable cause for an arrest." Warren went on to find that the Fourth Amendment protection against unreasonable searches and seizures applied as much to stops and frisks as to arrests and searches: "We therefore reject the notions that the Fourth Amendment does not come into play at all as a limitation upon police conduct if the officers stop short of something called a 'technical arrest' or a 'full-blown search.'" Warren then answers the question of how a Fourth Amendment intrusion is to be justified, with a "reasonable person" standard:

> The scheme of the Fourth Amendment becomes meaningful only when it is assured that at some point the conduct of those charged with enforcing the laws can be subjected to the more detached, neutral scrutiny of a judge who must evaluate the reasonableness of

a particular search or seizure in light of the particular circumstances. And in making that assessment it is imperative that the facts be judged against an objective standard: would the facts available to the officer at the moment of the seizure or the search "warrant a man of reasonable caution in the belief" that the action taken was appropriate?

Warren recognized that the government has a general interest in crime detection and concluded, based on that interest, that "a police officer may in appropriate circumstances and in an appropriate manner approach a person for purposes of investigating possibly criminal behavior even though there is no probable cause to make an arrest." Furthermore, he added that "It does not follow that because an officer may lawfully arrest a person only when he is apprised of facts sufficient to warrant a belief that the person has committed or is committing a crime, the officer is equally unjustified, absent that kind of evidence, in making any intrusions short of an arrest."

Putting all this together, the US Supreme Court has ruled that police officers may make instant decisions based on what they believe is a situation threatening to their own safety or the public's and that they may act on those decisions without evidence that a crime has been committed, which evidence would be required to justify an arrest. This means that police officers have discretion to use violence without evidence that a crime has or will be committed.

POLICE REFORM AND ITS DIFFICULTIES

George Floyd's death and the protests that followed motivated many to reconsider police reform. Police reform should not be confused with actions to simply abolish or defund police departments. **Police reform** in the context of what have appeared to be racially biased killings is a call for resources and protocols for the peaceful resolution of police-suspect confrontations, when the suspect may be mentally ill or challenged, or simply afraid. Such reform requires improvement in police-community relations, so that police officers know some members of the community and the community as a whole trusts the police officers assigned to it and is willing to cooperate with them to ensure its peace and safety. In many cases, police departments may require further training and be willing to work with social workers to attend to situations that are more matters of mental health than crime.

There are several obstacles to such police reform. First, there cannot be uniform police reform throughout the United States. Although the federal Department of Justice can issue guidelines and conduct investigations in cases that it deems merit it, the 18,000 US police departments and agencies are mainly responsible to state and local authorities. Second, police unions tend to be protective of their members and have both strong local influence as well as national influence in terms of law-and-order and public-safety political rhetoric. In keeping with this, individual police officers may work under the expectation of a certain predetermined number of arrests. Also, US police departments in the early twenty-first century have become increasingly militaristic, with access to grants for the purchase of weapons and armored vehicles used in war and a self-image as warriors rather than community service providers. Finally, police officers are overall very popular in the United States, which is evident in the high number of television shows and movies that feature them as the "good guys." And that means it is difficult to convince the public that police departments need to be reformed to further racial justice.

Despite the obstacles to police reform, by the 1980s and 1990s, more cities adopted community-policing approaches, which were supported by the federal government in the Violent Crime Control and Law Enforcement Act in 1994. This act authorized $8.8 billion to be spent over six years through the Office of Community Oriented Policing Services (COPS). During the Obama administration, ten US cities reported the successful enactment of community-policing programs. Moreover, most police officers who participated in these programs were enthusiastic about them.

The experience of the police department in Camden, New Jersey, provides an encouraging example of community policing. Camden had a population of 74,000 in 2013. The city was in a budgetary crisis and had the highest crime rates in the United States. The mayor fired the entire police force and rehired half of them at reduced pay. The rehires were told that their jobs would be more like working in the Peace Corp than the US Special Forces. Both crime and complaints of police violence decreased and the following incident received wide attention in 2015:

> The officers encountered the man on the sidewalk outside. Instead of shooting him or trying to disarm him, they walked with him for several minutes. "Drop the knife. Sir, drop the knife," one of the officers said repeatedly.
>
> They tried to disable him with a stun gun, but that failed. Still, the officers managed to tackle the man to the ground and disarm him, apparently without causing serious injury.
>
> "There is not a shadow of a doubt in my mind that six months prior to that, we would have shot and killed that man," said [Chief of Police] Scott Thomson, who retired last year. "That was a watershed moment for our organization. And that was a moment in time that really signaled to me that the cops got it right."

QUESTIONS FOR THINKING, DISCUSSION, AND WRITING

1. Let's assume that cocaine use in any form is justifiably illegal. Is there a moral issue in the different treatment of crack and powder cocaine by the US criminal justice system and police who make arrests? Do you think law-abiding citizens should be concerned about racial differences in how criminals are treated? Why or why not, given that they are criminals?

2. Discuss a famous high-profile police killing, other than the George Floyd case, that you found morally objectionable. (Look up the name of the person killed online for further information.) Or, discuss why such killings are not moral issues in your opinion.

3. Explain the gaps in the guilt of police officers who kill unarmed suspects provided by the US Supreme Court rulings discussed in this chapter. How do you assess these rulings in moral terms?

4. Explain how the structure of policing in the United States impedes whole-scale reform.

5. For what kinds of stops by police would community policing prevent violence? To what kinds of stops would it not apply?

SOURCES

Abramson, Jerry. "10 Cities Making Real Progress Since the Launch of the 21st Century Policing Task Force." White House/President Barack Obama, May 18, 2015, https://obama whitehouse.archives.gov/blog/2015/05/18/10-cities-making-real-progress-launch-21st -century-policing-task-force.

Adams, Richard E., William M. Rohe, Thomas A. Arcury. "Implementing Community-Oriented Policing: Organizational Change and Street Officer Attitudes." Crime and Delinquency, July 1, 2002, https://www.ojp.gov/ncjrs/virtual-library/abstracts/implementing -community-oriented-policing-organizational-change-and.

Arango, Tim. "Derek Chauvin Is Sentenced to 22 and a Half Years for Murder of George Floyd." *New York Times*, June 25, 2021, https://www.nytimes.com/2021/06/25/us/derek -chauvin-22-and-a-half-years-george-floyd.html.

Bittner, E. "Quasi-Military Organization of Police." In *Police and Society: Touchstone Readings*, Victor E. Kappeler, ed., *National Criminal Justice Reference Service* (NCJRS), NCJ-151401 (1995): 173–84, https://www.ojp.gov/ncjrs/virtual-library/abstracts/quasi-military-organi zation-police-police-and-society-touchstone.

Breslauer, Brenda, Kit Ramgopal, Kenzi Abou-Sabe, and Stephanie Gosk. "Camden, N.J., Disbanded Its Police Force: Here's What Happened Next." NBC News, June 22, 2020, https://www.nbcnews.com/news/us-news/new-jersey-city-disbanded-its-police-force-here -s-what-n1231677; see also this Twitter photo of Camden during the George Floyd protests, https://twitter.com/CamdenCountyPD/status/1266882383980216320?s=19.

"Derek Chauvin Guilty: A Look at High-Profile Cases over Killings by US Police." King5 .com, April 20, 2021, https://www.king5.com/article/news/nation-world/high-profile -police-killings-us/507-7693bcc4-492a-46f5-8c69-6159d2a13efc.

Discover Policing. "Types of Law Enforcement Agencies." https://www.discoverpolicing.org/ explore-the- field/types-of-law-enforcement-agencies/.

"Fatal Force." *Washington Post*, September 10, 2021, https://www.washingtonpost.com/graphics /investigations/police-shootings-database/.

Graham v. Connor, 490 U.S. 389 (1989), https://www.oyez.org/cases/1988/87-6571.

Lawrence, Sarah, and Bobby McCarthy, "What Works in Community Policing." Chief Justice Earl Warren Institute on Law and Social Policy, University of California, Berkeley School of Law, November 2013, https://www.law.berkeley.edu/files/What_Works_in_Community _Policing.pdf.

"Lists of Killings by Law Enforcement Officers in the United States." Wikipedia, July 13, 2020, https://en.wikipedia.org/wiki/Lists_of_killings_by_law_enforcement_officers_in_the_United_States.

NYU, Education and Social Sciences. "Powder vs. Crack: NYU Study Identifies Arrest Risk Disparity for Cocaine Use." February 19, 2015, https://www.nyu.edu/about/news-publications/news/2015/february/-powder-vs-crack-nyu-study-identifies-arrest-risk-disparity-for-cocaine-use.html.

Plumhoff et al. v. Rickard, US Supreme Court, October Term, 2014, https://www.supremecourt.gov/opinions/13pdf/12-1117_1bn5.pdf.

Sentencing Project. "Crack Cocaine Sentencing Policy: Unjustified and Unreasonable." https://www.prisonpolicy.org/scans/sp/1003.pdf.

Tennessee v. Garner, 471 U.S. 1 (1985), FindLaw, 7–12, https://caselaw.findlaw.com/us-supreme-court/471/1.html

Terry v. Ohio, 392 U.S. 1 (1968), no. 67, https://supreme.justia.com/cases/federal/us/392/1/

Videos

ABC News YouTube. "George Floyd: A Man, a Moment, America Changed." April 24, 2020, https://www.youtube.com/watch?v=kszgl-VkDM0.

Marshall, Madeline. "Why America's Police Look Like Soldiers, Why Are the Police Bringing Military Assault Rifles to Protests?" Vox.com, June 25, 2020, https://www.vox.com/2020/6/25/21303538/american-police-soldiers-1033-program.

Woodruff, Judy, and Hari Sreenivasan. "What Happened When Camden Started Rethinking Policing to Build Trust." PBS News Hour, June 30, 2017, https://www.pbs.org/newshour/show/happened-camden-started-rethinking-policing-build-trust.

11

Dignity, Income, and Wealth

Homeless man with dog. Getty Images: juefraphoto.

In chapter 1, we discussed the moral system of deontology or duty ethics, as set forth by Immanuel Kant. Kant had two formulations of his categorical imperative: that duties were absolute obligations centered on intentions and that we ought never to treat human beings as means to ends because they are ends in themselves with intrinsic value. Kant also made an important distinction between price and dignity. According to Kant, most things that are not human beings have prices, which means they can be exchanged with other things that have prices. However, individual human beings have **dignity** or absolute worth that makes them valuable and irreplaceable to themselves and others. This difference between price and dignity is useful for understanding social and legal rules to help those who need help, even if nothing unjust, illegal, or immoral has been done to them so that they do need help. The idea or intuition of human dignity has motivated safety-net programs or entitlements to aid in capitalistic countries where people are assumed to be responsible for their own economic conditions.

Programs such as old-age pensions and medical payments, free food, special aid to poor children, compensation for the victims of disaster, unemployment payments, and even the idea of guaranteed income are promoted politically with no mention of dignity or even rights. But the underlying assumption is that there is a value of human life that requires more than merely being alive biologically, which everyone in a community should seek to uphold. The idea of dignity is useful for morally evaluating **entitlements** or government-supported policies that help those whose material circumstances, as measured in prices such as their income and wealth, insult their dignity without such help. The first section of this chapter is a discussion of economic dignity for racial minorities—among others. A discussion of employment and income follows next and the chapter concludes with a section on wealth.

RACIAL MINORITIES AND ECONOMIC DIGNITY

Dignity is a universal human absolute because every human being has intrinsic worth, worth in being a human being. **Economic dignity** is a specific aspect of human dignity, which means being able to afford the necessities of life in a given society. The poor person in a poor country, the rich person in a poor country, the poor person in a rich country, and the rich person in a rich country all have the same absolute human dignity. However, dignity can be recognized, experienced, and insulted in different ways. Economic dignity is a relative quality because necessities and their cost vary. On a global level, very poor people in rich societies may experience economic indignities, but in poor societies, those with comparable resources may not experience the same indignities. For example, a person with only one outfit, surviving on one meal a day, might feel ashamed or be socially devalued in the United States, which insults their dignity. But in a country where the average income is one-sixtieth of the American average, that insult to dignity might not be experienced.

Racial minorities in the United States are more likely to experience economic indignities than white groups because they are more likely to be poor than whites. In February 2021, the Urban Institute projected an overall US poverty rate of 13.7 percent, or one in seven Americans. White non-Hispanic Americans had a poverty rate of 9.6 percent; black non-Hispanic, 18.1 percent; and Hispanic, 21.9 percent. Because whites are the majority at about 60 percent of the population, the number of white poor people is the largest, followed by Hispanics and blacks. However, the poor proportion within the Hispanic population is highest, followed by blacks. Affirmative action–type programs have proven vastly unpopular and legally unsustainable, so the most politically viable antipoverty programs would need to be racially inclusive. In sheer numbers, such programs would improve conditions for larger numbers of whites than Hispanics or blacks. Therefore, there is unlikely to be a strong white backlash against such programs if nonwhites benefit more in numbers relative to their groups.

Poverty itself is a relative lack of income and wealth. **Income** is the amount of money a person regularly earns or is paid from other sources. **Wealth** is the total monetary value of what a person owns, made up of cash, savings, investments, and material possessions, especially equity in real estate (how much the real estate is worth minus what is owed on it). **Net worth** is the sum of a person's wealth minus all of their debts.

Poor people throughout the world spend more of their time helping one another than do poor people in rich Western nations. A society like the United States, which is based on nuclear families, often in single-parent households, has less extended family and local community resources for help with the conditions of poverty. Among the poor, generally, and poor people of color, in particular, some groups suffer more than others. Children living in poverty have limited opportunities to develop their potential and, because they are children, may not understand their circumstances. The elderly, prison inmates, and those with disabilities have limits on their mobility, which can affect their agency. But homeless people are the most disadvantaged of the poor because their basic human functioning is criminalized.

There are many subgroups among homeless people—families, mothers with children, teenage runaways, drug addicts and alcoholics, veterans, those who are mentally ill, those who "couch surf," and those who are only temporarily homeless because they have been evicted while unemployed but will likely find employment soon. It is not known exactly how many Americans are homeless. Most counts of homeless people focus on those who have used shelter services, but there are many more who do not stay in shelters but live in temporary camps, anywhere, or in urban areas, under bridges, and on the streets. According to 2017 figures from the National Alliance to End Homelessness, 553,742 are homeless on any given night. From 2016 to 2017, homelessness increased nationally by 0.7 percent, with the largest increases among unaccompanied children and young adults. Some experts have claimed that there are three or more million homeless people in the United States.

A person is **homeless** if they do not have a permanent dwelling in which they can sleep. As a result, normal bodily functions, such as eating, going to the bathroom, and sleeping are performed in public, as is loitering. Many jurisdictions have criminalized these behaviors with penalties ranging from fines, jail time, or brutal eviction from temporary dwellings. Such "crimes of misery" garner little sympathy from housed people who are often frightened and repelled or simply annoyed by the sight of homeless people in public. Since about 2007, most local solutions to homelessness have involved the provision of housing. Giving a homeless person a free place to live, likely at taxpayer expense, may seem like an ultimate act of public charity. However, some social and political theorists have provided deeper explanations, which go beyond human misery, to explain why homelessness is unjust. In a now-classic essay, first published in 1991–1992, legal and political philosopher Jeremy Waldron analyzed homelessness in terms of fundamental rights to freedom. He wrote:

> Homelessness is partly about property and law, and freedom provides the connecting term that makes those categories relevant. By considering not only what a person is allowed to do, but where he is allowed to do it, we can see a system of property for what it is: rules that provide freedom and prosperity for some by imposing restrictions on others.

Waldron's insight is that within a system of property, freedom entails both what a person is allowed to do and where they may do it. Homelessness shows how the system of property restricts the freedom of those who become homeless because they have no legitimate claims to property. This restriction on the freedom of homeless people emphasizes the freedom of those who do have legitimate claims to property, and it shows how something as abstract as freedom is connected to an economic system of property ownership and claims. Without a claim to property, through ownership, renting, permission, or inheritance/gift, the most basic freedoms of human functioning are unavailable for those who are homeless.

Dignity is also at issue in homelessness, not only because it is undignified to perform certain bodily functions in public, but because those indignities are compounded by preexisting prejudice against people of color. African Americans make up more than 40 percent of the population of homeless people, although they are 13 percent of the overall population. Indeed, histories of explicit racial discrimination and legacies of undignified stereotypes in the present compound the condition of homelessness for most nonwhite racial and ethnic groups (see figure 11.1). This is not merely a matter of being without a permanent dwelling or dealing with existence in public. Rather, all homeless people of color are subject to ongoing disparagement and contempt, simply because they are black, Latinx, or Native American. Homelessness of people of color is also connected to issues of income and wealth, through institutional racism that has made homeownership more difficult—as we will see in the third section of this chapter.

EMPLOYMENT AND INCOME

Most Americans and most members of minority groups get most of their income from employment, which is to say that they earn it. Unemployment rates have hovered around 9–10 percent during downturns in the economy such as the Great Recession of 2008–2009 and disruptions caused during the COVID-19 pandemic. The Census Bureau report on income, poverty, and health insurance coverage in 2019 reveals impressive growth in median household income relative to 2008, across

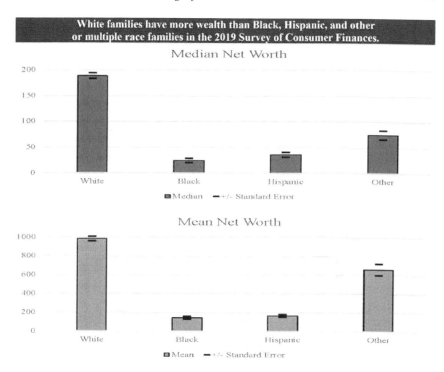

Figure 11.1 Family net worth in thousands of dollars according to the 2019 Survey of Consumer Finances. Note that the mean is higher than the median, because it is the average or most common value, influenced more by higher numbers than the median. Source: Neil Bhutta, Andrew C. Chang, Lisa J. Dettling, and Joanne W. Hsu (2020). "Disparities in Wealth by Race and Ethnicity in the 2019 Survey of Consumer Finances," FEDS Notes. Washington: Board of Governors of the Federal Reserve System, September 28, 2020, https://doi.org/10.17016/2380-7172.2797. https://www.federal reserve.gov/econres/notes/feds-notes/disparities-in-wealth-by-race-and-ethnicity-in-the -2019-survey-of-consumer-finances-20200928.htm.

all racial and ethnic groups. Still, income gaps persist. According to the US Census, median (number separating higher from lower half of a set of figures) household income increased by 10.6 percent among Asian households (from $88,774 to $98,174), 8.5 percent among black households (from $42,447 to $46,073), 7.1 percent among Hispanic households (from $52,382 to $56,113), and 5.7 percent among non-Hispanic white households (from $71,922 to $76,057). The starkest difference is between black and white households.

According to the Pew Research Center, the tight labor market or higher demand for labor coming out of the COVID-19 pandemic in 2020, narrowed the unemployment gap between whites and people of color. Nevertheless, racial gaps in unemployment have been historically consistent for several deep structural reasons involving institutions, policies, and attitudes. Black unemployment has fairly consistently been about twice that of whites, despite economic booms and busts. Without structural changes, the aggregate unemployment rate would need to be about 1 percent to close the racial gap between black and white men and 1.75 percent to close the gap between white and black and Hispanic women. An economy with full employment such as that is unlikely to be achieved in a free market, capitalistic society.

Why do people of color earn less money than white people in the United States? The answer lies in their disproportionate lack of degrees in higher education (see chapter 12) and the resulting nature of available employment. Attainable jobs are not solidly middle class. Apart from unskilled labor across industries and service sectors, people of color are disproportionately employed as frontline workers, who overlap with essential workers. During the early days of the COVID-19 pandemic, **essential workers** were recognized as those necessary to keep infrastructure functioning. They included police officers, fire responders, medical first responders, doctors, nurses, delivery people, grocery and pharmacy workers, defense workers, janitors, and scores of other kinds of workers in utilities, transportation, agriculture, and childcare. Except for doctors, their pay was about $27/hour and they made up 70 percent of the pre-COVID workforce. **Frontline workers**, who are part of the essential-worker workforce, disproportionately have socioeconomically disadvantaged backgrounds; they make up about one-third of the total workforce, including healthcare workers, store cashiers, food processors, janitors, maintenance workers, and truck drivers; they earn about $22/hour. Higher-paying jobs in management and occupations that do not require physical labor are disproportionately filled by Asians and whites. Thus, 54 percent of employed Asians work in management, professional, and related occupations, compared to 41 percent of employed whites, 31 percent of employed blacks, and 22 percent of employed Hispanics.

Statistics alone do not convey the suffering attending extreme poverty in the United States. We have already considered the existential burdens of those who are homeless. Many others among the "working poor" barely make ends meet and often have to choose among necessities: Food or medicine? Transportation or rent? Sleep and recreation or a third job? Some of these pressures would be eased if there were a **guaranteed income** or a fixed amount of money that either everyone or some preselected income group received. Social experiments with guaranteed income in Europe and Canada have had mixed results, although overall, a greater sense of well-being has been reported. However, given the political controversies of plans to help homeless people, aid to families with dependent children, and universal health insurance, guaranteed income policies have not gained much traction in the United States.

WEALTH

An individual or family's wealth consists of accumulated net worth, sometimes over generations. Differences in wealth among Americans vary significantly according to race and ethnicity.

In the Federal Reserve System 2019 survey, white families had the highest level of both median and mean family wealth: $188,200 and $983,400. Black families' median and mean wealth was less than 15 percent that of white families, at $24,100 and $142,500. Hispanic families' median and mean wealth was $36,100 and $165,500, respectively. The group including those identifying as Asian, American Indian, Alaska Native, Native Hawaiian, Pacific Islander, "some other race," as well as those reporting more than one racial identification, had lower wealth than white families, but higher wealth than black and Hispanic families. For each of the four race/ethnicity groups, the mean was higher than the median, reflecting the concentration of wealth at the top of the wealth distribution within each group. That is, each racial and ethnic group has different wealth stratifications within it. This is important to note for minority groups, because some may assume that groups different from their own have uniform economic conditions. However, for an average sense of difference, the median or the number that divides the upper half from the lower half is probably a better indicator than the mean.

In addition to differences in income, savings and investments account for much of the racial and ethnic wealth discrepancies. Practically, for many Americans, homeownership is the greatest source of wealth because a home is a passive investment that usually increases in value over time and mortgages are paid off over time. There is a persistent gap in homeownership between American blacks and whites. Before the COVID-19 pandemic, only 40 percent of blacks owned their own homes, compared to over 51 percent of Hispanics and 76 percent of whites. Native Hawaiian and Pacific Islanders and Asians had a homeownership rate of over 61 percent. The gap between black and white homeownership was wide even in cities with the largest proportion of black households. The Urban Institute has found that current obstacles to black homeownership vary according to location. In 2019, they proposed a multifaceted approach that involves: policy solutions for specific localities; removing housing supply constraints, equitable financing, outreach to renters and millennials, and a focus on sustainable homeownership and upkeep. It's not surprising that the Urban Institute advocates a location-specific approach because it is well known that although housing prices can be calculated in national trends, specific price ranges and the amount of property on the market vary greatly by state, city, township, and neighborhood.

In addition to local differences, the racial homeownership gap has general characteristics. Young white people buying their first homes are often helped by parents. Part of the reason white parents are wealthier than parents of color is because of the factor of homeownership over generations. Not only has black income consistently been lower than white income, but the ability to accumulate wealth through homeownership has met obstacles of neighborhood prejudice and so-called **redlining** whereby banks and mortgage companies give less favorable rates to purchasers buying in black neighborhoods. Another factor has been **gentrification**, when white middle-class buyers bid up the cost of homes in minority neighborhoods, driving out their initial occupants. Thus, while according to the Fair Housing Act of 1964 discrimination in housing is illegal, black people have faced obstacles to home buying that white people have not faced.

In addition to social and economic practices, the US Supreme Court has upheld practices that have antiblack discriminatory housing effects. There was a moratorium on renter evictions during the COVID-19 pandemic. When it was set to expire, the Biden administration sought to extend it. But in *Alabama Association of Realtors v. Department of Health and Human Services*, the US Supreme Court ruled in August 2021 that it could not be extended because, as a policy, it exceeded the authority of the Centers for Disease Control and Prevention (CDC) that had initiated it. According to the Brookings Institution, this decision was consistent with a history of US Supreme Court rulings that have increased the suffering of black Americans, although the direct intent of such rulings has been to preserve democratic institutional structures, such as states' rights and differences in government agencies' powers. As a result, evictions are likely to separate family members and increase COVID-19 transmission in their community. Black neighborhoods have already had disproportionately high numbers of evictions, as well as high COVID-19 transmission. Brookings suggests that effective measures to benefit African Americans need to be achieved through federal legislation.

QUESTIONS FOR THINKING, DISCUSSION, AND WRITING

1. Explain how dignity as posited by Kant comes down to little things, as described in the NWDignityLeads video. How can poverty be an insult to human dignity?
2. Explain how homelessness is worse for people of color than white people in the United States and how this is another form of antiblack institutional racism.
3. Do you think discrepancies in income according to race are morally wrong? Why or why not? How would you evaluate a guaranteed income policy in moral terms?
4. Explain how family wealth has been connected to homeownership in different ways for white and nonwhite families in the United States.
5. Do you think differences in wealth are a moral wrong, as associated with race? Why or why not?

SOURCES

Bhutta, Neil, Andrew C. Chang, Lisa J. Dettling, Joanne W. Hsu, and Julia Hewitt. "Disparities in Wealth by Race and Ethnicity in the 2019 Survey of Consumer Finances." FEDS Notes, Board of Governors of the Federal Reserve System, September 28, 2020, https://www.federalreserve.gov/econres/notes/feds-notes/disparities-in-wealth-by-race-and-ethnicity-in-the-2019-survey-of-consumer-finances-20200928.htm.

Choi, Jung Hyun, Alanna McCargo, Michael Neal, Laurie Goodman, and Caitlin Young. "Explaining the Black-White Homeownership Gap, a Closer Look at Disparities across

Local Markets." Research Report, Urban Institute, October 2019 (updated November 2019), https://www.urban.org/sites/default/files/publication/100204/building_black_own ership_bridges_1.pdf.

Giannarelli, Linda, Laura Wheaton, and Katie Shantz. "2021 Poverty Projections: One in Seven Americans Are Projected to Have Resources below the Poverty Level in 2021." Urban Institute, February 2021, https://www.urban.org/sites/default/files/publication /103656/2021-poverty-projections.pdf.

Guo, Eileen. "Universal Basic Income Is Here—It Just Looks Different from What You Expected, How the Pandemic Took the Concept of Universal Basic Income Out of Silicon Valley's Hands—and Turned It into Something Far More Radical." *MIT Technology Review*, May 7, 2021, https://www.technologyreview.com/2021/05/07/1024674/ubi-guaranteed -income-pandemic/.

McNicholas, Celine, and Margaret Poydock. "Who Are Essential Workers? A Comprehensive Look at Their Wages, Demographics, and Unionization Rates." Economic Policy Institute, May 19, 2020, https://www.epi.org/blog/who-are-essential-workers-a-comprehensive-look -at-their-wages-demographics-and-unionization-rates/.

Mitchell, Bruce, and Juan Franco. "Home Owners' Loan Corporation 'Redlining' Maps: The Persistent Structure of Segregation and Economic Inequality." 2018, dataspace.princeton .edu, https://dataspace.princeton.edu/handle/88435/dsp01dj52w776n.

Molteni, Megan. "Why Meatpacking Plants Have Become Covid-19 Hot Spots." *Wired*, May 7, 2020, https://www.wired.com/story/why-meatpacking-plants-have-become-covid -19-hot-spots/.

National Alliance to End Homelessness. "Racial Inequality in Homelessness, by the Numbers." June 1, 2020, https://endhomelessness.org/resource/racial-inequalities-homelessness -numbers/.

National Alliance to End Homelessness. "The State of Homelessness in America." https://end homelessness.org/homelessness-in-america/homelessness-statistics/state-of-homelessness -report-legacy/ (consulted September 2021).

Romer, Carl, and Kristen Broady. "In Overturning the Eviction Moratorium, the Supreme Court Continues Its History of Harming Black Households." The Avenue, Brookings, September 14, 2021, https://www.brookings.edu/blog/the-avenue/2021/09/14/in-overturning -the-eviction-moratorium-the-supreme-court-continues-its-history-of-harming-black -households/?utm_campaign=Brookings%20Brief&utm_medium=email&utm_content =159977144&utm_source=hs_email.

US Bureau of Labor Statistics. "Labor Force Characteristics by Race and Ethnicity, 2018." Oct. 2019, https://www.bls.gov/opub/reports/race-and-ethnicity/2018/home.htm.

Waldron, Jeremy. "Homelessness and the Issue of Freedom." Originally published in 39 *UCLA Law Review* 295 (1991–1992), https://constcourt.ge/files/2/Journal2019.1/Jeremy -Waldron-2019.1eng.pdf (quotation from p. 14).

Wilson, Valerie. "Racial Disparities in Income and Poverty Remain Largely Unchanged Amid Strong Income Growth in 2019." Working Economics Blog, Economic Policy Institute, September 16, 2020, https://www.epi.org/blog/racial-disparities-in-income-and-poverty -remain-largely-unchanged-amid-strong-income-growth-in-2019/.

Wood, Allan. "The Final Form of Kant's Practical Philosophy in Kant's Ethical Thought." In *Kant's Metaphysics of Morals: Interpretive Essays*, Mark Timmons, ed. Oxford: Oxford University Press, 2002, pp. 5–10.

Videos

Aaronson, Stephanie, Mitchell Barnes, and Wendy Edelberg. "A Hot Labor Market Won't Eliminate Racial and Ethnic Unemployment Gaps." Think Tank, Pew Research.org, September 2, 2021, https://www.pewresearch.org/fact-tank/2013/08/21/through-good-times -and-bad-black-unemployment-is-consistently-double-that-of-whites/.

Connley, Courtney. "Why the Homeownership Gap between White and Black Americans Is Larger Today Than It Was Over 50 Years Ago." Make It, CNBC, Aug. 21, 2020, https:// www.cnbc.com/2020/08/21/why-the-homeownership-gap-between-white-and-black -americans-is-larger-today-than-it-was-over-50-years-ago.html.

National Alliance to End Homelessness. "Racial Equity and Emergency Shelter: Access and Outcomes." Toolkits and Training Materials, October 14, 2020, https://endhomelessness .org/resource/racial-equity-and-emergency-shelter-access-and-outcomes/.

NWDignityLeads. "Dignity—Little Things Make a Big Difference." January 8, 2012, YouTube, https://www.youtube.com/watch?v=ueLqAJRxKpQ.

PBS. "New Deal I: FDR's First 100 Days." Collection: Ken Burns in the Classroom, PBS Learning Media, https://ny.pbslearningmedia.org/resource/new-deal-i-fdr-first-100-days -video/ken-burns-the-roosevelts/.

12

Education

African descent female graduate and friends on college campus. Getty Images: fstop123.

Our word "education" derives from the Latin word "educare," which means "to bring up." Another Latin word, "educere," means "to bring forth." Putting these together, in Latin we have *"Educit obstertrix, educate nutrix, institute pedagogues, docet magister"* or, "The midwife brings forth, the nurse brings up, the tutor trains, and the master teaches." Others have said that education means "to lead forth" or extract the best in the student. In Plato's dialogue *Meno*, Socrates (c. 470–399 BC) tried to prove that education was the bringing forth of *innate knowledge* or inherited truths that the child already had. The medieval philosopher Thomas Aquinas (1225–1274) objected to these passive views of the student. When asked, "Can one man teach another?" his answer was, "Yes, provided that the student goes through a process of thought which is similar to that of his teacher." Aquinas meant that knowledge learned in education was not passive but active.

Today, education is a process of both teaching and learning for its own sake and teaching and learning so that the student is equipped to successfully enter society in different ways. For instance, in the United States, K–12 education usually includes history and literature, as well as civics classes that provide information about how to function as a citizen. Higher education provides more specialized knowledge and introduction to new subjects, which enhance employment prospects; it can also lead to graduate professional degrees that enable employment in the professions. Education thus has an important role of **certification** or officially recording that a student has gone through a specific study of learning about something or practical training for doing something. These two parts of learning or studying, and training or doing, are the key components of a modern process of education and both are now options for certification for racial and ethnic minority groups. But history teaches us that training has taken precedence over studying for these groups. If training without studying limits human flourishing, the choice of only training and certification is a moral matter—for everyone but especially for minorities.

Training is easy enough to understand because it has practical value and certification, for instance, a medical degree, a degree in accounting, or just a plain college degree. But studying in what has come to be called "the liberal arts" or humanities in American higher education is not as clearly understood. In ancient Greece, education in general, philosophical discussion, and political activity were leisure activities. **Leisure** in the ancient world was not what we would count as recreation today. While recreation now is important for pleasure and relaxation, it is not considered a serious adult activity on its own. Leisure in the ancient world consisted of activities pursued by those who did not have to do manual labor to survive. Those with leisure were free, well-born, somewhat affluent men. Women, slaves, and "mechanics" or workers had no leisure. Leisure was presented as an ideal in ancient Athens, although some have claimed that it was politically elitist and subject to pushback from workers at the time.

To this day, even worthwhile activities of leisure that are not accessible to everyone are criticized as implicitly harmful to those who cannot pursue them and useless apart from symbolizing class status. For example, the high arts in the United States, such as opera, symphonic music, and museum art, are supported by wealthy patrons. Middle-class people may be part of the audience but for working-class or poor people who cannot attend or do not regard them as pleasurable, they are useless. The academic discipline of philosophy, as well as literature, are instances of leisure studies in higher education and some might object to them in the same way—as elitist and useless. It is important to sort out these issues of elitism and usefulness in modern education, again because human well-being is at stake, which makes it a moral matter, especially for racial and ethnic minorities who do not have the same access as white students.

We saw in chapter 7 that 25 percent of African Americans have college degrees, compared to about 40 percent of whites. And it was also evident that although there may be race-neutral opportunities for higher education, the ability to take advantage of those opportunities, or access to them, is not race-neutral. New programs suggest that equal access is now an important political and social topic. For example, at the start of the fall 2021 school year, every kindergarten pupil in New York City received $100 for a college fund. By the time a student graduates from high school, assuming a 5 percent return a year, that fund will have grown to $3,000. Parents and pupils can also add to the fund. Research suggests that even though these funds will not cover college tuition, knowing that there is some money available for college results in stronger intentions to attend college. Similar programs have been instituted throughout the United States.

The first part of this chapter is about the structure of the US educational system. Next, we will consider the study versus training/leisure versus work components of education and how they are related to racial and ethnic minorities. The third part is about the recent political and cultural debate about the content of high school and college education, which is focused on the 1619 Project and critical race theory.

THE STRUCTURE OF THE US EDUCATIONAL SYSTEM

Like police departments in our federal system, there is no national educational system. Primary and secondary education is now divided into about one hundred thousand school districts, over a fivefold degree of localization compared to police departments, which number about 18,000 (see chapter 10). Public schools are tied to specific neighborhoods and 87 percent of the 56.4 million US school-age students attend them, while 10 percent attend private and foundation-funded schools, and 3 percent are homeschooled. State laws make education compulsory between the ages of five and eight to sixteen and eighteen, depending on the state. At a total cost of $1.3 trillion, most of which comes from states and localities, the United States has the most expensive primary and secondary educational system in the world. But the overall knowledge and skills of American fifteen-year-olds, in reading, literacy, mathematics, and science, is thirty-first in the world. So before even considering differences related to race and ethnicity, we should note that US K–12 education has broad problems.

Pertaining to differences in race and ethnicity, not all K–12 school districts have the same resources. This situation is the direct result of funding via school taxes.

Wealthier, white neighborhoods have higher-priced housing, which results in higher school tax revenue. Poor and nonwhite neighborhood school districts have much lower revenue. Some have stressed the importance of monetary resources for good schools, in building upkeep, teacher qualifications, and cultural and learning materials. Thus, racially and ethnically segregated housing patterns directly underlie inadequate resources for black and brown K–12 students. (See also chapter 14.) However, monetary resources are not the only factor in the quality of education. A lack of diversity in the nature of history that is taught, low expectations on the part of white teachers, and destabilizing factors in homes also contribute. The net effect is that there is a **racial achievement gap**, as measured by significantly different scores on standardized tests by black and white middle school pupils.

Man Hung et al. in their study of achievement data for white and black students from 2008 to 2013, covering data from 2,868 school districts for grades three to eight, in mathematics and English language, found surprising factors that were predictive of achievement gaps. Economic inequality, racial inequality, and household adult education were most strongly associated with achievement gaps. Pupil-teacher ratios and funds allocated per student were less predictive of achievement gaps. It is reassuring that pupil-teacher ratios or class size are not as important as many believe and interesting that for schools mainly populated by students of color, funding alone is unlikely to close achievement gaps. The researchers reasoned that in highly educated, competitive communities, parents using adult education resources experience racism and stress that hampers their children's performance in school. This finding was surprising concerning the family benefits from adult education by minority parents. It seems more intuitive that a parent's pursuit of education would inspire their children to higher achievement in school. However, it does make sense that parental stress associated with adult education in a competitive environment could hinder pupil achievement because it is well known that children are sensitive to the stress experienced by their parents. It may also be that if pupils see adults in their household pursuing education, they may feel that it is less necessary for them to take educational demands seriously because they can catch up later. (The study by Hung et al. did not seek data for this hypothesis or put it forward as an interpretation.)

The structure of US higher education is even more complex than that of K–12 education, and it plays varied roles throughout society. The schools include selective elite universities, public universities, private liberal arts colleges, historically black colleges and universities, Hispanic-serving colleges, Native American colleges, community colleges, and for-profit, distance-learning colleges. Eight of the top ten colleges and universities in the world are in the United States (the remaining two are Oxford and Cambridge in the United Kingdom). There are 6,606 institutions of higher education in the United States, of which 4,360 grant degrees from 2,863 four-year schools and 1,538 are community colleges.

Higher education enrollment tends to fluctuate with the broader economy, often increasing at lower-cost institutions during recessions because unemployment can make further education an attractive option if it's difficult to find a job. The total operating costs of US higher education are about $600 billion with $600 billion in endowment or funds and investments in reserve, plus the value of their real estate. In the whole US yearly economy of about $20 trillion, the expenses of higher education are less than half that of the K–12 system and this aligns with the fact that only about 40 percent of Americans have college degrees. Higher education also supports health care through academic medical centers and research. Research institutions are major employers in forty-four US states and employ close to one million researchers and trainees.

LEISURE VERSUS WORK

Primary and secondary school education is mainly compulsory while higher education is optional. People attend college for a variety of reasons and pragmatic concerns about upward socioeconomic mobility may be the main one. This brings us back to the studying versus training or leisure versus work issue discussed at the outset of this chapter. The college enrollment rate for eighteen- to twenty-four-year-olds attending two- and four-year institutions increased within racial and ethnic groups between 2000 and 2018 for blacks, Hispanics, and whites and remained constant for Asians who already led enrollment. The 2018 enrollments were: Asian 59 percent, white 42 percent, black 37 percent, and Hispanic 36 percent.

We saw in chapter 7 that in 2015–2016, approximately 45 percent of all undergraduate students identified as nonwhite, compared with 29.6 percent in 1995–1996. This seems like a significant improvement in nonwhite college attendance, overall. But it is important to keep two things in mind: Not every college has 45 percent nonwhite students because elite institutions and many public institutions in predominantly white states, as well as colleges in predominantly white regions, have far lower percentages of minority students. Second, many nonwhite students of color are the first in their families to attend college.

Some nonwhite students in college may not have experienced study for its own sake or experienced the value of intellectual activity in its own right. They may therefore enroll in college with a focus on certification toward better-paying employment when they graduate. Still, their admission to college may be encouraged by administrators because of the benefits of diversity (see chapter 7). Ideas of diversity from a white majority perspective can be traced back to John Dewey (1859–1952), the great (white) American philosopher, educator, and psychologist. In "Ethical Principles Underlying Education," Dewey wrote: "The school cannot be a preparation for social life excepting as it reproduces, within itself, the typical conditions of social life." Dewey was advocating racial and ethnic plurality or diversity in education, but mere plurality does not get us to equality within institutions or to equal aims for nonwhite and white students.

There is a history of not only ideas of nonwhite intellectual inferiority (see chapters 3 and 4) but deliberate separate training for manual work for African Americans. The late nineteenth-century debate between Booker T. Washington (1856–1915) and W. E. B. Du Bois (1868–1963), the most influential African American public intellectuals of their day, was about this issue. Washington, an **accommodationist**, thought that African Americans should accept discrimination and segregation and better their conditions through hard work, seeking employment in building trades and crafts, industry, and agriculture. Du Bois, by contrast, advocated civil rights activism and college training of an elite group of African Americans who he called "the talented tenth." The role of the talented tenth did not address the intellectual activity of the other 90 percent.

Anna J. Cooper (1858–1964), influential African American educator, activist, writer, and high school principal, did strongly advocate for humanities or liberal arts education for all black pupils. Cooper emphasized the importance of liberal arts education, in ways still relevant today. **Critical reasoning skills** can be taught so that students can deliberately analyze and solve problems using logic and evidence. Philosophy deepens those skills. History helps everyone understand their own and others' present place in the world. Literature broadens consciousness to include experiences that one may never have in one's own life. Altogether, education in the humanities, while it may not seem to be directly relevant to earning a living, betters the quality of life itself, besides being enjoyable in its own right.

CONTROVERSIAL CONTENT

Continuing from Dewey's emphasis on plurality, he also deserves credit for the core idea of multicultural education as a need to accept students as they are already part of communities outside of the classroom. Dewey was speaking mainly about K–12 education, but his insights have been applied to college education and scholarly work. The cultural backgrounds of all students should be part of the education of all students. This means that curricula on all levels should be taught by faculty from all groups, with content that represents the history and place in society of members of all groups. During the COVID-19 pandemic, two multicultural subjects, which were already routinely taught in many high schools and colleges, rose to prominence in national controversy in the United States: the *New York Times* 1619 Project and critical race theory.

The 1619 Project, first published by the *New York Times* four hundred years after the first slave ship containing twenty Africans landed in the colony of Virginia, has been presented as popular history, suitable for readers on all levels. The core idea is that real American history begins with slavery, and not with the Declaration of Independence, Revolutionary War, or the US Constitution. The major theme of the project has been set forth as follows:

> Out of slavery—and the anti-black racism it required—grew nearly everything that has truly made America exceptional: its economic might, its industrial power, its electoral system, its diet and popular music, the inequities of its public health and education, its astonishing penchant for violence, its income inequality, the example it sets for the world as a land of freedom and equality, its slang, its legal system and the endemic racial fears and hatreds that continue to plague it to this day. The seeds of all that were planted long before our official birth date, in 1776, when the men known as our founders formally declared independence from Britain.
>
> The goal of The 1619 Project is to reframe American history by considering what it would mean to regard 1619 as our nation's birth year. Doing so requires us to place the consequences of slavery and the contributions of black Americans at the very center of the story we tell ourselves about who we are as a country.

Notice that the 1619 Project aims to relocate the history of the United States in an originary black perspective that it is claimed should become reality for all Americans. What this would mean is that "the story we tell ourselves about who we are as a country" could not claim the founding ideals of freedom, justice, and individual rights. The controversy arising from teaching this project has swirled around whether traditional American ideals, as tied to official history, need to be jettisoned. However, it is not the ideals themselves that the 1619 Project attacks, but the use of those ideals to claim that they are embedded in actual American history.

President Trump issued an executive order in September 2020 that excluded from federal contracts "any diversity and inclusion training interpreted as containing 'Divisive Concepts.'" Divisive concepts were held to include "race or sex stereotyping," and "race or sex scapegoating," as well as critical race theory. **Critical race theory** was begun by Derrick Bell (1930–2011) and other legal scholars in the 1970s who aimed to analyze the ways that racial discrimination was, both historically and reaching into the present, an integral part of the US legal system. Critical race theorists could uncontroversially point to past laws enforcing slavery and racial discrimination, but their analyses of contemporary institutional racism that resulted from legally protected structures, such as the US prison system (see chapter 9), were often subjects for theoretical debate among those same academic scholars. In response to Trump's executive order, some immediately pointed out that critical race theory was not a training but a somewhat rarified scholarly pursuit, usually reserved for graduate school, but at most taught to some college students. Nevertheless, as with objections to the 1619 Project, there was immediate outcry on state and local levels against its being taught in K–12 schools.

Thus, both the 1619 Project and critical race theory became lightning rods for political and cultural controversy in an already divided country. Those opposed to these projects, often without understanding what they are, viewed them as threats to core patriotic values that they wanted taught to schoolchildren as tradition required. But sorting out the misunderstanding in these debates, as well as claims integral to critical race theory, are a prime example of the value of intellectual activity for its own sake, which has an even longer tradition in higher education.

QUESTIONS FOR THINKING, DISCUSSION, AND WRITING

1. Based on the discussion in the beginning of this chapter, how do you define education and what are your reasons for that definition?
2. How might the achievement gap be the result of something other than school resources?
3. Why might African American college students focus more on studies and certification for better jobs than intellectual activity for its own sake? What do you think is the value of intellectual activity for human well-being?
4. Explain the purpose of the 1619 Project and evaluate its importance.
5. Is critical race theory in itself a moral matter? What about its inclusion in school curricula, is that a moral matter?

SOURCES

Bernard, Tara Siegel. "Seeding Accounts for Kindergartners and Hoping to Grow College Graduates: New York City Is Giving Every Public School Kindergartner $100 in a College Savings Account. Here's Why Every Penny Matters." *New York Times*, October 12, 2021, https://www.nytimes.com/2021/10/11/your-money/529-savings-plans-baby-bonds.html.

Dewey, John. *Moral Principles in Education, II: The Moral Training Given by the School Community.* Chicago, IL: Houghton Mifflin, 1909 (1897a, EW5: 61–62), https://www.gutenberg.org/files/25172/25172-h/25172-h.htm.

"Education in the United States." Wikipedia, https://en.wikipedia.org/wiki/Education_in_the_United_States.

Field, Kelly. "'Can Critical Race Theory and Patriotism Coexist in Classrooms? Political Polarization Has Damaged the Standing of Civics and History,' said Paul Carrese, an Arizona State University Professor." The Hechinger Report, CNBC News, May 28, 2021, 6:00 AM EDT, https://www.nbcnews.com/news/us-news/can-critical-race-theory-patriotism-coexist-classrooms-n1268824.

George, Janel. "A Lesson on Critical Race Theory." Human Rights, American Bar Association, January 11, 2021, https://www.americanbar.org/groups/crsj/publications/human_rights_magazine_home/civil-rights-reimagining-policing/a-lesson-on-critical-race-theory/.

Gines, Kathryn T. "Anna Julia Cooper." *The Stanford Encyclopedia of Philosophy* (Summer 2015 Edition), Edward N. Zalta, ed., https://plato.stanford.edu/archives/sum2015/entries/anna-julia-cooper/.

Hung, Man, William A. Smith, Maren W. Voss, Jeremy D. Franklin, Yushan Gu, and Jerry Bounsanga. "Exploring Student Achievement Gaps in School Districts Across the United States." *Education and Urban Society* 52, no. 2 (2020): 175–93, DOI: 10.1177/001312 4519833442.

National Center for Education Statistics. "Back to School Statistics." Educational Institutions, Expenditures, Fast Facts, https://nces.ed.gov/fastfacts/display.asp?id=372#PK12_enrollment; https://nces.ed.gov/fastfacts/display.asp?id=84, consulted August 18, 2020.

National Center for Educational Statistics. "College Enrollment Rates by Race." 2021, https://nces.ed.gov/programs/coe/pdf/coe_cpb.pdf.

Organisation for Economic Co-operation and Development (OECD), "Education at a Glance." 2021, https://www.oecd.org/education/education-at-a-glance/.

PBS, Frontline. "The Debate between W. E. B. Du Bois and Booker T. Washington." February 10, 1998, https://www.pbs.org/wgbh/frontline/article/debate-w-e-b-du-bois-and-booker-t-washington/.

Silverstein, Jake. "Why We Published the 1619 Project." *New York Times*, December 20, 2019, https://www.nytimes.com/interactive/2019/12/20/magazine/1619-intro.html.

Study Lecture Notes. "The Etymology of Education." http://studylecturenotes.com/etymological-meaning-of-education/.

Sylvester, Charles. "The Classical Idea of Leisure: Cultural Ideal or Class Prejudice?" *Leisure Sciences* 2 (1999): 3–16, DOI: 10.1080/014904099273255.

Videos

"Booker T. Washington vs. W. E. B. Du Bois." PBS. Season 2019, Episode 5215, 26m 47s, https://www.pbs.org/video/booker-t-washington-vs-web-dubois-grnfaf/.

"'Critical Race Theory Is Simply the Latest Bogeyman.' Inside the Fight over What Kids Learn about America's History." Time.com, https://time.com/6075193/critical-race-theory-debate/.

"The 1619 Project Details the Legacy of Slavery in America." PBS Newshour. August 18, 2019, 4:44 PM EDT, https://www.pbs.org/newshour/show/the-1619-project-details-the-legacy-of-slavery-in-america.

13

Health and Disability

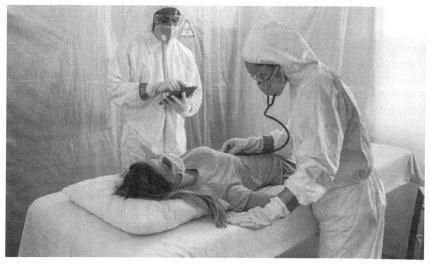

Doctors with bacteriological protection suits attending a patient. Getty Images: doble-d.

Outside of vampire stories and science fiction, we are all mortals. If we are fortunate, we will die in our beds at some ripe old age, with memories of a life well-spent, surrounded by loved ones. Those who study longevity posit an ideal of a long healthy life followed by a short period of illness before death. In reality, many die before their time from illnesses that could have been prevented and others carry on with pain and discomfort. Twenty-six percent of Americans are disabled, a proportion that rises if mental illness is included. While disability in itself is not necessarily unhealthy, it is an obstacle to conforming to norms for optimal functioning, as well as self-care. Obviously, good mental and physical health, with optimal functioning, is the best way to go through life. But even for healthy biological creatures, things break down and we get sick.

In advanced industrial societies, sickness is a matter of modern medicine, a condition that intersects with the medical system and insurance for entry into the medical system. Still, people can do a lot for themselves to prevent illness, and during the COVID-19 pandemic, there has been increased attention paid to wellness or self-care as a way of supporting both physical and mental health and preventing illness. A certain amount of **autonomy**, or the ability to design and set goals, or rule one's own life, is necessary for wellness. Knowledge is required for informed autonomy and the basics of good health practices can be taught to schoolchildren. Recent research has also found indirect correlations between higher education and good health because higher education is believed to strengthen autonomy, as well as lead to better paying jobs that in themselves result in better health.

The poor are more likely to be ill, both for lack of access to the medical system and lack of the autonomy or material resources necessary to preserve wellness. They may also have less time to focus on wellness or self-care. Racial and ethnic minorities are less likely to have high school and college degrees and more likely to be poor. The addition of stress from discrimination and obstacles to opportunities in life has meant that they have more illnesses and die younger than white people.

Some progressive thinkers now claim that good health or at least access to needed medical care is a **human right** that everyone deserves to have, simply because they are human. Insofar as medical care and medical insurance cost money in a capitalistic system, this claim is controversial, because not everyone has the right to the same amounts of money. Again, ethnic and racial minorities have less money and access to the medical system than white people. Some potential moral issues about racial and ethnic minorities are relevant here—income and wealth, institutional racism, education, autonomy, and underlying wellness. These are moral issues when they deepen inequality and affect important aspects of well-being in ways that individuals are neither responsible for nor deserve. That is, the victims are innocent. Also, in political terms the government could do something about the inequalities in health that are related to nonwhite race and ethnicity, if equality in society is an important value.

The first section of this chapter is about disparities in the health of whites and racial and ethnic minorities in the United States. The second section is about wellness and food, and the third section focuses on physical and mental disabilities as they intersect with racial and ethnic identities.

DISPARITIES IN RACIAL AND ETHNIC HEALTH

During the COVID-19 pandemic the CDC reported higher rates of illness and death among nonwhites, compared to white Americans (see table 13.1). This heightened risk was explained in terms of **comorbidities** or preexisting disease conditions that COVID-19 made worse. Such preexisting conditions are in normal times higher among nonwhite racial and ethnic groups.

Race and ethnicity are risk markers for other underlying conditions that impact health. As "risk markers," being Native American, black, or Hispanic meant that a person was almost three times more likely to be hospitalized from COVID-19 and almost twice as likely to die. The COVID-19 pandemic acted like a spotlight (or X-ray) for many inequalities in the United States, which are associated with race and ethnicity. In the normality that was taken for granted before the pandemic, the conditions that became comorbid and mortal were already unequal. For example, the rate of diabetes among blacks and Hispanics compared to whites was almost twice as high (see figure 13.1).

Table 13.1 CDC, Risk for COVID-19 Infection, Hospitalization, and Death by Race/Ethnicity.

Rate ratios compared to White, Non-Hispanic persons	American Indian or Alaska Native, Non-Hispanic persons	Asian, Non-Hispanic persons	Black or African American, Non-Hispanic persons	Hispanic or Latino persons
Cases	1.7x	0.7x	1.1x	1.9x
Hospitalization	3.5x	1.0x	2.8x	2.8x
Death	2.4x	1.0x	2.0x	2.3x

Race and ethnicity are risk markers for other underlying conditions that impact health. Source: CDC, https://www.cdc.gov/coronavirus/2019-ncov/covid-data/investigations-discovery/hospitalization-death-by-race-ethnicity.html.

Percentage of Adults Aged 18 Years or Older With Diagnosed Diabetes, by Racial or Ethnic Group, United States, 2017–2018.

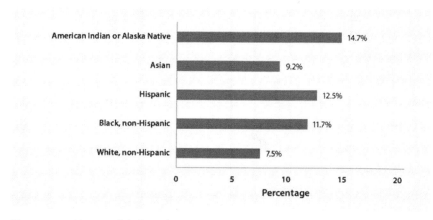

Figure 13.1 Diagnosed diabetes by race and ethnicity. Note that percentages are age-adjusted to the 2000 US standard population. Figure adapted from CDC's National Diabetes Statistics Report 2020. Data Sources: CDC's National Health Interview Survey, 2017–2018, and the Indian Health Service National Data Warehouse, 2017 (American Indian or Alaska Native data), https://www.cdc.gov/diabetes/pdfs/data/statistics/national-diabetes-statistics-report.pdf.

More broadly, over the twentieth century, differences in life expectancy between white and black men did not decline. In 2018, life expectancy associated with race varied according to US states, with an average difference of about five years between black and white Americans.

Treatment for serious illnesses has also been unequal for minorities, especially African Americans. The US federal human science agency, the CDC, has a shameful history of antiblack racism, going back at least to the infamous Tuskegee syphilis study that it took over in the 1950s. In that study, without their consent, black males with syphilis were deliberately not treated—when treatment was available—so that the progression of the disease could be observed. The CDC was also passive regarding lead in drinking water in Washington, DC. However, the CDC is not directly to blame for current race disparities in health care because it is an advisory agency, primarily. Still, critics contend that over the years, the CDC has not advocated strongly enough for medical equality. Black people throughout the United States have been underdiagnosed and undertreated by doctors and in medical facilities throughout the United States, particularly for heart disease. A myth still prevails among medical trainees that black people do not experience pain as severely as white people.

Many of the race-based differences in serious illness have lifestyle or medical neglect origins. That is, there is nothing biological about race that is associated with higher illness or lower longevity. Nevertheless, the so-called black heart drug, BiDil, made headlines in 2005. BiDil was first rejected by the Federal Drug Administration (FDA) because it was a combination of two drugs. However, in the research sample it was found that a subgroup of African American subjects improved with the drug and it was later approved for that reason. But it is misleading to think of BiDil as a black drug in any racial-biological sense. BiDil is a vasodilator that corrects nitric oxide deficiency in heart patients. But there is nothing biological about race, per se, that identifies black people as more likely to benefit from BiDil than anyone else. Indeed, heart disease itself is often largely the effect of social, environmental, and lifestyle factors such as exercise, smoking, stress, and nutrition.

WELLNESS AND FOOD

Good health requires good nutrition, especially fresh fruits and vegetables. Disparities in health among minority groups have been directly linked to lifestyle factors of exercise and food. The history and health issues of the Pima Indians dramatically show that minority-related health differences are connected to what people eat. The US National Institute of Diabetes and Digestive and Kidney Diseases conducted research on the Pima Indians in Arizona for over thirty years. Half had diabetes by 2010 and 95 percent were overweight. Their traditional lifestyle had been disrupted over the nineteenth century when American farmers appropriated their water supply. Pima communities could no longer irrigate their agriculture, and from a diet of 15 percent fat, with considerable starch and fiber, their diet changed to 40 percent fat from food provided by the US government which mainly consisted of lard, sugar, and white flour. They also lost the activities related to farming. By contrast, a Pima population in Mexico had a much lower rate of obesity and diabetes. This group ate less fat, ate more starch, and was more physically active. The Arizona and Mexican Pima Indians had the same ancestral origins and were genetically very similar, so this is an example of how lifestyle affects obesity and with that clinical health. In recent years, these issues have been addressed through prevention, particularly in K–12 education (see video).

Many black and brown communities across the United States, particularly in urban areas, are now **food deserts**, because residents do not have access to affordable, nutritious food or know about its importance for their health. Instead, fast food, which is designed to be addictive by activating human receptors for salt, sugar, and fat, is cheap and handy. By 1999, half of Americans were overweight and over 40 million were obese, including children. On the one hand, many are now concerned about *fat shaming* or making people feel bad because they are overweight. But on the other hand, being overweight and obesity are known to be causal factors in several life-threatening illnesses, including diabetes, heart disease, kidney disease, and stroke.

In 2009, then First Lady Michelle Obama launched a kitchen garden with guides for individual home projects. The White House Garden became part of her Let's Move! Project in 2010, because exercise is another important factor for wellness. The Obamas left the White House in 2017, and the national conversation on nutrition and wellness may have become muted. Nevertheless, the American public has known for many decades that nutritious fresh food and exercise are not merely lifestyle choices, but essential components of good health (see video).

By summer 2021, Black Yard Farm Cooperative was established to promote "food sovereignty" for the largely nonwhite communities in Harlem and the Bronx in New York City. The founder's slogan is "Food is medicine," and they focus on crops that are relevant to the cultures of the city residents they serve: lima beans, collard greens, callaloo, hot peppers, and different varieties of rice. In the Bronx, obesity affects almost 32 percent of inhabitants. Throughout the United States, among black non-Hispanic Americans older than age twenty, 39 percent of men and 56 percent of women are obese. While the slogan "Food Is Medicine" may sound political or what used to be called "new age," it is not difficult to connect the dots: People of color have higher rates of all major diseases, and they are more likely to live in food deserts than other groups. Malnutrition from lack of fresh goods contributes to obesity and other illnesses.

DISABILITIES AND MENTAL ILLNESS

One in four Americans and one in nine working-age adults has a disability. The rate for working-age adults further varies by race and ethnicity. African Americans are the most likely to have a disability (14 percent) followed by non-Hispanic whites (11 percent), Latinos (8 percent), and Asians (5 percent). This disparity results from a complex interaction of socioeconomic and environmental characteristics. The likelihood of having a disability increases with age. Six percent of young adults ages eighteen to twenty have a disability, compared with 22 percent of adults near retirement, ages sixty-one to sixty-five. Chronic medical conditions such as diabetes, high blood pressure, back pain, anxiety, or depression can lead to functional limitations over time. In addition, the cumulative effects of inadequate nutrition and health care, or unsafe working conditions and other risk factors, such as continuous stress, increase the risk of disability over the life span. The lifetime disparities in disabilities by race widen with age. At ages eighteen to twenty, African Americans are slightly more likely to have a disability than non-Hispanic whites (7 percent compared to 6 percent), but among those sixty-one to sixty-five, the disparity grows to 50 percent (30 percent compared to 20 percent). Younger Latinos have a lower rate of disability than non-Hispanic whites. But by age fifty-five, the rates are equivalent (15 percent) and older Latinos (sixty-one to sixty-five) are more likely to have a disability than non-Hispanic whites (23 percent compared to 20 percent).

Mental illness disables a person and prevents them from carrying on with responsibilities and obligations. They may disturb others, be a danger to themselves or others, show an inability to care about others, or lack an ability to reason logically or attend to reality. A mentally ill person is not the same as someone who psychologists call "worried well." The worried well may experience life disruptions that cause grief, sadness, or anxiety in their lives, they may have "bad days" emotionally, or they may worry more than is rationally required. However, the worried well fall within psychological averages for moods and behavior that rule out mental illness.

Mental health care, including talk therapy, counseling, and psychotropic medications that alter brain functioning and mood, is in short supply in the United States. There is a short supply of both diagnosis and treatment. Many people who would like to get mental health treatment for themselves and their loved ones are afraid of being judged. According to "America's Mental Health 2018," a report issued by Cohen Veterans Network and the National Council for Mental Wellbeing, based on a study of five thousand adults, the main problem was simple access to mental health care. Seventy-six percent of respondents claimed that mental health was as important as physical health. Over 56 percent sought or wanted help but did not believe that services were available to them. High cost and insufficient insurance coverage were primary barriers. Over three-quarters did not think that mental health services were available for everyone and almost half reported having to choose between paying for mental health care and buying everyday necessities.

Access to mental health care is better in some states than in others. Texas, Wisconsin, and Georgia were the lowest in providers, facilities, and funding, whereas Pennsylvania, New York, and Minnesota were at the top. But even in states with relatively high overall access, underserved populations may have obstacles to access and minorities may be misdiagnosed. For instance, African Americans have been repeatedly incorrectly diagnosed with schizophrenia, when in fact their illness is depression.

The COVID-19 pandemic has complicated this issue. Columbia University psychiatrists and psychologists report that they are preparing for a "tsunami" of delayed responses to the COVID-19 pandemic in communities already underserved before the pandemic. These researchers and clinicians refer to a "mental-health desert," comparable to the food desert in the black and brown communities near the university. Projects include public information campaigns and outreach to community leaders such as ministers, teachers, and also hair salons and barbershops. Research indicates that mental health deterioration after trauma, such as a prolonged pandemic, is more severe in those already suffering from depression and post-traumatic stress disorder (PTSD). Food insecurity also contributes to mental health problems.

We have discussed food nutrition throughout this chapter, but it is very important to keep in mind that not having enough to eat remains a problem throughout the United States. Like other health issues, food insecurity disproportionately affects racial and ethnic minorities. Research of over 74,000 households during the COVID-19 pandemic reported the following:

> Black households were more likely to report that they could not afford to buy more food; Asian and Hispanic households were more likely to be afraid to go out to buy food; Asian households were more likely to face transportation issues when purchasing food; while White households were more likely to report that stores did not have the food they wanted.

Cost, fear, inconvenience, and preference thus presented barriers to getting enough food, depending on race or ethnicity.

QUESTIONS FOR THINKING, DISCUSSION, AND WRITING

1. *This is a thought question because medical information is confidential.* Consider the state of your health, mental and physical. Did any of the information or discussion in this chapter resonate with you?
2. How is health generally skewed against minorities—what are the statistics? What happened during the COVID-19 pandemic?
3. Explain how race-related medical issues have social causes. Use BiDil and the Pima Indians as examples.
4. What is a food desert and what can be done about it, individually?
5. Explain the difference between the mentally ill and the worried well. Do you think this is a sharp line?

SOURCES

CDC. "Risk for COVID-19 Infection, Hospitalization, and Death by Race/Ethnicity." CDC, September 9, https://www.cdc.gov/coronavirus/2019-ncov/covid-data/investigations-discov ery/hospitalization-death-by-race-ethnicity.html.

Centers for Disease Control and Prevention. Disability and Health Data System (DHDS). May 24, 2018, cited August 27, 2018, https://www.cdc.gov/ncbddd/disabilityandhealth/ dhds/index.html.

Gara, M. A., S. Minsky, S. M. Silverstein, T. Miskimen, S. M. Strakowski. "A Naturalistic Study of Racial Disparities in Diagnoses at an Outpatient Behavioral Health Clinic." *Psychiatric Services* 70, no. (2019): 130–34, https://pubmed.ncbi.nlm.nih.gov/30526340/.

Hahn, R. A., and B. I. Truman. "Education Improves Public Health and Promotes Health Equity." *International Journal of Health Services* 45, no. 4 (2015): 657–78. https://journals .sagepub.com/doi/10.1177/0020731415585986.

Krimsky, Sheldon. "The Short Life of a Race Drug." *The Lancet*, January 14, 2012, https:// www.thelancet.com/journals/lancet/article/PIIS0140-6736(12)60052-X/fulltext.

Krosnick, A. "The Diabetes and Obesity Epidemic among the Pima Indians." *New Jersey Medicine: The Journal of the Medical Society of New Jersey* 97, no. 8 (August 2000): 31–37, https://pubmed.ncbi.nlm.nih.gov/10959174/.

Melillo, Wendy. "Why Are the Pima Indians Sick? Studies on Arizona Tribe Show Excessive Rates of Diabetes, Obesity and Kidney Disease." *Washington Post*, March 30, 1993, https://www.washingtonpost.com/archive/lifestyle/wellness/1993/03/30/why-are-the-pima -indians-sick-studies-on-arizona-tribe-show-excessive-rates-of-diabetes-obesity-and-kidney -disease/1f978958-e73b-483a-9af9-47d9efdad534/.

Morales, D. X., S. A. Morales, and T. F. Beltran. "Racial/Ethnic Disparities in Household Food Insecurity During the COVID-19 Pandemic: A Nationally Representative Study." *Journal of Racial and Ethnic Health Disparities* 8 (2021): 1300–314, https://doi .org/10.1007/s40615-020-00892-7.

Moss, Michael. "The Extraordinary Science of Addictive Junk Food." *New York Times Magazine*, February 20, 2013, https://www.nytimes.com/2013/02/24/magazine/the-extraordi nary-science-of-junk-food.html.

National Center for Health Statistics (NCHS). "NCHS Data on Racial and Ethnic Disparities." NCHS Factsheet, March 2020, https://www.cdc.gov/nchs/about/factsheets/ factsheet_disparities.htm.

National Disability Institute. "Financial Inequality, Disability, Race and Poverty in America." part 3, https://www.nationaldisabilityinstitute.org/wp-content/uploads/2019/02/disability -race-poverty-in-america.pdf.

Okoro, C. A., N. D. Hollis, A. C. Cyrus, and Blake S. Griffin. "Prevalence of Disabilities and Health Care Access by Disability Status and Type among Adults—United States." 2016, https://www.cdc.gov/mmwr/volumes/67/wr/mm6732a3.htm.

"Records Reveal CDC Sent Germ Strains to Iraq in 1980s." Associated Press, *Washington Times*, October 1, 2002, https://www.washingtontimes.com/ news/2002/oct/1/20021001 -091445-2576r/. For sources on the other errors listed, see the notes in Wikipedia, "Centers for Disease Control and Prevention," https://en.wikipedia.org/wiki/Centers_for_Disease_ Control_and_Prevention, June 14, 2020.

Rooks, R. N, E. M. Simonsick, L. M. Klesges, A. B. Newman, H. N. Ayonayon, and T. B. Harris. "Racial Disparities in Health Care Access and Cardiovascular Disease Indicators in Black and White Older Adults in the Health ABC Study." *Journal of Aging Health* 20, no. 6 (2008): 599–614, https://www.researchgate.net/publication/5226134_Racial_Dis parities_in_Health_Care_Access_and_Cardiovascular_Disease_Indicators_in_Black_and_ White_Older_Adults_in_the_Health_ABC_Study.

Sabin, Janice A. "How We Fail Black Patients in Pain." Association of American Medical Colleges (AAMC), January 6, 2020, https://www.aamc.org/news-insights/how-we-fail -black-patients-pain.

Shear, Michael D. "'They Let Us Down': 5 Takeaways on the C.D.C.'s Coronavirus Response." *New York Times*, June 3, 2020, https://www.nytimes.com/2020/06/03/us/cdc -virus-takeaways.html.

Tayag, Yasmin. "Meet the Black Farmers Fighting Food Deserts in New York, Black Yard Farm Cooperative Is Producing Fresh Food to Promote Food Sovereignty in Harlem and the Bronx." VICE News, September 9, 2021, https://www.vice.com/en/article/4ave8q/meet -the-black-farmers-fighting-food-deserts-in-new-york.

Weinhouse, Beth. "The Mental Weight of COVID-19." *Columbia Magazine*, Fall 2021, https://magazine.columbia.edu/article/mental-weight-covid-19.

Welsh, Jennifer. "Race and Life Expectancy in All 50 States." Live Science, March 5, 2012, https://www.livescience.com/18835-race-lifespan-states.html.

Wood, Paul, Joy Burwell, Kaitlyn Rawlett, and Weber Shandwick. "New Study Reveals Lack of Access as Root Cause for Mental Health Crisis in America," National Council for Mental Wellbeing, https://www.cohenveteransnetwork.org/wp-content/uploads/2018/10/ Press-Release-Americas-Mental-Health-2018-FINAL.pdf.

Videos

Gatalica, Daniel. "Native Americans Fight Historical Discrimination to Lower Diabetes, Obesity Rates." Cronkite News, January 7, 2020, https://www.indianz.com/News/2020/01/07/ native-americans-fight-historical-discri.asp.

Let's Move! "Inside the White House: The Kitchen Garden." https://letsmove.obamawhite house.archives.gov/gardening-guide.

Lieberman, Jeffrey, "Imagine There Was No Stigma to Mental Illness." TEDx, January 18, 2016, https://www.linkedin.com/pulse/imagine-stigma-mental-illness-jeffrey-lieberman.

IV

SOCIAL DISRUPTIONS

Social disruptions are episodes or conditions that run counter to general rules and practices that keep society together over time. Violent episodes of social disruption affect all racial and ethnic groups, whereas everyday racism is a disruption that the white majority may not notice, although it continually affects people of color. Chapter 14 addresses everyday racism with a focus on continuing racial segregation where people live. The racist aspect of place segregation endures in other social institutions, but members of racial and ethnic minority groups are not passive. Self-segregation and minority professional organizations are examples of coping skills. However, microaggression, white privilege, and white status can permeate all aspects of inter-racial life.

In chapter 15, hate speech is discussed in the context of First Amendment rights. Hate crimes are forms of action that are narrowly defined in the United States. While the connections between hate speech and hate actions are difficult to block legally in democracies, the idea of speech that incites may be a bridge between hate speech and hate crimes. Chapter 16 addresses contemporary protests from both the left and right and takes up the question of whether progressive protests are merely expressive, or effective in bringing about egalitarian change.

14

Everyday Racism

Street under subway railroad with restaurants and shops with sidewalk in the Bronx, downtown Fordham area. Getty Images: ablokhin.

Everyday racism divides people based on race and interferes with the ability of nonwhites to interact with whites as equals. Human equality is disrupted as a result. Such racism is "every day" and humdrum because it is accepted as normal by many white Americans, even though it is often disturbing for people of color. Many Americans believe that the battle against racism in the United States ended with the formal equality granted to minorities during the civil rights legislation of the 1960s. However, most people of color and their advocates claim that racism persists, both institutionally and between individuals and groups. We discussed police killings of unarmed young black men in chapter 10, but many white Americans believe that these are unusual occurrences perpetrated by "bad apples." Throughout this book, almost every chapter has focused on racism that shapes life in different segments of society, with the understanding that racism presents ongoing moral problems. And yet, normal life, even early post-pandemic normal life, goes on. People of color work, go to school, consume goods and entertainment, and use public amenities, so that racism does not seem to be constantly stage front. And yet, it is still there, often in quite subtle background ways that surprise people when they erupt into crises.

This chapter is dedicated to **everyday racism**, patterns of racially divisive behavior, and reactions to them, and the often-small slights, assumptions, and inconveniences that affect people of color, because they are people of color. Much of everyday racism keeps people of color physically and psychologically apart from white people in interactions that come before the friendship and marriage racial divisions discussed in chapter 2. Segregated housing, whether by choice or economic necessity, is a perceptible example of such distance. At the same time, these separations based on race form opportunities for tighter associations and mutual aid within nonwhite groups. A large number of nonwhite associations, especially in the professions, is an example of both the assertion of positive identities and survival tactics that people of color have found necessary in white-dominant institutions.

Ordinary, everyday, humdrum racism in society occurs through socially acceptable customs of behavior that favor white people, even when oppression, prejudice, or discrimination are not blatant. Where people live, according to their race, is a major factor of everyday life that is associated with race. The first section of this chapter is about current place segregation in the United States. The second section is about microaggression, white privilege, and white status, which are all factors of person-to-person racist interactions that shape the distribution of power, authority, and rewards, in ways that people take for granted and white people may not even notice. However, people of color are not passive given such disruptions to their daily lives. In the third section, several survival tactics against everyday racism are discussed.

PLACE SEGREGATION

Consider a 2020 "This Day in History" entry by the editors of History.com about an incident now thirty-five years in the past:

> On December 20, 1986, three Black men are attacked by a group of white teenagers yelling racial slurs in Howard Beach, a predominately white, middle-class, Italian-American neighborhood in Queens, New York. Earlier that night, the men were driving from Brooklyn to Queens, when their car broke down near Howard Beach. They walked several miles to a pizza parlor in Howard Beach, where they asked to use a phone to call for assistance. After being told there was no phone available, they ordered some pizza. When the men left the pizzeria, they were confronted by the gang of teens. One of the men, Michael Griffith, 23, was chased into traffic on the Belt Parkway and died after

being hit by a car. A second man, Cedric Sandiford, was severely beaten, while the third man, Timothy Grimes, outran the assailants and escaped without serious injury.

Now, consider this account of an incident in May 2020:

> Black birdwatcher Christian Cooper was thrust into the national spotlight when a white woman he encountered in New York's Central Park called the police after he asked that she leash her dog in accordance with park rules. (Dogs can disturb sensitive ecosystems and have contributed to the extinction of at least eight bird species.) "An African American man is threatening my life," she can be heard saying to a 911 operator in a now-viral video.

Both the Howard Beach hate crime and the woman's 911 call on the black bird-watcher were explicitly racist. But the background conditions that enabled them to erupt were more subtle. Because of now normal customs and behavior patterns that were shaped by white dominance in US society, black people are not expected to be in, or occupy, certain places. Howard Beach was a racially segregated residential area in 1986, and it may have been assumed that there were no black bird-watchers in designated bird-watching areas in Central Park in 2020.

The 1968 Fair Housing Act expanded on previous acts and prohibited discrimination concerning the sale, rental, and financing of housing based on race, religion, national origin, or sex; the act was later amended to include handicap and family status. However, over half a century later, US housing is more segregated than ever. Black critical race theorist Patricia Williams reported buying a house in 1997, only to have her down payment and mortgage costs go up as soon as she checked the race box for "black." The reason given was that property values in the neighborhood had suddenly gone down. Williams concluded that her application as a black person had caused the bank to reassess the value of the entire neighborhood!

US residential segregation increased from 1990 to 2019 so that over 80 percent of US cities had segregated housing. Detroit is the most segregated American city, followed by Hialeah, Florida, Newark, Chicago, Milwaukee, and Cleveland. Only two out of 113 cities with populations of at least 200,000 were integrated—Colorado Springs, Colorado, and Port St. Lucie, Florida. Paradoxically, residential segregation has increased as the United States has grown more racially and ethnically diverse. The reason is that within areas that have diverse populations, people of distinct races and ethnicity live together in neighborhood enclaves. These enclaves are often quite specific as to nationality and religion, as well as income and race. Thus, American cities now contain neighborhoods with hundreds of distinct groups, in addition to the traditional divisions between blacks and whites, such as Cubans in Miami, Japanese and Korean enclaves in California, and Chinatown and Jewish communities in Manhattan. If housing is segregated, then so is primary and secondary school education (see chapter 12). Most observers believe that racially integrated schools and neighborhoods are essential for good relations between races, as well as income, career, and higher educational opportunities for children of color.

However, racial integration of neighborhoods might not always be the best solution toward social justice. Philosopher Tommie Shelby and others have suggested that middle-class black people who can afford to live in all or mostly white neighborhoods might prefer living in poor black neighborhoods, to contribute to a rise in quality of life in those neighborhoods and avoid white discrimination and prejudice in mostly white neighborhoods. When middle-class or affluent whites move into poor nonwhite neighborhoods, it's considered **gentrification**, because their presence raises real estate prices, not only for housing but commercially, as the result of new businesses that serve them. White gentrification tends to be resented because it is seen as financially opportunistic—getting a bargain for houses or apartments. But if middle-class blacks move into poor black neighborhoods, they may be welcomed for "giving back." The same would be true of other middle-class minorities moving into poor neighborhoods populated by those of their ethnicity.

Place is more than where people live because it extends to where they feel comfortable going outside of their homes and neighborhoods. Comfort includes feeling safe and believing that one has the skills to occupy a place. For a long time in US history, the majority of African Americans lived in rural areas, mainly in the South. But with the Great Migration from 1916 to 1970, as many as six million moved to cities in the North and West. Their descendants took up urban life, often in poverty. American affluence often brings with it expectations of physical activity that include hunting, fishing, sailing, tennis, and excursions into natural areas. For reasons of lifestyle habits, suspicion by white habitues of nonwhite newcomers, and lack of money and leisure time, many African Americans have not availed themselves of these pastimes. Recently, enthusiasm has grown for breaking out of that tradition. For instance, when the white-woman black-bird-watcher incident became famous, a group called "Black Birders" announced a week to celebrate recognition and representation of black people studying nature. The COVID-19 pandemic made it evident that minority neighborhoods had less access to coastlines, fresh air, and areas free of industrial pollution, which has revitalized public concern about **environmental racism**, or less desirable environments for people of color.

MICROAGGRESSION, WHITE PRIVILEGE, AND WHITE STATUS

The concept of *microaggression* captures the asymmetry of what is normal for a dominant white majority but disruptive to people of color. Columbia University psychologist Derald Sue and his research team have defined **microaggressions** as everyday acts and patterns of behavior that are harmful to people of color, regardless of the perpetrator's intentions. Here is their full definition from the abstract of an article that introduced the concept:

> Racial microaggressions are brief and commonplace daily verbal, behavioral, or environmental indignities, whether intentional or unintentional, that communicate hostile, derogatory, or negative racial slights and insults toward people of color. Perpetrators of

microaggressions are often unaware that they engage in such communications when they interact with racial/ethnic minorities. A taxonomy of racial microaggressions in everyday life was created through a review of the social psychological literature on aversive racism, from formulations regarding the manifestation and impact of everyday racism, and from reading numerous personal narratives of counselors (both White and those of color) on their racial/cultural awakening. Microaggressions seem to appear in three forms: microassault, microinsult, and microinvalidation. Almost all interracial encounters are prone to microaggressions.

An example of *microassault* would be uninvited bodily touching, after a white person indicates that a person of color's hair or clothing is somehow unusual. A *microinsult* would be disparaging a person by putting down the culture of the group to which it is assumed they belong. A *microinvalidation* might be failing to acknowledge a person or persons of color in a majority white professional meeting. Sue, who is Asian, along with other Asians, famously uses the example of white people asking, "Where are you from?" When the answer provides the name of a location in the United States, the speaker persists with "No, where are you really from?" as though someone who looks Asian cannot be a native American.

Microaggressions are possible because of **white privilege**. In 1989, white American feminist Peggy McIntosh published an article about her "invisible knapsack" containing items of white privilege, or perks and rights that white people enjoyed, that people of color did not have. She wrote: "I was taught to see racism only in individual acts of meanness, not in invisible systems conferring dominance on my group." Many of the privileges McIntosh documented are still evident today, so they are worth listing, to see exactly what has not changed:

1. I can if I wish to arrange to be in the company of people of my race most of the time.
2. If I should need to move, I can be pretty sure of renting or purchasing housing in an area that I can afford and in which I want to live.
3. I can be pretty sure that my neighbors in such a location will be neutral or pleasant to me.
4. I can go shopping alone most of the time, pretty well assured that I will not be followed or harassed.
5. I can turn on the television or open the front page of the paper and see people of my race widely represented.
6. When I am told about our national heritage or about "civilization," I am shown that people of my color made it what it is.
7. I can be sure that my children will be given curricular materials that testify to the existence of their race.
8. If I want to, I can be pretty sure of finding a publisher for this piece on white privilege.
9. I can go into a music shop and count on finding the music of my race represented, into a supermarket and find the staple foods which fit with my

cultural traditions, into a hairdresser's shop and find someone who can cut my hair.

10. Whether I use checks, credit cards, or cash, I can count on my skin color not to work against the appearance of financial reliability.
11. I can arrange to protect my children most of the time from people who might not like them.
12. I can wear or dress in second-hand clothes, or not answer letters, without having people attribute these choices to the bad morals, the poverty, or the illiteracy of my race.
13. I can speak in public to a powerful male group without putting my race on trial.
14. I can do well in a challenging situation without being called a credit to my race.
15. I am never asked to speak for all the people of my racial group.
16. I can remain oblivious of the language and customs of persons of color who constitute the world's majority without feeling in my culture any penalty for such oblivion.
17. I can criticize our government and talk about how much I fear its policies and behavior without being seen as a cultural outsider.
18. I can be pretty sure that if I ask to talk to "the person in charge," I will be facing a person of my race.
19. If a traffic cop pulls me over or if the IRS audits my tax return, I can be sure I haven't been singled out because of my race.
20. I can easily buy posters, postcards, picture books, greeting cards, dolls, toys, and children's magazines featuring people of my race.
21. I can go home from most meetings of organizations I belong to feeling somewhat tied in, rather than isolated, out-of-place, outnumbered, unheard, held at a distance, or feared.
22. I can take a job with an affirmative action employer without having coworkers on the job suspect that I got it because of race.
23. I can choose public accommodation without fearing that people of my race cannot get in or will be mistreated in the places I have chosen.
24. I can be sure that if I need legal or medical help, my race will not work against me.
25. If my day, week, or year is going badly, I need not ask of each negative episode or situation whether it has racial overtones.
26. I can choose blemish cover or bandages in "flesh" color and have them more or less match my skin.

Some of McIntosh's listed white privileges are more than privileges because they are contrasted to violations of the rights of nonwhite people. Others of these privileges derive simply from being born visibly racially white, and they are more issues of **status** or stable rank, than privilege. The modern social construction of human races began as hierarchies that put whites at the top, as superior and thereby higher in racial status than other races. (See chapter 3.) Poor white people may deny being privileged, but their whiteness itself is a high racial status.

ANTIRACIST COPING STRATEGIES

Just as everyday racism is normal for white people, coping with it has become part of everyday life for people of color. This is evident in organizations, self-segregation, and parental recognition of the dangers black children may face from police officers.

Much of individual life in society is mediated by affiliations with organizations—professional groups, social groups, and special interest groups. The racial composition of these groups has been asymmetrical in the United States. Over much of American history, whites were dominant, as well as more numerous than any other group. For an organization to be all-white, it did not have to proclaim itself as such, but merely exclude nonwhites. Except for extreme forms of white supremacy, the exclusion did not have to be made explicit by the name of the organization. However, many organizations that serve people of color and mainly have nonwhite membership explicitly assert their race or ethnicity. The groups serve purposes unrelated to race, but they are named by their race or identity, such as the National Association of Black Accountants and the Hispanic Organization of Toxicologists.

In her 1998 book, *Why Are All the Black Kids Sitting Together in the Cafeteria?*, Beverly Daniel Tatum takes up self-segregation by race of middle school students to discuss broader underlying issues that draw them together. While onlookers might ask the question of the title because they think that the black kids sitting together are displaying hostility toward whites, Tatum interprets it as "affirming their identities, building community, and cultivating leadership," in anticipation of adulthood. Tatum is also sensitive to issues of exclusion faced by children who self-segregate, such as name-calling, teacher neglect, and not seeing their group history prominently represented in curricula. Insofar as students who self-segregate support one another, their self-segregation resembles an antiracist coping strategy.

In higher education, where minorities have less student involvement and higher dropout rates than traditional students, nonwhite Greek-letter groups or sororities and fraternities, while recently garnering a negative reputation for having rituals, have been found to increase student involvement and develop leadership skills in college and beyond. The findings apply to both predominantly white schools and those with high percentages of student diversity.

To talk about coping strategies for racism implies that there is racism to be defended against or negotiated. The worldwide televised killing of George Floyd set off many disclosures of how the parents of black children have been coping with their fears of unprovoked police violence against their children. "The Talk" was explored in a two-hour video on PBS. Quite simply, "The Talk" is a cautionary conversation that parents of black children, particularly sons, have with their children. The child is instructed, with the utmost seriousness, about how to behave if stopped by police officers. It is impressed upon the child that they must keep their hands visible, follow orders, and generally act in a polite and compliant way. This protocol is presented as necessary, even if the child who is stopped has done nothing wrong and should not have been stopped. Most American children, especially middle-class children, including black middle-class children, are taught in school and at home that authority figures will treat them fairly, regardless of race. Their parents generally seek to bolster their self-confidence about who they are in the world. But the necessity for "The Talk" and its prevalence shows that black children cannot have that confidence in encounters with police officers, especially white police officers. This danger from police officers is now part of US everyday racism and "The Talk" has become an antiracist strategy for coping with it. (See PBS SoCal video.)

Also, in the wake of George Floyd's murder, the Black Lives Matter movement achieved national prominence. It had been formed via social media as #BlackLives Matter in 2012, after the acquittal of George Zimmerman for killing Trayvon Martin in Florida. Since its inception, "Black Lives Matter" has been a controversial title or slogan. Its initial intention seemed to be a reminder, or simple assertion, that the lives of black people, that is, whether they live or die, are important. Unjust killings of innocent and unarmed black people and an apparent public indifference and failure to change the circumstances enabling such killings made the assertion a necessary intervention. Thus, the slogan "Black Lives Matter" could have initially been a coping strategy. But it was not universally received as such. Reactions to the words "Black Lives Matter" included counter-assertions such as "All Lives Matter" and "Blue Lives Matter" ("blue" referring to police officers). The counter-assertions and perhaps misunderstandings—assuming that they were not claiming that black lives do not matter—underscore the everyday nature of police killings of innocent, unarmed black men, and with that, the same atmosphere of fear that prompts "The Talk." In other words, preparing for sudden unjustified police violence is now part of everyday racism for black people in American life and the everyday way of dealing with it, by black people, begins with recognition within families of this everyday danger.

QUESTIONS FOR THINKING, DISCUSSION, AND WRITING

1. What are the advantages and disadvantages of minorities living in enclaves limited to members of their own groups? What moral imperatives may be involved?
2. What are some of the implications of race-related places in terms of human activities and recreation? What is the moral issue involved?
3. Do you think that black people and other minorities in the United States need antiracist coping strategies? Or, are they being paranoid? Give reasons for your answer.

4. Discuss how microaggression, white privilege, and ongoing white status, while accepted as part of humdrum everyday life, are intense and disruptive for those who suffer from them. What can we say about practices that are uneventful for some but disruptive for others?
5. Consult Peggy McIntosh's 1989 list of twenty-six US white privileges. Which are no longer only white privileges, and which remain?

SOURCES

Bardella, Kurt. "Op-Ed: The Question Every Asian American Hates to Be Asked: 'Where Are You From?'" *Los Angeles Times*, March 22, 2021, https://www.latimes.com/opinion/story/2021-03-22/op-ed-the-question-every-asian-american-hates-where-are-you-from.

Editors, History.Com. "Man Chased to His Death in Howard Beach Hate-Crime." This Day in History, December 20, 1986, https://www.history.com/this-day-in-history/man-chased-to-his-death-in-howard-beach-hate-crime.

Espinoza-Kulick, Mario Alberto Viveros, Maura Fennelly, Kevin Beck, and Ernesto Castañeda. "Ethnic Enclaves." January 2020. Retrieved April 21, 2021, https://www.researchgate.net/publication/344468963_Ethnic_Enclaves.

Kimbrough, Walter M., and Philo A. Hutcheson. "Organizations on Black Students' Involvement in Collegiate Activities and Their Development of Leadership Skills." *Journal of Negro Education* 67, no. 2 (Spring 1998): 96–105, https://doi.org/10.2307/2668220.

McIntosh, Peggy. "White Privilege: Unpacking the Invisible Knapsack." Peace and Freedom, July/August 1989, https://psychology.umbc.edu/files/2016/10/White-Privilege_McIntosh-1989.pdf.

Mock, Jillian. "'Black Birders Week' Promotes Diversity and Takes on Racism in the Outdoors." *Audubon Magazine*, June 1, 2020, https://www.audubon.org/news/black-birders-week-promotes-diversity-and-takes-racism-outdoors.

PBS, Frontline, Patricia Williams from "The Du Bois Institute's 'A Conversation on Race,' 1997," audio excerpts, https://www.pbs.org/wgbh/pages/frontline/shows/race/audio/pwilliams.html.

Rowland-Shea, Jenny, Sahir Doshi, Shanna Edberg, and Robert Fanger. "The Nature Gap Confronting Racial and Economic Disparities in the Destruction and Protection of Nature in America." Center for American Progress, July 21, 2020, https://www.americanprogress.org/issues/green/reports/2020/07/21/487787/the-nature-gap/.

Sampathkumar, Mythili. "The Joys and Challenges of Exploring Nature while Black." Fix Solutions Lab, June 10, 2021, https://grist.org/fix/the-joys-and-challenges-of-exploring-nature-while-black/.

Semuels, Alana. "The U.S. Is Increasingly Diverse, So Why Is Segregation Getting Worse?" *Time*, June 21, 2021, https://time.com/6074243/segregation-america-increasing/.

Shelby, Tommie. "Integration, Inequality, and Imperatives of Justice: A Review Essay." *Philosophy and Public Affairs* 42, no. 3 (2014): 1–33, https://www.tommieshelby.com/uploads/4/5/1/0/45107805/integration_and_inequality.pdf.

Sue, Derald Wing, Christina M. Capodilupo, Gina C. Torino, Jennifer M. Bucceri, Aisha M. B. Holder, Kevin L. Nadal, and Marta Esquilin. "Racial Microaggressions in Everyday

Life: Implications for Clinical Practice." *American Psychologist* 62, no. 4 (May–June 2007): 271–86, https://psycnet.apa.org/buy/2007-07130-001.

Tatum, Beverly Daniel. *Why Are All the Black Kids Sitting Together in the Cafeteria?: And Other Conversations about Race.* Penguin, 1998/2017/2021.

Wilkerson, Isabel. *The Warmth of Other Suns: The Epic Story of America's Great Migration.* Random House, 2010, DOI: 10.1093/OBO/9780199756384-0257.

Videos

Alvoid, Tiffany. "Eliminating Microaggressions: The Next Level of Inclusion." TEDx Oakland December 9, 2019, YouTube, https://www.youtube.com/watch?v=cPqVit6TJjw.

Melton, Marissa. "US Ranger on Mission to Attract More African Americans to National Parks." March 30, 2021, OWN News, https://www.voanews.com/a/usa_us-ranger-mission-attract-more-african-americans-national-parks/6203926.html.

Natividad, Ivan. "The Roots of Structural Racism: How American Racism Is Rooted in Residential Segregation." Berkeley News, June 21, 2021, https://news.berkeley.edu/2021/06/21/how-american-racism-is-rooted-in-residential-segregation/.

PBS SoCal. "The Talk—Race in America." 2021, Public Media Group of Southern California, https://www.pbssocal.org/shows/talk-race-america/special/talk-race-america-talk-race-america.

15

Hate Speech and Hate Crimes

Definition of Neo-Nazism. Getty Images: Devonyu.

According to Christianity, hate itself is a deadly sin. Most religions view hate in similar ways. In secular society, also, hate is a vice, a morally bad disposition or character trait. Let us assume at the outset that hate is morally bad, and race-based hate is at least as bad, maybe worse. What is hate as a quality of what some people say and of the crimes they commit? Hate is an emotion, a combination of feelings of extreme dislike and intentions to do harm, that persists for some time against a target. Philosopher J. L. A. Garcia has located the core of racism itself as hatred in the hearts and minds of individuals, regardless of whether or not they act on their feelings and beliefs.

Targets of hate can be individuals or whole groups of people in which each member of the group is imagined as having the qualities or traits that make them hated. The qualities or traits vary with the nature of the target. In racial and ethnic hate, the hated quality is something believed to be characteristic of a specific race or ethnic group. Sometimes racial and ethnic hatred exists irrationally on its own, according to distortions in individual hearts and minds. But other times, racial and ethnic hatred masks greed and theft. In *The Souls of White Folk*, written in 1920, African American scholar W. E. B. Du Bois described white individuals' expressions of hatred of black people as arising from psychological depths.

> I see again and again, often and still more often, a writing of human hatred, a deep and passionate hatred, vast by the very vagueness of its expression. Down through the green waters, on the bottom of the world, where men move to and fro, I have seen a man—an educated gentleman—grow livid with anger because a little, silent, black woman was sitting by herself in a Pullman car. He was a white man. I have seen a great, grown man curse a little child, who had wandered into the wrong waiting room, searching for its mother: "Here, you damned black__" He was White. In Central Park I have seen the upper lip of a quiet, peaceful man curl back in a tigerish snarl of rage because black folk rode by in a motor car.

Du Bois also directly referred to mass attitudes of racial hatred in American history:

> For two or more centuries America has marched proudly in the van of human hatred,— making bonfires of human flesh and laughing at them hideously and making the insulting of millions more than a matter of dislike,—rather a great religion.

Du Bois knew that in 1919, sixty-six African American men and women were lynched in the US South and 250 died in urban riots in the North and Arkansas during the so-called Red Summer of that year. In his big picture view, Du Bois saw the global race relations of colonization as massive European exploitation of Asians and Africans, which World War I, the "War to end all wars," would not end.

> The World War was primarily the jealous and avaricious struggle for the largest share in exploiting darker races. As such it is and must be but the prelude to the armed and indignant protest of these despised and raped peoples. . . . Is, then, this war the end of wars? Can it be the end, so long as sits enthroned, even in the souls of those who cry peace, the despising and robbing of darker peoples? If Europe hugs this delusion, then this is not the end of world war,—it is but the beginning!

Du Bois viewed white supremacy as both the cause and justification (as rationalization by some whites) for white exploitation and crimes against people of color. In the early twentieth century, the ideas of hate speech and hate crimes had not yet fully made their way into broad awareness and public policy. Today, people debate the suppression or permission of hate speech in terms of free speech rights. In the United States at this time, the legal definition of a hate crime is very narrow and hate crimes are under-reported. Hate crimes are often horrifying and universally condemned, but a case still has to be made that hate crimes deserve more severe punishment than the same crimes committed without hate. The first part of the chapter is about hate speech, the second about hate crimes, and the third about reporting and punishing hate crimes.

HATE SPEECH

Hate speech is written or spoken language that expresses hatred for a specific group, usually a group that is already vulnerable in some way. In this context, hate speech targets racial and ethnic minorities. Many democratic countries have laws against hate speech. For instance, according to the Canadian constitution, while freedom of expression is protected, this freedom extends to listeners, as well as speakers. The result is that there are legal penalties for both speech that incites action against a specific group and speech that incites hatred.

Invalidation of a minority group's experience, such as denial of the Nazi Holocaust against Jews—which is historically documented to have resulted in the death of six million Jews—is also a punishable violation of law. Sixteen European countries and Israel have laws against Holocaust denial speech. However, when such laws have been proposed in the United States and the United Kingdom, opposition has been fierce in defense of free speech. Free speech includes both a right to freedom of belief and freedom to express one's beliefs, without government censorship. These are foundational moral and legal rights in democracies and in the United States are associated with Amendment I of the Constitution:

> Congress shall make no law respecting an establishment of religion or prohibiting the free exercise thereof; or abridging the freedom of speech, or of the press; or the right of the people peaceably to assemble, and to petition the Government for a redress of grievances.

There are, of course, exceptions to such rights and those committing them may be criminally prosecuted: obscenity, fighting words, child pornography, perjury, blackmail, incitement to imminent lawless action, true threats, and solicitations to commit crimes. Some scholars have argued that spoken treason is also unprotected. Civil penalties can result from defamation (including libel and slander) and copyright infringement.

The principle behind free speech rights is partly deontological or absolute and partly utilitarian. Free speech rights are absolute, justified by the nature of what they are. Free speech rights are also justified by the utilitarian principle that greater harm will result from restricting free speech than protecting it. Nevertheless, people are harmed by racial hate speech, as they are harmed by all forms of racism.

The United Nations has attempted to resolve the tension between the right to free speech and the harmful consequences of racial hate speech. In "United Nations Strategy and Plan of Action on Hate Speech," the UN has declared:

> Addressing hate speech does not mean limiting or prohibiting freedom of speech. It means keeping hate speech from escalating into something more dangerous, particularly incitement to discrimination, hostility and violence, which is prohibited under international law.

The UN's target of incitement is defined as follows:

> **Incitement** is a very dangerous form of speech, because it explicitly and deliberately aims at triggering discrimination, hostility and violence, which may also lead to or include terrorism or atrocity crimes. Hate speech that does not reach the threshold of incitement is not something that international law requires States to prohibit. It is important to underline that even when not prohibited, hate speech may be harmful.

If hate incitement is what the law should stop, and not hate speech itself, it follows that beliefs leading to hate speech should not be controlled by law, because beliefs are both private and everyone is recognized to have a right to their beliefs. However, negative beliefs about a group often lead to speech as an expression of those beliefs. And hate speech from the mouths of activists can very easily become a form of incitement. This suggests that hate speech by certain people who are already in positions to lead action might be the right target. But how are such people to be identified before they have succeeded in inciting harm to members of a group? The unfortunate conclusion is that hate speech cannot be controlled in democratic contexts where people have freedom of speech, until after their speech has led to actual harm. It follows from this that further back in the causal sequence, in education, is where the harm resulting from incitement should be addressed. People do not form their beliefs in a vacuum but learn from an early age which kinds of beliefs are true or likely to be true. Indeed, the UN turns to education as the ultimate solution to the problem of controlling hate speech:

> UN entities should take action in formal and informal education to implement SDG4 [Sustainable Development Goal4], promote the values and skills of Global Citizenship Education, and enhance Media and Information Literacy.

HATE CRIMES

When the law deals with serious criminal issues, it is surprisingly psychological. A suspect's intention has to be established and they have to have a plausible motive.

An intention or **intent** in law to do an action means that the action is deliberate. A *plausible motive* is a reason or cause for the action. If X does something that kills Y, to be guilty of murder, X must act deliberately and be motivated to kill Y or benefit from Y's death. If the gun accidentally goes off and X has no reason to want Y dead, the death itself would a **homicide**, but not murder. US Supreme Court Justice Oliver Wendell Holmes Jr. (1841–1935) famously said, "Even a dog knows the difference between being stumbled over and being kicked." Moreover, the accused must be sane enough to know the difference between right and wrong when they committed the crime and also when they are tried. This importance of motive, intent, and sanity for conviction of serious crimes is the ***mens rea*** or the "guilty mind" according to criminal law.

Mens rea must be present in every element of a crime and the more blameworthy the crime, the more serious the crime and the greater the penalty. The Modern Penal Code (MPC) specifies four degrees of blame with associated punishment:

1. Acting purposely—the defendant had an underlying conscious object to act (X shot Y "in cold blood").
2. Acting knowingly—the defendant is practically certain that the conduct will cause a particular result (X knew the gun was loaded and X was a good shot).
3. Acting recklessly—the defendant consciously disregarded a substantial and unjustified risk (X was playing Russian Roulette by pointing a gun at someone's head).
4. Acting negligently—the defendant was not aware of the risk but should have been aware of the risk (X did not know the gun was loaded in playing Russian Roulette but should have known, by checking).

These legal *mens rea* requirements, like the definition of *mens rea*, are not only psychological but they parallel our moral judgments when no crime has been committed, but action is morally wrong. Moral blame requires that the wrongdoer knows what they were doing and intended to do it for a morally bad reason, with disregard for the risk of bad consequences. For example, suppose a friend betrays their friend's confidence out of long-standing envy and the betrayed friend, who is known to suffer from depression, attempts suicide when they find out. We would blame the disloyal friend, perhaps not wholly for the suicide attempt, but for precipitating it.

The FBI began investigating hate crimes during World War I. Traditionally, hate crimes were limited to racial bias and left to local investigation. After the passage of the 1964 Civil Rights Act, the FBI focused on violations of the constitutional rights of racial minorities, and in 2009 biases of actual or perceived sexual orientation, gender identity, disability, and gender were added. Consider now how the US Federal Bureau of Investigation (FBI) defines a hate crime:

A **hate crime** is a traditional offense like murder, arson, or vandalism with an added element of bias. For the purposes of collecting statistics, the FBI has defined a hate crime as a "criminal offense against a person or property motivated in whole or in part by an offender's bias against a race, religion, disability, sexual orientation, ethnicity, gender, or gender identity." Hate itself is not a crime—and the FBI is mindful of protecting freedom of speech and other civil liberties.

Notice the importance of a *mens rea* element of bias or hate in the motivation for committing a crime. But hate itself is protected as part of the right to freedom of speech. Therefore, in a hate crime, the hate has to be a motive for that particular crime. For example, if an antiblack, racist motorist gets into a road rage dispute with a black driver and kills them, the criminal act is not necessarily a hate crime if they kill them because their fender is dented, but not specifically because they are black. Racism has to be a direct motive for the crime itself—the racist motorist would have to kill the black person because they were black for it to be a hate crime. Nevertheless, the idea of hate crimes has had traction on state levels, in addition to the federal government. Since 1979, over forty US states have passed hate crime laws.

REPORTING AND PUNISHING HATE CRIMES

All crime is disturbing for what it says about criminals and its effects on their victims. Hate crimes are especially heinous and unlikely to decrease without broad knowledge about their occurrence and strong moral condemnation. But before those who commit hate crimes can be punished, or even for cogent discussion of whether the element of hate should increase punishment, it is necessary to be told how many hate crimes there are, and, before that, hate crimes need to be accurately reported. For 2019, the FBI reported that 15,588 law enforcement agencies participated in the Hate Crime Statistics Program and 2,172 reported 7,314 hate crime incidents involving 8,559 offenses. There were fifty-one murders, which included twenty-two Mexicans killed in a Walmart in El Paso, Texas. Observers and statisticians have claimed that the FBI under-reports hate crimes because it depends on reports coming to it from local jurisdictions, and some of these jurisdictions, including cities, simply do not participate. As a result of nonreporting and other structural factors, many believe that race-based hate crimes or racial-bias crimes are under-reported throughout the United States, beginning on local levels.

Researchers comparing local crime projects with reports in local newspapers have concluded that hate crimes are almost uniformly under-reported in local media, especially newspapers. A 2021 study published in *The Lancet* compared official death statistics with reports of police homicides. The evidence showed that between 1980 and 2019, there were about 30,8000 deaths from police violence, although the US National Vital Statistics System (NVSS) reported only about 17,000. Rates were highest among non-Hispanic black victims and Hispanic people of any race. As discussed in chapter 10, police legal responsibility, including punishment for biased homicides against people of color, cannot be taken for granted. However, the NVSS under-reporting comes not only from police furnishing incomplete information about cause of death to coroners, but coroners knowingly failing to report police involvement in deaths, because they have close working relationships with police officers. For instance, George Floyd's death was at first recorded as due to drugs and heart failure. Such failure to document, and, in many cases, with it a failure to punish police officers who are at least partly motivated by bias in homicides against people of color, is morally wrong in at least three ways: the "bias," here included under "hate," is morally wrong; failure to report the homicides is morally wrong because it is a form of lying; failure to comply with reporting requirements is a betrayal of trust and obligations that come with holding a public office.

In principle, the failure to report hate crimes accurately should itself be punished. But in practice, not everyone is convinced that hate crimes should be punished more severely than the same crimes committed without hate or racial bias. Professor of Criminal Justice Brian Levin has written that justification for hate crime legislation, as well as compliance in reporting, requires clear definition of what the criminal conduct is, evidence that laws against hate crimes are in accord with the criminal justice system, and demonstration that hate crimes are worse than the same crimes from different motives. Some may object that it is sufficient to punish an individual for their actual crime committed, without adding to the punishment based on their state of mind or beliefs. However, as Levin points out, there are consequences to hate crimes that make them worse than the same crimes committed without hate. The effects on victims are often more severe, both in the extent of their physical injuries and psychological trauma that persists to disrupt their lives for years afterward. Those who commit hate crimes often do so in groups, ganging up on one victim. This makes the crime worse because the victim's options for self-defense are restricted, in addition to the moral cowardice of such bullying. Also, hate crime perpetrators are often serial offenders, and serial crimes usually merit harsher punishment. Hate crimes are also disruptive to the community in causing protests and public unrest and they may be followed by "copycat crimes of the same nature." For instance, after the 1986 Howard Beach homicide, the New York City Police Department reported as many similar crimes in the month following as in the previous three months.

All the consequences of hate crimes, which are more destructive than the consequences of the same crimes committed without racial hate or bias, merit harsher punishment. In addition, there is an important logical structure to hate crimes as a cause of community disruption that pertains to racism, generally. A hate crime harms or kills individuals, not for anything they have done or are, but mainly because they appear to belong to a specific racial or ethnic group. This element of racism affects all members of the same group, as though it were happening to them, because they share the race or ethnicity of the victim. Hate crimes thereby have the effect of communicating the existence of racial stereotypes as a form of vulnerability. They result in mass fear for members of minority groups who have been targets and such fear in itself is a disruption to the whole of normal life for members of the targeted group. Although the George Floyd case has focused national attention on African American victims of hate crimes, nearly 3,800 incidents of hate, abuse, and discrimination against Asian Americans have been reported since March 2020, as part of hate-motivated reactions to the COVID-19 pandemic (see American Bar Association video).

QUESTIONS FOR THINKING, DISCUSSION, AND WRITING

1. Explain why it is difficult to control hate speech in the United States.
2. Do you think there is a causal connection between belief, speech, and action? Why is this difficult to regulate and what is the solution?
3. What is the legal *mens rea* element in the FBI's narrow definition of hate crimes?
4. Why do you think it is important that hate crimes be accurately reported?
5. What are your moral views on how the hatred in a hate crime should be punished, in addition to usual criminal punishments?

SOURCES

Balsamo, Michael. "Hate Crimes in US Reach Highest Level in More Than a Decade." November 16, 2020, https://apnews.com/article/hate-crimes-rise-FBI-data-ebbcadca8458aba96575da905650120d.

Davani, Aida Mostafazadeh, Leigh Yeh, Mohammad Atari, Brendan Kennedy, Gwenyth Portillo-Wightman, Elaine Gonzalez, Natalie Delong, Rhea Bhatia, Arineh Mirinjian, Xiang Ren, and Morteza Dehghani. "Reporting the Unreported: Event Extraction for Analyzing the Local Representation of Hate Crimes." Computer Science, Computation and History, Cornell University, September 4, 2019, 1–16, https://arxiv.org/pdf/1909.02126.pdf.

Du Bois, W. E. B. "The Souls of White Folk." In *Darkwater*, 1920, pp. 44–58, quotes from pp. 56 and 57, https://cominsitu.files.wordpress.com/2019/02/du-bois-the-souls-of-white-folk.pdf.

FBI. Hate Crimes, Civil Rights. "What We Investigate," https://www.fbi.gov/investigate/civil-rights/hate-crimes, and "2019 Hate Crime Statistics," https://ucr.fbi.gov/hate-crime/2019.

Freedom Forum Institute. "Which Types of Speech Are Not Protected by the First Amendment?" https://www.freedomforuminstitute.org/about/faq/which-types-of-speech-are-not-protected-by-the-first-amendment/.

Garcia, J. L. A. "The Heart of Racism." *Journal of Social Philosophy*, first published March 1996, https://doi.org/10.1111/j.1467-9833.1996.tb00225.x.

Justice Canada. Section 2(b) Freedom of expression, Government of Canada, https://www.jus tice.gc.ca/eng/csj-sjc/rfc-dlc/ccrf-ccdl/check/art2b.html and "Public Incitement of Hatred, Justice Law Website, Government of Canada, https://laws-lois.justice.gc.ca/eng/acts/c-46/ section-319.html.

Larson, Carlton F. W. "The Forgotten Constitutional Law of Treason and the Enemy Combatant Problem." *University of Pennsylvania Law Review* 154 (2006): 863–926, https:// scholarship.law.upenn.edu/cgi/viewcontent.cgi?article=1303&context=penn_law_review.

Legal Information Institute. "mens rea," Cornell Law School, https://www.law.cornell.edu/ wex/mens_rea.

Levin, Brian. "Hate Crimes: Worse by Definition." *Journal of Contemporary Criminal Justice.* first published February 1, 1999, Research Article, https://journals.sagepub.com/doi/10.1 177/1043986299015001002.

Naghavi, Mohsen, et al. "Fatal Police Violence by Race and State in the USA, 1980–2019: a Network Meta-Regression." *The Lancet* 398 (October 2, 2021): 1239–255, https://www .thelancet.com/journals/lancet/article/PIIS0140-6736(21)01609-3/fulltext.

United Nations. "United Nations Strategy and Plan of Action on Hate Speech." https://www .un.org/en/genocideprevention/documents/UN%20Strategy%20and%20Plan%20of%20 Action%20on%20Hate%20Speech%2018%20June%20SYNOPSIS.pdf.

Videos

American Bar Association (ABA). "Hate Crimes Are Growing More Violent: Realities, Challenges, Remedies." ABA Section of Civil Rights and Social Justice, panel discussion, December 8, 2020, https://www.americanbar.org/groups/crsj/events_cle/recent/hate -crimes-are-growing-more-violent/.

Attorney General Mark R. Herring. "No Hate VA with the Attorney General of Virginia: COVID-19 and the Rise of Anti-Asian Hate." https://www.oag.state.va.us/programs -initiatives/no-hate-va.

Reason TV. "The 3 Rules of Hate Speech: Free Speech Rules." Episode 2, YouTube, February 19, 2019, https://www.youtube.com/watch?v=Ea2ntXnCD_M.

16

Protests from Left and Right

Portland, Oregon, USA, June 12, 2020: Passers-by stop and take a look at the boarded-up Apple Store in downtown Portland's Pioneer Place, which has become unofficial canvases for peaceful protest. Artists have also joined to promote peace over violence. Getty Images: hapabapa.

Protests resemble free speech in exercising a universally recognized democratic right, the right to assemble or get together in the same place. And like free speech in the United States, they are supposed to be legally protected, unless they are violent and incur criminal penalties. This is both a moral and legal norm because nonviolent protests are generally approved of by a wider audience and in democratic countries are not expected to be put down with government force. The content of democratic protests is also usually moral because protesters show up to physically demonstrate their opposition to an injustice that may be lawful as things stand, or to demand just changes in existing law.

The model for lawful, nonviolent moral protest in the twentieth century was provided by India, the world's second-oldest democracy—the United States is the oldest—with the highest population of 1.4 billion in 2021. Mohandas Karamchand Gandhi (1869–1948) created and led this model of mass, peaceful, moral protest, which was his life's work, ethically, spiritually, and in practice. After studying law in England, Gandhi first went to South Africa, at the time a British colony, where he became an activist advocate for the rights of Indians living there. By using civil disobedience with nonviolent protest demonstrations, he was able to mobilize thousands toward reform of racially discriminatory laws against Indians. After Gandhi returned to India in 1915, he applied the same principles to the Indian National Congress political party. The goal was the independence of India from Great Britain.

Gandhi changed the strategy and tactics of the Indian National Congress party from lawyers' legal reform projects involving changes in legislation and court decisions, to mass protests and **civil disobedience** or the refusal to comply with certain laws or to pay certain taxes and fines. Because there was a clear, large goal—independence from Great Britain—Gandhi's protests were coherently connected within the same movement for independence. Gandhi led millions to protest and go on strike, and many were jailed. Gandhi himself rejected violence based on Hindu religious rules against harming living creatures. Nonviolence was also a very effective strategy. The British military could have defeated violent insurrection, but they withdrew when confronted with a peaceful protest that was morally right—the people of India were eventually recognized to have a collective right to national independence.

Successful peaceful protests share certain qualities: spectacle, expression, demonstration, moral conviction, and sometimes pathos. The element of **spectacle** is the public show put on by members of the movement for those who already share the same cause and the members of the wider public who may join them. French sociologist Jean Baudrillard and other social critics have criticized political spectacles for taking the place of informed citizen participation and conversation. But the spectacle as protest has the democratic force of participants bodily—typically by marching—taking action. Even standing in one place together is a form of action. Not everyone has the ability or inclination to read, absorb, and discuss political issues and ideas. But almost everyone can get out and show themselves. Such action is a way to express feelings, goals, and frustration.

The physical exertion required for mass participation has the appearance of sincerity and many are sincere. Protests and demonstrations can also be celebratory and even festive. Political participants know that they are visibly part of something bigger than themselves. Onlookers can be brought to understand, from the demonstration, what is being opposed, who is opposing it, and what their general intent is. Moral conviction is communicated when injustice is described in simple terms. Pathos is enacted when authorities react violently against peaceful protesters.

Just one of Gandhi's many protests illustrates the components of his model. In 1930, Gandhi embarked on a public protest against British law requiring Indians to buy British salt, instead of producing their own. In the Salt Satyagraha or Dandi

March, Gandhi led a 241-mile march to the west coast of Gujarat, where protesters collected handfuls of salt from the Arabian Sea. Others joined him and the demonstration continued for two months. Gandhi was jailed for announcing an intention to march on the Dharasana salt works as were, eventually, sixty thousand of his followers. The spectacle was of the marchers and their growing numbers who had joined Gandhi in the march as he spread his message along the way. Their sincerity was evident in the length of the march. The demonstration was both the growing number of protesters and the actual gathering of salt in India. The participants expressed both their opposition to British law and the importance of salt in their lives. The moral cause was the right of poor people to obtain a necessity of life from resources in their own country. Pathos was generated when British troops responded brutally and protesters did not resist. The Salt Satyagraha was a major turning point for Gandhi's movement. Gandhi represented the Indian National Congress at roundtable discussion in London in 1931. And his movement for Indian independence grew.

Gandhi used nonviolence in leading protests because, as part of his Hindu religion, he believed it was wrong to harm living creatures. He may also have realized that being morally right was an important tactical resource. Gandhi's ultimate success through nonviolent methods was emulated by Martin Luther King Jr. in the US civil rights movement of the 1950s and 1960s. More theoretically, research supports the idea that peaceful protest for moral reasons is more likely to be successful than violent or even patriotic protest. In their 2017 study, Matthew Feinberg et al. recognized that protests by social movements vary in both their tactics and public support. They found that extreme tactics that are disruptive or destructive, such as inflammatory speech, blocking traffic, and damaging property, may attract more publicity than more peaceful tactics. However, they also found that such extreme tactics decrease popular support for the movement because members of the public cannot identify with protesters.

Extreme tactics create drama and enlarge the spectacle, which attracts instant media attention. But if members of the larger audience, who otherwise agree with the aims and principles of the movement become alienated because they do not want to be associated with such tactics, then the use of extreme tactics may have gone too far. On the other hand, it is not always clear what is extreme. US Congressman and civil rights activist John Lewis (1940–2020) was famous for advocating that aspirations for equality get people in "good trouble." But in *Uncivil Disobedience: Studies in Violence and Democratic Politics*, Jennet Kirkpatrick chronicles the moral wrong of violent and terroristic protests, even though they may be undertaken for a cause that participants dearly believe is highly moral. Kirkpatrick argues that respect for law should be as much a democratic ideal as the right of people to protest.

The first section of this chapter is about recent US protests from the political left and the second section considers recent protests from the right. These sections aim to understand recent racial and ethnic protests in the United States in terms of spectacle, expressivity, demonstration, moral message, and pathos. They can then be evaluated in terms of their effectiveness as protests. However, not every successful protest accomplishes the legal and social changes sought by members of its movement. The last section of the chapter is a discussion of the effectiveness of protests for achieving such change.

PROTESTS FROM THE LEFT

Racial and ethnic protests from the US left have succeeded when their aims are clear and attainable as specific goals. The elements of sincerity and pathos have also been important, and their overall messages have been moral. Sometimes they have succeeded in directly changing laws, as with the US civil rights movements. Other times, they have resulted in broad changes in public attitudes that have then resulted in legal changes. And still other times, they remain works in progress. To highlight these elements, let's consider the 1965 attack on civil rights activists in Selma, Alabama, the 2006 immigration protests, and the 2020 Geroge Floyd protests. (See videos for reference.)

- On "Bloody Sunday," March 7, 1965, John Lewis, who was then leader of the Student Nonviolent Coordinating Committee (SNCC), and Reverend Hosea Williams of the Southern Christian Leadership Conference (SCLC) led a march in support of black voting rights. Protesters crossed the Edmund Pettus Bridge to be confronted by state and county officers who ordered them to stop and turn back. The marchers disobeyed and were attacked by troopers on horseback. Many were hospitalized for their injuries. Images were broadcast nationally and support for the civil rights movement increased. Martin Luther King Jr. invited supporters to Selma and the Voting Rights Act of 1965 was passed in June. The demonstration on "Bloody Sunday" was successful. A moral message was broadcast, and public support followed the element of pathos.
- In 2006, over half a million Hispanic Americans and their allies participated in immigration protests. It began in Chicago where 100,000 demonstrated against a US Senate bill that would have made it a crime to aid illegal immigrants with food, housing, or medical care. There were demonstrations in 150 cities in thirty-nine states. On May 1, a demonstration called "Day without Immigrants" was organized in Los Angles where half a million rallied in support of a path to citizenship for undocumented immigrants.

  The necessity of immigrants for past and ongoing US prosperity is not in dispute. Each presidential administration since 2006 has promised to solve the problem of a consistent and humane refugee policy and find a solution to the status of those who were brought to the United States illegally when they were children, and who have since made productive and constructive lives here. But so far, protests have not precipitated coherent immigration legislation. (See chapter 6.)
- Perhaps billions viewed bystanders' video recordings of George Floyd's death from a police officer's knee on his neck on May 25, 2020, in Minneapolis, Min-

nesota. Protests erupted in cities throughout the United States and spread internationally. The overwhelming majority of these protests and the millions who participated were nonviolent, but there were also clashes with police, as well as ongoing police killings of unarmed black men. The George Floyd protests were notable for occurring during the COVID-19 pandemic, although they were not important sources of contagion, perhaps because many were outdoors. Many areas with protests were otherwise in pandemic lockdown, so the protests may have been an important expressive outlet for those who participated. The broad outrage at George Floyd's death was evident in the multicultural and multiracial demographics of protesters. White people joined in large numbers, as did those of all ages.

The George Floyd protests made many Americans aware of unjust police behavior, but as discussed in chapter 10, the localization of 18,000 US police departments and the inability of Congress to agree on national reform legislation leaves the problem as yet unsolved (in October 2021) with no clear path forward. The George Floyd protests had elements of both moral outrage and pathos.

PROTESTS FROM THE RIGHT

Protests from the US right are less frequent than those from the left. Although they are often presented to be about race and ethnicity only in objecting to progressive left protests, some are understood by wider audiences to be assertions of white racial dominance and superiority. Such protests stand less on moral grounds than patriotic ones. If the models for left protests are the movement causes of Mahatma Gandhi and Martin Luther King Jr., the models for recent right protests have been more militant, invoking both the Confederacy of the US Civil War and the Revolutionary War itself. Their aims are not so much progressive but **regressive**—they want to go back to periods of history they view as more favorable to their racial and ethnic groups. Because these protests often erupt in violence, they succeed in getting a lot of media attention but fail in advancing their movement's causes in ways that could change laws or the structure of government. Instead, they face government opposition. Only history will be able to tell us whether such protests change public opinion enough in their favor so that elections are affected and laws and government structures are changed that way. Looking ahead to such influence, we should keep in mind the Charlottesville rally and the January 6, 2021, riot at the US Capitol. (See videos for reference.)

- During an August weekend in Charlottesville, Virginia, hundreds of white supremacists came together to protest the removal of Confederate statues. On Friday evening, they marched through the University of Virginia campus, carrying torches and chanting: "You will not replace us. Jews will not replace us." (These words referred to an anti-Semitic conspiracy theory that rich and powerful Jews were planning to increase the immigration of people of color to replace white Americans.) On Saturday morning, members of this group met with locals who had been objecting all summer to the removal of the statue. Some were armed with homemade weapons and one had a gun. A fight broke out with counter-protesters, one of whom was severely beaten. Many of the white supremacists fled, but one returned and drove through a crowd, killing thirty-two-year-old Heather Heyer. There was mass condemnation and many residents of Charlottesville became aware of racism in their communities for the first time. Two African Americans joined the city council and an African American mayor was elected. The statue of Robert E. Lee was eventually removed. The Charlottesville rally gained local and national attention, but for the protesters, their motivation of hate and threats and use of violence backfired.

- On January 6, 2020, after months of false accounts of voter fraud in the election of President Biden, a rally of right-wing and white supremacist groups formed near the US Capitol. A part of that group advanced to the Capitol. What happened next has been variably called a riot, a protest gone wrong, an insurrection, or an attempted coup. President Trump, who many believe incited the violent events at his "Save America" rally before the violent protest, was impeached for the second time as a result of those events.

  The mob battled capitol police and broke into the Capitol Building. Many carried homemade weapons. One officer died, a second committed suicide, and many more were injured. Vice President Mike Pence was targeted and those who put up a noose threatened to hang him because, although Republicans had lost the election, he intended to preside over the counting of electoral votes. The rioters were eventually expelled, FBI arrests ensued over weeks and months following, and congressional investigations were formed to both find out how security had been breached and determine connections between riot organizers and some members of Congress and the Trump administration.

  The violent events of January 6, 2021, have yet to find their full description in American history but there is no evidence that this protest has been credibly defended by anyone. As of October 2021, the disputes in the aftermath have been between Republicans who deny its violence and Trump's involvement, and Democrats and other critics who insist that such Republicans ought to condemn the January 6 riot and abandon Trump as the leader of their political party.

DO PROTESTS WORK?

All protests work in the limited sense of creating public spectacles. And many draw people into political life who would not otherwise participate. But protests are a form of rhetoric or persuasive speech that is enacted to bring attention to a cause. Unless their aims are very specific, and they are well-organized events, they may remain inspirational and aspirational, but self-contained as only protests. For example, the Occupy Movement began in November 2011 as Occupy Wall Street (OWS) in Zuccotti Park in Manhattan's financial district. Their slogan "We are the 99 percent," referred to recent huge increases in income inequality in the United States. Participants physically occupied the park by camping there until police drove them out. OWS spread throughout the United States. But although the attention to income inequality grew, the Occupy Movement itself, which was disorganized, lacked connections to political officials or candidates, and did not present specific goals, dissipated. In retrospect, it can be seen as a mainly expressive form of protest. However, as the famous scholar and activist Noam Chomsky put it: "You have to go on, have to form the structures that will be sustained, that will go on through hard times and can win major victories."

Thus, of course, all is not lost concerning OWS, or for that matter, the immigration and George Floyd protests, despite the slowness and reluctance to effect large-scale reform. The mass of voters needs to become aware that something is a social problem before the problem can be addressed with new laws that people will obey or before needed government funding will be made available. However, attention itself can become absorbed in a bubble, along with the rhetoric of protests. Righteous protesters may exhaust their energy in public demonstrations. Unless people beyond the protests, throughout society, change their ideas and political behavior through how they vote, even huge protests may remain bubbles, both self-contained and suspended above reality.

However, recent research does indicate that civil rights protests have lasting effects on attitudes. For a study published in 2018, Soumyajit Mazumder surveyed 150,000 respondents from US counties and found that whites from counties where there had been historical civil rights protests were more likely to identify as Democrats. These whites also were in favor of affirmative action and decades later were less likely to express racial resentment against black people. That is, the protests they experienced had become part of their collective history, with enduring results. Mazumder's study also highlights the local, experiential nature of protests and politics in the United States. People form their broad political opinions on controversial topics as a result of their own experience and that experience is necessarily local because most individuals live and work locally.

QUESTIONS FOR THINKING, DISCUSSION, AND WRITING

1. Explain the elements of protests and apply them to these questions. Was Gandhi an idealist or a pragmatist? Given his success, does it matter, and why?
2. What are the individual virtues and vices involved in US protests from the left? Explain.

3. What are the individual virtues and vices involved in US protests from the right? Explain.

4. Of all the protests described here, which is your favorite one? Describe and argue in favor of its moral justification.

5. Explain how the very nature of protests creates an open question of whether any given one will "work"?

SOURCES

Baudrillard, Jean. *In the Shadow of the Silent Majorities*. New York: Semiotext(e), 1983.

Chomsky, Noam. *Occupy*. Zuccotti Park Press, 2012, quotation from p. 34.

Feinberg, Matthew, Robb Willer, and Chloe Kovacheff. "Extreme Protest Tactics Reduce Popular Support for Social Movements." Rotman School of Management Working Paper No. 2911177, February 3, 2017, https://papers.ssrn.com/sol3/papers.cfm?abstract_id=2911177.

Kirkpatrick, Jennet. *Uncivil Disobedience: Studies in Violence and Democratic Politics*. Princeton, NJ: Princeton University Press, 2009.

Mazumder, Soumyajit. "The Persistent Effect of U.S. Civil Rights Protests on Political Attitudes." *American Journal of Political Science* 62, no. 4 (2018): 922–35, http://www.jstor.org/stable/26598792.

Pletcher, Kenneth. "Salt March." Indian History, *Encyclopedia Britannica*, https://www.britannica.com/event/Salt-March.

Videos

"Do You Remember the 2006 Immigration Protests?" *Los Angeles Times*, April 27, 2016, https://www.latimes.com/86927904-132.html.

Equal Justice Initiative. "Bloody Sunday: Civil Rights Activists Brutally Attacked in Selma." On this Day in History, March 7, 1965, https://calendar.eji.org/racial-injustice/mar/7.

Khavin, Dmitriy, Haley Willis, Evan Hill, Natalie Reneau, Drew Jordan, Cora Engelbrecht, Christiaan Triebert, Stella Cooper, Malachy Browne, and David Botti. "Day of Rage: An In-Depth Look at How a Mob Stormed the Capitol." *New York Times*, June 30, 2021, https://www.nytimes.com/video/us/politics/100000007606996/capitol-riot-trump-supporters.html.

PBS News Hour. "A Year Ago, the Charlottesville Rally Shined a Light on White Supremacists and Sparked Overdue Conversations." August 10, 2018, https://www.pbs.org/newshour/show/a-year-ago-the-charlottesville-rally-shined-a-light-on-white-supremacists-and-sparked-overdue-conversations.

PIB India. "Dandi March to Break the Salt Laws." YouTube, August 27, 2019, https://www.youtube.com/watch?v=oY0aACSyW2Q.

Porter, Dawn. "John Lewis: Good Trouble." 2020 documentary film directed by Dawn Porter, YouTube, July 3, 2020, https://www.youtube.com/watch?v=Iyl-GY1_sG0.

Silverstein, Jason. "The Global Impact of George Floyd: How Black Lives Matter Protests Shaped Movements around the World." CBS News, June 4, 2021, https://www.cbsnews.com/news/george-floyd-black-lives-matter-impact/.

V

IDENTITY AND REPRESENTATION

Identity has two parts: how people view themselves as individuals and group members and how others view them. In a society with problems of race relations, the two parts rarely line up and this gives rise to further conflict, some of which produces greater understanding and progress toward social equality.

Chapter 17 first considers mixed-race identities that are particularly fraught for people with some black ancestry. While the "one-drop rule" holding that any black ancestry results in a person being completely black is not as rigorously enforced as in the past, mixed or multiracial people continue to have contested identities. On the one hand, their freedom to choose their identities has been emphasized, but on the other hand, group loyalty and calls for black solidarity may undermine the freedom of such choices. Chapter 18, in considering connections between culture and race, first takes up the complexities of Jewish identities that have since World War II been considered no more than a matter of religious affiliation, although many Jews do not observe Judaism. Indigenous identities, unlike those of other racial and ethnic minorities, have been asserted in resistance to assimilation or participation in the dominant culture. Cosmopolitan ideals would stress fluidity and harmonious interactions among all racial and ethnic identities. However, in a mass consumer culture, cosmopolitan choices may be superficial and bland or prize exotic people and objects in ways that reassert dominance.

Chapter 19 adds to the complexity of understanding identities with the idea of multiple oppressions. That is, in real life, people are not only members of a racial or ethnic group but may also experience disadvantage due to gender or income. Intersectionality first became famous for demanding recognition of the multiple oppressions experienced by black women. But scholars have also used intersectional methods to examine overlooked robust identities, such as black males in a racist society and Latina women. Chapter 20 takes up identities in terms of their public representation in media. Topics include Latina representation, Asian American representation, and memorials for African Americans and Native Americans. In chapter 21, both intersectionality and representation are examined in American sport that has mirrored racism in society. But lately, star athletes of color have spoken out more strongly, in revealing their vulnerabilities and protesting racial injustice.

17

Mixed Race

Portrait of multigeneration family group. Getty Images: monkeybusinessimages.

In the United States, those who are mixed race or multiracial have been a subject of tension and sometimes intense conflict. The irony about such intensity is that the idea of mixed race presupposes the idea of race, which itself has had the validity of its biological foundation hollowed out by recent science. If science provides no foundation for human races, it follows logically that it can provide no foundation for mixed race or mixed races. However, just as monoracial differences and identities are strong social realities, based at least on **phenotypes** or inherited traits of physical appearance, the same can be said about mixed race. If social race is real, which it is, then so is mixed race. Race is an idea imposed on people or chosen by them, which lacks the objective biological foundation it is commonly assumed to have (see chapter 4). That is what it means to say that race is a social construction. It follows from this that mixed race or the identity of mixed race is a combination of social constructions. In that sense, mixed race is also a social construction.

In American discussions of race, black and white racial identity is **binary**. Either a person is black or else they are white. To be white, a person must look white and have no known black ancestry. But to be black, it is enough if a person just has a black appearance or any black ancestry. Racial blackness is defined as the **logical contradictory** of racial whiteness, which means that someone must be black or white and cannot be both. The existence of mixed black and white people belies that binary. We also need to remember that mixed black and white individuals are not all there is to mixed race. Other racial and ethnic groups have produced mixed- or multiracial individuals, including Asian/white, Native American/black, Asian/black, Hispanic/black, Hispanic/white, and so forth. If all the racial and ethnic categories specified by the US census are assumed to have mixed individuals—which is a safe assumption—then the categories yield every possible combination of the five racial groups—white, black or African American, American Indian or Alaska Native, Asian, and Native Hawaiian or other Pacific Islander—plus "some other race," and, Hispanic-non-Hispanic ethnicity. Mathematically, this requires **factorials** of the number of races that can be mixed or the number of possibilities in every possible combination, including how identities in a mixture are arranged. The arrangements of racial identities are important because people who are mixed emphasize different races in their mixture. People with black and white ancestry might emphasize either one, for instance, and here there are two possibilities based on factorial 2. But if a person is black, Asian, and white, there are six possibilities for factorial 3, considering both mixtures and arrangements: black-Asian-white, Asian-black-white, white-Asian-black, black-white-Asian, Asian-black-white, and white-black-Asian. Since there are five US census racial categories and a sixth for "some other race," plus Hispanic-non-Hispanic, we might consider factorial 7. The total of that is 5,040 combinations!

Are there really 5,040 combinations for US mixed-racial identities? Logically there are, but whether people exist for each of them has not been researched. Even the five racial categories of the census yield 120 different combinations, without considering how each combination is arranged. The number of racially combined types of people who are mixed is important because racial identities are generally assumed to be visible and easily understood. Most people believe they can tell what race a person is by looking at them or the "box" they check on a form. If 120 racial possibilities instead of five or six, or even seven, were recognized, then what race a person is would no longer be socially intelligible. While there are no moral or medical reasons why a person's race should be evident, the system of race as a social construction, with norms for behavior that accompany it, requires clear and accessible identification by race. There are two reasons for this—vulnerability and status. Nonwhites or people of color are generally more vulnerable than whites, experiencing a variety of social disadvantages that include racism and entitlements to respect. White people have the highest status in a system of race, and the differences between whites and nonwhites are important to recognize for that reason (see chapter 14).

The first section of this chapter is about mixed race and social construction. The second section is about important aspects of the "one-drop rule" for US black identity. The third section is about the moral aspects of mixed-race identity.

MIXED RACE AND SOCIAL CONSTRUCTION

How can human biology result in physical traits that are considered racial in society, without there being a biological foundation for race itself? We saw in chapter 4 that contemporary science has found no evidence for a natural taxonomy or system of human races. There is greater variety in the traits considered racial traits within any of the major races than between them. The traits considered racial are physical traits, but they are each inherited separately and they are no different from other inherited traits. That is, there is nothing "racial" about them apart from identities in society. Now-bogus theories of race arose during the age of discovery, colonization, and chattel slavery. Europeans were brought into contact with people who looked very different from them and that fact of appearance seemed to make the existence of human races self-evident. For instance, slaves brought to the US South from Africa looked strikingly different from white settlers and planters. But this perceived contrast itself was not a natural phenomenon, but the result of people being brought together in a situation where they were not considered equal from the beginning. Naturally, skin shades associated with race are **clines**, because without human travel and relocation, skin shades associated with races vary gradually and continuously, as the distance from the equator increases or decreases.

The idea of whiteness was bound up with initial situations of dominance through discovery, colonization, and slavery. Whites asymmetrically benefited from resulting arrangements and the idea of race justified white dominance by positing nonwhites as humanly inferior to them. Racial whiteness was also mythologized as pure and elevated in itself. And because the idea of race was first presented as biological, white purity was associated with inheritance. Families could only be considered white if they were purely white, with no nonwhite members or ancestors. If white family members had children with nonwhites, those children, especially when their mothers were black slaves, were not considered members of the white family.

The story of Thomas Jefferson (1743–1826), third president of the United States, and his female slave Sally Hemings shows how the idea of a white family worked from early US history onward. Sally Hemings was a teenage slave who Jefferson inherited from his wife's estate. She was said to already be racially mixed. Over the years, Jefferson was believed to have fathered at least six of her children, although modern DNA analysis is ambiguous about whether it was Jefferson or his nephew who was their father. At any rate, Jefferson freed all of Hemings children, also mentioning her sons Madison and Eston in his will, and he did not free any other family units. The Jefferson family rejected the story of the paternity of Sally Hemings's children over many subsequent generations. However, in January 2000, the Thomas Jefferson Foundation Research Committee reported that known evidence—from a DNA study, original documents, written and oral historical accounts, and statistical data—indicated a high probability that Thomas Jefferson was the father of Eston Hemings, and that he was likely the father of all six of Sally Hemings's children listed in the records of Monticello, Jefferson's estate.

Eston Hemings, who had been freed after Jefferson's death, moved to Ohio and eventually settled in Wisconsin with his wife and children. They were a white family and changed their name to "Jefferson." Ironically, a white family was able to claim prestigious Jeffersonian heritage through their black forebear, Sally Hemings. The official white Jefferson family, headquartered at Monticello, has since welcomed members of different branches of descendants from Sally Hemings. However, the time it took to acknowledge these family members shows how important ideas of racial purity have been in US history. The importance of these ideas and of the system of race that was limited to a small number of fixed races is also evident in the history of the US census itself.

Since the first US census of 1790, those counted have been identified by race. But the options for racial identification have continually changed, particularly for those who are mixed race. From 1790 to 1950, census takers determined the race of the Americans they counted, sometimes based on how they were perceived in their community or using calculations based on their amount of "black blood." This idea of the amount of "black blood" was based on fractions of inheritance, such as one-half white and one-half Chinese, or one-fourth black and three-fourths white, and so forth. The Pew Research Center has reproduced instructions to census takers from 1930 (see figure 17.1).

The racial determination based on "blood" is a **genealogical** method referring to the race or races of the parents or grandparents of a person and not what they actually inherited from them. What a person inherits from parents or grandparents, that is, which inherited traits are the traits considered racial, requires DNA analysis and matching, which of course did not exist until well into the twentieth century.

By 1960, census respondents were permitted to choose their own race on census forms, but without instructions for how they were to determine their race. Since 2000, respondents have been permitted to select more than one race. Census racial categories are important for equitable political districting and entitlement programs, as well as personal identity. The first census in 1790 had only three racial categories: free whites, all other free persons, and slaves; "Mulatto" was added in 1850. According to Pew and the US census, in 2010, there were sixty-three possible race categories—six for single races and fifty-seven for combined. Nine million respondents or 2.9 percent chose more than one category. But an additional census question of "ancestry or ethnic origin" yields 4.3 percent or over thirteen million with two-race ancestry.

The two-race ancestry group more than doubled after 1980, when the question was first asked, and researchers agree that the US mixed-race population is trending

Instructions to 1930 Census Takers on Counting People by Race

PERSONAL DESCRIPTION

149. Column 11. Sex.—Write "M" for male and "F" for female, as indicated in the notes at the bottom of the schedule.

150. Column 12. Color or race.—Write "W" for white; "Neg" for Negro; "Mex" for Mexican; "In" for Indian; "Ch" for Chinese; "Jp" for Japanese; "Fil" for Filipino; "Hin" for Hindu; and "Kor" for Korean. For a person of any other race, write the race in full.

151. Negroes.—A person of mixed white and Negro blood should be returned as a Negro, no matter how small the percentage of Negro blood. Both black and mulatto persons are to be returned as Negroes, without distinction. A person of mixed Indian and Negro blood should be returned a Negro, unless the Indian blood predominates and the status as an Indian is generally accepted in the community.

152. Indians.—A person of mixed white and Indian blood should be returned as Indian, except where the percentage of Indian blood is very small, or where he is regarded as a white person by those in the community where he lives. (See par. 151 for mixed Indian and Negro.)

153. For a person reported as Indian in column 12, report is to be made in column 19 as to whether "full blood" or "mixed blood," and in column 20 the name of the tribe is to be reported. For Indians, columns 19 and 20 are thus to be used to indicate the degree of Indian blood and the tribe, instead of the birthplace of father and mother.

Source: U.S. Census Bureau

Figure 17.1 1930 US census takers instructions. Source: Pew Research Center, https://www.pewresearch.org/st_2015-06-11 _multiracial-americans_01-01/).

upward. By the time of the 2020 census, 33.8 million people in the United States identified as multiracial, a 276 percent increase over 2010 and about 10 percent of the total population. As the US mixed-race population increases, the question of how mixed race will be regarded remains open. As we will soon see, the persistence of the one-drop rule suggests that both official and popular attitudes remain slow to change toward recognition of mixed-race identities.

THE IMPORTANCE OF THE ONE-DROP RULE

In terms of black and white racial identity, white purity has been protected through the racial myths and traditions of the white American family. But those with black identity have had to pay the price for such purity through the so-called **one-drop rule** or idea that one drop of "black blood"—itself a bogus concept because blood is not biologically or scientifically associated with race—determines that a person is all black.

The three towering nineteenth-century African American public intellectuals and activists—Frederick Douglass (1817–1895), Booker T. Washington, and W. E. B. Du Bois (see chapter 12)—were mixed race, with black mothers and white fathers. But there was never any question about their identity as black. Today, popular culture abounds with celebrities, ranging from Clark Gable to Jennifer Beals, who are known to have black ancestry and, although they may be called "biracial" or "multiracial," most nowadays identify as black and are considered black by both black and white people. If they are described as biracial or multiracial, it is presented as an interesting factoid, especially "surprising" if a biracial or multiracial person looks white. Mixed-race identities among those who are famous tend to be announced as something that makes them unusual or exotic. Rarely is there a discussion of the ongoing one-drop rule or a demonstration of how it is still being applied. But a demonstration occurred when Barack Obama was a candidate and after he was elected president.

If we consider the official presidential bioguide, Obama was the first African American president. End of story:

> Born in Honolulu, Hawaii, August 4, 1961; obtained early education in Jakarta, Indonesia, and Hawaii; continued education at Occidental College, Los Angeles, Calif.; received a B.A. in 1983 from Columbia University, New York City; worked as a community organizer in Chicago, Ill.; studied law at Harvard University, where he became the first African American president of the Harvard Law Review, and received J.D. in 1991; lecturer on constitutional law, University of Chicago; member, Illinois State Senate 1997–2004; elected as a Democrat to the US Senate in 2004, and served from January 3, 2005, to November 16, 2008, when he resigned from office, having been elected president; elected as the 44th President of the United States on November 4, 2008.

This account does not explicitly say Obama was the first black president but implies it in saying he was the first African American president of the *Harvard Law Review*, with a further implication that his race had not changed between 1991 and 2008.

But Obama's race did change, perhaps more than once, during those years. In his 2004 autobiography, *Dreams from My Father*, Obama described his development of black identity in late adolescence. But when he first became a candidate for president, he did not proclaim his black identity but presented himself as a symbol of American unity, because his father was a black man from Kenya and his mother was a white woman from Kansas. Throughout his candidacy, he was claimed by African Americans. And during his victory speech, he identified with a 106-year-old black women who voted for him in Atlanta. Thus, although Obama was not a descendant of slaves as are many African Americans, but a descendant of an African who had studied in Hawaii, he became the first African American president, which erased both his biracial and immigrant heritage, not to mention his multicultural background of education in Indonesia and upbringing by white grandparents in Hawaii. Thus, on the highest and most powerful levels, the one-drop rule overrides mixed race.

MORAL ASPECTS OF MIXED-RACE IDENTITY

In 1991, American mixed-race psychologist Maria P. P. Root published a "Bill of Rights for People of Mixed Heritage" that many continue to find relevant. Root did not say where these rights came from. They are not anywhere set forth as legal rights or humanitarian rights and no known religion puts them forth. We can understand them as moral humanitarian rights for people of mixed heritage (including parents, grandparents, and other forebears of different races) who live in societies that are arranged on the assumption that each individual is a member of just one race and has just one heritage. As moral rights, Root's "bill" prescribes what mixed people ought to expect from others who are not mixed. Root's "bill" does not address how mixed people should themselves relate to those who are not mixed or to members of groups other than their own who are also mixed. But if mixed people have these rights, then monoracial people are morally obligated to respect them and act accordingly. We should note that although Root refers to "mixed heritage," not "mixed race," and uses the word "ethnicity," and not "race," she has been widely interpreted to be referring to mixed race and race. Let's consider Root's rights, before further discussion of their implications:

Bill of Rights for People of Mixed Heritage
I Have the Right . . .
Not to justify my existence in this world.
Not to keep the races separate within me.
Not to justify my ethnic legitimacy.
Not to be responsible for people's discomfort with my physical or ethnic ambiguity.
I Have the Right . . .
To identify myself differently than strangers expect me to identify.
To identify myself differently than how my parents identify me.
To identify myself differently than my brothers and sisters.
To identify myself differently in different situations.
I Have the Right . . .
To create a vocabulary to communication about being multiracial or multiethnic.
To change my identity over my lifetime—and more than once.
To have loyalties and identification with more than one group of people.
To freely choose whom I befriend and love.

Some of Root's rights would seem to belong to everyone, regardless of race or mixed race. They are simply human rights: "Not to justify my existence in this

world"; "Not to keep the races separate within me"; "To have loyalties and identification with more than one group of people"; "To freely chose whom I befriend and
love." These rights are all straightforward and usually taken for granted. For instance,
the right "not to keep the races separate in me," speaks to a right to experience oneself
as a whole, fully integrated person. To assert that people of mixed heritage have such
rights is to assert that insofar as these are universal human rights and those of mixed
heritage are human, it would be discriminatory to deny them these rights. More directly, the right to ask that others not discriminate based on race and include mixed
race as what may not be discriminated against is stated as the right "Not to justify
my ethnic legitimacy." That is, if people with one race or ethnicity do not have to
justify their racial or ethnic identity, then people with more than one race or ethnicity should be treated the same way. The right to have loyalties and identification with
more than one group of people must in this context mean, "more than one racial
or ethnic group of people." In a society where racial or ethnic loyalty is customarily
given to one group, this would be a special right for mixed-race people.

Additional rights put forth by Root speak to creativity, autonomy, and something
new to the world that mixed-race people have perhaps special rights to experience
and then contribute to others. Included here are rights to: have acceptance for racial
or ethnic ambiguity in appearance; have racial or ethnic identities different from
family members; invent new ways of describing racial experience; surprise strangers
about what one's race or ethnicity is; change how one identifies racially and ethnically, over a lifetime. The moral aspect of these rights is that others who are not
mixed should recognize them and not punish those who exercise them.

For some, several of Root's rights might be morally problematic. Most people
value family solidarity and conformity to the general identity of the family. Loyalty
to more than one racial group may be questioned when group goals are opposed
and politicized. Some African Americans have insisted on practices of racial solidarity, given the vulnerabilities of black experience and identity. As a result, they
consider it principled and even obligatory that everyone with known black ancestry
identifies as black. For instance, in *Challenging Multiracial Identity*, Ranier Spencer
has claimed that multiracial identity is superficially lauded in media and fashion as
a form of racial exploitation to distract the public from the real problems of African Americans. Also, the idea of changing one's racial identity over time may raise
questions about why the person wants to make such changes and whether they are
self-serving in doing so, depending on what they gain from a racial identity in a
given situation. For instance, passing for white by mixed-race people has traditionally been considered disloyal and deceptive. More recently, passing for black by
people who are white has evoked outrage and fury in "cancel culture." In 2020,
Jessica Krug, a white Jewish woman who grew up in Kansas City resigned from the
faculty of George Washington University after severe public condemnation when
she admitted that she had falsely claimed to be black. Krug's life and work had
been devoted to African American, Caribbean, and Hispanic culture, but she had
no black ancestry. If Krug had been mixed race with black ancestry, her choice of

a black identity would not have been questioned. But why should black ancestry have been so important when genealogy does not establish race and race itself lacks an objective scientific foundation?

QUESTIONS FOR THINKING, DISCUSSION, AND WRITING

1. Explain how if race is a social construction, mixed race must be also.
2. What is the irony of how Eston Jefferson's descendants claimed their Jeffersonian identity and how is it related to the history of racial categories in the US census?
3. What does the racial categorization of Barack Obama and his own identification suggest about mixed-race identities in the United States?
4. Select two rights for multiracial Americans according to Root, with which you agree and provide moral reasoning.
5. Select two rights for multiracial Americans according to Root, with which you or those you may know disagree and provide moral reasoning.

SOURCES

Calculator Soup. "Factorial Factor n!" https://www.calculatorsoup.com/calculators/discrete mathematics/factorials.php.

CNN. "Famous Biracial and Black People." August 1, 2016, https://www.cnn.com/2014/02/11/ living/gallery/famous-biracial-people/index.html.

Gordon-Reed, Annette. *The Hemingses of Monticello: An American Family.* New York: W.W. Norton, 2008.

Jefferson Monticello. "Thomas Jefferson and Sally Hemings, A Brief Account." https://www .monticello.org/thomas-jefferson/jefferson-slavery/thomas-jefferson-and-sally-hemings-a -brief-account/.

Marks, Jonathan. Interview transcript, background to "Race: The Power of an Illusion," PBS, https://www.pbs.org/race/000_About/002_04-background-01-08.htm.

Mixed/Remixed, Admin. "A Reminder of the Bill of Rights for People of Mixed Heritage by Maria P. P. Root." January 17, 2017, http://www.mixedremixed.org/reminder-bill-rights -people-mixed-heritage-maria-p-p-root/.

NBC Washington Staff. "GW Professor Resigns after Falsely Claiming Black Identity." September 9, 2020, https://www.nbcwashington.com/news/gw-professor-resigns-after-falsely -claiming-black-identity/2414247/.

Obama, Barack. *Dreams from My Father: A Story of Race and Inheritance.* New York: Three Rivers Press, 2002.

Parker, Kim, Juliana Menasce Horowitz, Rich Morin, and Mark Hugo Lopez. "Chapter 1: Race and Multiracial Americans in the U.S. Census." Multiracial in America, Report, Pew Research Center, June 11, 2015, https://www.pewresearch.org/social-trends/2015/06/11/ chapter-1-race-and-multiracial-americans-in-the-u-s-census/.

Spencer, Ranier. *Challenging Multiracial Identity.* Boulder, CO: Lynne Rienner, 2006.

Thomson, Katherine. "Obama Victory Speech." https://www.huffpost.com/entry/obama-victory-speech_n_141194.
US Census. "Race." Reviewed October 2021, updated annually, https://www.census.gov/quickfacts/fact/note/US/RHI625219.
US Census. "Race." https://www.census.gov/library/stories/2021/08/improved-race-ethnicity-measures-reveal-united-states-population-much-more-multiracial.html.
US Congress, Barack Obama, Official biography. Available at https://bioguide.congress.gov/search/bio/O000167, 2008.
Zack, Naomi. *Race and Mixed Race*. Philadelphia, PA: Temple University Press, 1993.

Videos

BBC Three. "Things Not to Say to Someone of Mixed Race." YouTube, January 17, 2017, https://www.youtube.com/watch?v=g8sY29iN0-c.
Donnella, Leah. "All Mixed Up: What Do We Call People of Multiple Backgrounds?" Code Switch, NPR, NYC, August 25, 2016, https://www.npr.org/sections/codeswitch/2016/08/25/455470334/all-mixed-up-what-do-we-call-people-of-multiple-backgrounds.
Schmitt, Annabelle. "Why Mixed Race Babies Aren't the Answer to Racism." TEDx Talks, February 24, 2020, https://www.youtube.com/watch?v=lcMcvDZU3T8.

18

Race, Ethnicity, and Culture

Orthodox Lelov Jews at synagogue. Getty Images: Philippe Lissac.

The word "ethnicity" is sometimes used as a euphemism for "race," for instance when white people include black and Asian people in discussions of "different ethnicities." But unlike race, there has never been an explicit definition of ethnicity. Ethnicity can be based on language, appearance, religion, nationality, or the culture of a group. At this time, the US census counts five races: white, black or African American, American Indian or Alaska Native, Asian, Native Hawaiian or other Pacific Islander. A sixth category of "some other race" is used for respondents who do not identify with any of these five, and the ethnicity of Hispanic or non-Hispanic must be checked.

Many people assume that differences in race are differences in inherited traits, whereas differences in ethnicity are differences in culture. However, members of ethnic groups may be **racialized** or treated as nonwhite races in the course of oppression or discrimination. After 9/11, many Middle Eastern and North African Americans were racialized in practice, that is, treated as members of a race who could be recognized by their physical appearances. That could lead to harsh US round-up and expulsion antiterrorist policies, as well as "rendition" to countries that allowed for torture in interrogation. In reverse, some Hispanic/Latinx Americans, who are not officially designated as a race, have demanded recognition as a race to better combat racist practices against them by police and other authorities.

The assignment of biology to "race" and "culture" to "ethnicity" is relatively recent. Before the twentieth century, the idea of race included notions of inherited culture. For sociologists and anthropologists, the idea of ethnicity to represent everything about race that pertained to society and individual identities took up those aspects of the idea of race that were not biological. However, there is an important difference between races and ethnicities.

As discussed in chapter 4, the idea of race posited a universal system for sorting human beings into a few fixed categories. Race was thus an abstract system imposed on human reality. Ethnicity, in contrast, follows real human differences in history, geographical movement, and group customs and traditions. As such, the number of ethnicities is open-ended. In a 2002 paper for the Harvard Institute of Economic Research, 650 worldwide ethnic groups were identified. Countries in Europe and Northeast Asia are the most homogenous and Sub-Saharan African countries are the most diverse. Both North and South America are in the middle. Ethnic diversity in the United States tends to be concentrated in urban areas because many immigrant groups start in cities. In New York City, for example, eight hundred different languages are spoken in the metropolitan area, and in the public school system, 176 languages are spoken. If there are only 650 different ethnic groups worldwide, some of the different languages spoken in New York City must be associated with the same ethnic groups.

So long as it is fruitful to understand people in terms of ethnic groups, but not biological races, the cultural aspects of ethnicity will remain informative. There are different meanings of culture and different kinds of judgments associated with them. Here, we should distinguish between four: culture as part of race or ethnicity; culture as an anthropological field that studies how people live, including group traditions regarding marriage, food, religion, holidays, dress, and so forth; culture as attainment or accompaniment of social class; and culture as aesthetic products of art, music, dance, and craft, which are both popular and elite. Our focus here is on culture as part of race or ethnicity. Most of culture in this sense is respected and considered part of protected free choice in democratic societies. An exception would be if a cultural practice, for instance, polygamy or child marriage, is a crime in the wider society. A person or group's choice of their culture is protected in democratic societies because the expression and practice of culture are close to freedom of religion and free speech, including the right to assemble.

Ideas and judgments of culture have been closely tied to ideas about race in ways intended to mask either **essentialism** or the belief that there is one all-important trait that all members of a race share, or to cover up biological racial prejudice. When cultural identities are used as a substitute for racial identities, judgments about culture may mask judgments about race, either in beliefs in one's own group's racial superiority or in another group's racial inferiority. But own-group cultural affirmations may also express unity within the group to resist oppression.

Groups may strive to retain their cultures as a way of resisting racial oppression, as well as for their sincere attachment to traditional ways of living. This may involve beliefs and practices that are so different from those of dominant groups that traditionalists do not want to join the dominant group's society. This has been the case with indigenous cultures throughout the world. Normally, most cultures are inclusive and new members and practitioners can join. But goals for cultural retention among indigenous groups have made them wary of inauthentic uses of their cultural practices that distort their meaning.

Cosmopolitanism or knowledge of cultures different from one's own and ease in interacting with them has been developed as an ideal capable of relaxing tensions arising from the sheer facts of difference. However, in a mass consumer society such as the United States, the products of international cultures may be diluted or sanded down so that they approximate a general American norm. Many Americans crave foods from different cultures, but they have to seek them out beyond the bland arrays offered in the food courts of suburban shopping malls.

The first part of this chapter is about Jewish identity that is variably based on religion, ideas about race, and culture. The second part is about indigenous culture and issues of racial identity. The chapter concludes with an exploration of cosmopolitanism as a practical ideal.

COMPLEXITIES OF JEWISH IDENTITY

Jewish identity, particularly American Jewish identity, is complex, because it involves religion, race, ethnicity, and culture, in ways that are difficult to separate. There is also an additional factor of persecution, which is an important part of Jewish history. Throughout Western history, Jews were both persecuted for their religion in Christian countries and viewed as a race. This persecution and racialization came to a hideous conclusion with the Nazi program of **genocide** that was an explicit intention to kill all Jews in the world, resulting in six million deaths in World War II German concentration camps. The methods used by Nazis to persecute and vilify Jews and target them for genocide are now understood to be based on Hitler's study of the treatment of African Americans and Native Americans, as well as immigration and citizenship restrictions in the United States. Hitler admired these laws and policies in his manifesto, *Mein Kampf* (1925), and they were translated into the German anti-Semitic Nuremberg Race Laws (1935) after he came to power.

Following World War II, there was an international effort to condemn racism, to some degree generally, but specifically to condemn how Jews had been racialized in Germany. The result in many democratic countries, particularly the United States, was that Judaism came to be identified as a religion. Those who practiced the religion were considered *observant*. However, the customs and forms of in-group identity, as well as external anti-Semitism, continued to be based on Jewish cultural practices and in-group criteria for identity as Jewish, which had existed before both the German attempt at genocide and the subsequent designation of Jewishness as a religion. That is, anti-Semites continued to racialize Jews, and Jews themselves based their identity on appearance and inheritance that worked like racial identities, as well as ethnic culture. Religion remains the main aspect of Jewish identity, even among Jews who are not observant, suggesting that even religion is believed to be inherited. This interplay of components or aspects of Jewish identity has at times resulted in crises of identity swirling around the Jewish in-group question, "Who is a Jew?"

According to a 2013 poll conducted by the Pew Forum for Religious and Public Life, 78 percent of Jews said they were Jewish by religion, while 22 percent said they had no religion. Among those who claimed Judaism as religion, 68 percent said that a person could both not believe God exists and be Jewish. Twice as many religious Jews said that having a good sense of humor was an essential part of being Jewish as said that following Jewish law was. After noting the Pew data, Sarah Imhoff proposes five different criteria for Jewish identity: **halakha** or Jewish Law, Reform and Reconstruction movements, Christian theology concerning Jesus, genetics, and ethnicity.

According to Jewish law, if a person's mother is Jewish or they convert according to Jewish law, then they are Jewish. Reform and Reconstructionists reject halakhic law as binding and hold that "the past has a vote but not a veto," or that Jewish law is influential for ethical reasons but not decisive. Some Christians consider themselves Jewish because Jesus was Jewish. Not all Jews accept such claims from Christians, but some do, and this raises the question of who decides who is Jewish, which is a problem because rabbis often disagree. When Jews rely on genetic tests to claim Jewishness, because they believe their ancestors may have converted to Christianity, genetics thereby becomes a criterion for Jewish identity. But all that DNA testing can ensure is a similarity to other people known to have Jewish identity—there is no Jewish gene or DNA sequence. Ethnicity becomes a criterion of Jewish identity through food, music, language, rituals, and other aspects of culture.

None of these criteria taken separately, apart from halakhic law, are accepted by all Jews. And the requirement of a Jewish mother could be a matter of genetics, or maternal Jewish environment in the womb, or nourishment from a Jewish woman. Finally, many who identify as Jews do not specify how or on what basis they are Jewish but claim that they are "just Jewish." No one has the authority to deny or dispute such a claim, and Imhoff concludes that there may be a lesson here for other forms of religious identity. But that is to assume that Judaism is a religion. The claim of being "just Jewish" may have the same validity as religious identity (according to halakhic law or Christianity), descent, beliefs about race, or common culture. This raises the more general question of whether any racial or ethnic identity could be valid if someone says they "just are" the identity in question.

RESISTANT INDIGENOUS IDENTITY

The history of modern humans has been a process of migration, originally out of Africa, to what is now Europe, Asia, and the Americas. There were internal travels from Europe and Asia that are still research subjects for archeologists, anthropologists, and population geneticists. Contemporary indigenous peoples throughout the world are the longest-dwelling and original populations on all continents. Their traditional cultures are a major part of their identities and the Western idea of race that divides humankind into a few unchanging groups has been imposed on them from without, meeting resistance from within. The recent US story of Kennewick Man provides a dramatic narrative of such resistance and the tension between modern Western ideas of race and indigenous identities.

After the Columbia River flooded in Kennewick, Washington, in 1996, anthropologist James Chatters found human remains. Instead of his expectation that they were those of a recent crime victim, forensic evidence indicated that the remains were that of a middle-aged man with "Caucasoid" features who lived about 9,300 years ago. Chatters and other anthropologists thought that this "Kennewick Man" belonged to a European group who had traveled to the Americas before modern Native Americans.

Because of their age, the remains of Kennewick Man were placed under the jurisdiction of the Native American Graves Protection and Repatriation Act of 1990 and the Army Corps of Engineers removed them to a secure vault in the Burke Museum. The Umatilla Indians, tribes in Oregon, Washington, and Idaho, claimed Kennewick Man for reburial, but Chatters and colleagues sued for possession or access to the skeleton for further research. Armand Minthorn, speaking for the Umatillas, claimed that the age and place of the skeleton alone established it as Native American:

> If this individual is truly over 9,000 years old, that only substantiates our belief that he is Native American. From our oral histories, we know that our people have been part of this land since the beginning of time. We do not believe that our people migrated here from another continent, as the scientists do.
>
> We also do not agree with the notion that this individual is Caucasian. Scientists say that because the individual's head measurement does not match ours, he is not Native American. We believe that humans and animals change over time to adapt to their environment. And, our elders have told us that Indian people did not always look the way we look today.

After calling Kennewick Man "Caucasoid," anthropologists clarified that they were not making a racial designation, but they were just applying a *typology* or system of human types based on phenotypes—that is, physical traits or bodily resemblance. However, Caucausoid typology is evidence for racial whiteness. Minthorn claimed identity, not based on typology or race but on where people lived. Kennewick Man was a Umatilla ancestor because he had lived in the same place where Umatillas now lived. And, if he was Caucasoid, that did not mean he wasn't Umatilla, because Umatillas believed that their physical traits had changed over time. That is, in Western terms, they were claiming that they had been white in the past. (This claim is not impossible because humans have adapted the very traits considered racial over their evolutionary history.)

It's not surprising that further, finer-grained genetic research followed the initial discovery and typing of Kennewick Man. In September 2014, Smithsonian physical anthropologist Douglas Owsley reported that the Kennewick Man was related to Pacific groups such as the Ainu and Polynesians. And, in June 2015, Eske Willerslev and colleagues from the University of Copenhagen reported sequencing the genome of Kennewick Man and comparing DNA from a hand bone to worldwide genomic data that included the Ainu and Polynesians. They concluded that Kennewick Man is most closely related to modern Native Americans. In February 2017, Kennewick Man, who the Umatillas called "The Ancient One," was returned to the Umatilla Indians by the Burke Museum and buried by Umatilla Indians in a private ceremony at an undisclosed place.

Similar forms of indigenous resistance to racialization are evident throughout the world. Indigenous inhabitants of Australia were called "Aboriginals" after 1830 when white settlers took their name of "Australians" for themselves. Similar to the Umatilla Indians, they do not have an internal idea of race or racial typologies, but they have identified themselves based on family relations, rather than place. Family genealogy includes non-Aboriginals and Aboriginal identity is defined according to: family descent from Aboriginal ancestors, self-identification as Aboriginal, and acceptance by the Aboriginal community as an Aboriginal person. Australian references to ancestral and contemporary places over time is shared, as well as language and ecological practices, in a process called "tjukurrpa," which includes recognition of language groups the same and different from one's own. Māori people in New Zealand call the ongoing process of communication about descent and culture "whakapapa."

COSMOPOLITAN IDEALS

Cosmopolitanism is an ancient practice and ideal that has been revived in the context of modern racial and ethnic differences and tensions. Cosmopolitanism advises belonging to the whole human world and viewing those different from oneself and one's group or nation as worthy of tolerance, respect, and politeness. Many who advocate cosmopolitanism today view it as a moral doctrine. Taken absolutely, as "you must belong to the whole human world," cosmopolitanism is deontological. Because cosmopolitanism requires that individuals know about and experience the lives of groups or nations different from their own, it is also a form of virtue ethics. Utilitarianism is also relevant because the more people in the world who are cosmopolitans, the more extensive human well-being would be.

British-Ghanaian philosopher Kwame Anthony Appiah combines all three aspects of cosmopolitanism in his 2010 *Cosmopolitanism: Ethics in a World of Strangers*. Appiah (who is also the ethicist for the *New York Times Magazine*) calls for conversation across differences, a back and forth of speaking and listening. Cosmopolitan conversation does not require agreement but a willingness to accept that others have ideas different from one's own about how human beings should live. Appiah emphasizes that we should value not only human life in general but particular, actual persons. He argues that this kind of valuing should replace both claims for universal moral values and the idea of moral relativism that differences are too extreme to bridge and there can be no universal morality. There can be universal morality, but it is piecemeal and extremely contextualized, rather than the imposition of one set of values on people who do not share them.

The history of cosmopolitanism contains both efforts to reject the imposition of values and norms that do not fit, and tolerance or forbearance from imposing one's own values on others or judging them because they are different. Diogenes the Cynic of Sinope (c. 412–323 BC) replied when asked where he was from: "I am a citizen of the world [kosmopolitês]." Diogenes is here understood to be rejecting obligations to Sinopians (inhabitants of that Greek city) in favor of his own more expressive and free moral system—he preached free love and lived in a barrel. Roman statesman and philosopher Marcus Tullius Cicero (106–43 BC), by contrast, recognized obligations to both the world or cosmos and to Rome. Philosopher Immanuel Kant reconciled individual practice and both national and international cosmopolitan obligations by proposing "cosmopolitan law," according to which both nations and individuals have rights: Individuals have rights as "citizens of the earth," instead of citizens of specific nations; nations have rights over both other nations (to protect their sovereignty) and their own citizens. By the early twentieth century, cosmopolitan clubs formed by students on US college campuses had the goal of understanding differences in values, without imposing American imperialism and American values on others.

For many ordinary Westerners, the practice of cosmopolitanism occurs not through political philosophy, ethics, or belief in world citizenship, but through recreational travel and new foods both imported and eaten abroad. Josh Lew tells the story of the pineapple, which was so highly prized during the fifteenth to eighteen centuries that it was too expensive to eat. Although pineapples probably originated in South America, they could not be cultivated in Europe or the eastern US colonies. A pineapple in George Washington's day cost as much as $8,000 in today's dollars. But by the late 1800s, pineapples were mass-produced in Hawaii and could become a symbol of hospitality that were just freely given away.

Objects and people prized as "exotic" by Westerners for aesthetic appreciation, consumption, or recreation raise an interesting question: Why is it that such people or things may be part of cultures and categories that are otherwise dominated, crushed, or treated disrespectfully? Striking examples are the exoticization of Africa itself, from which black slaves were imported or the value placed on Native American artifacts and spirituality after near-genocide against them. A more subtle example is the contrast between the exploitation of animals in factory farming and the precious status of pets. There are several speculative answers to this interesting question. There may be a need for changes in aesthetics, consumption, and recreation to alleviate boredom, but there is a special "bite" to appreciating, eating, or playing with or in a place that is considered exotic. The fact that one society can do as it likes with the people and artifacts of another may constitute a sadistic element in the use and enjoyment of what is "exotic." Alternatively, apart from boredom, use and enjoyment of the exotic may express an innocent desire to venture beyond one's own culture. In that sense, the discrepancy between domination and enjoyment of people, animals, and objects belonging to the same culture may be resolved by the human ability to compartmentalize experiences or simply not see the discrepancy.

Some experiences and objects may be genuinely unusual and enjoyed as exotic, without a history of domination. Examples would be rare plants and animals or newly discovered places that are not thereby despoiled. But making something or someone exotic that has a history of domination is generally disrespectful. This is why the use of representations of Native Americans as mascots in US sports has been decried and all but terminated.

QUESTIONS FOR THINKING, DISCUSSION, AND WRITING

1. Explain how race, ethnicity, and culture are different, but connected, with an example from your own experience or the experience of people you know.
2. What can be learned, to apply to all identities, from the complexity of Jewish identity? Are there moral imperatives for someone grounded in Jewish identity?
3. How has Native Americans' culture enabled them to resist ideas of race? Do indigenous people have a moral right to reject Western scientific ideas of race and why or why not?
4. Kwame Anthony Appiah has recommended that Americans whose primary language is English watch a foreign film with subtitles, on occasion. How is that part of a cosmopolitan ideal? Do you think it's a moral obligation or a matter of taste, and why?
5. In what cosmopolitan activities have you recently participated or aim to participate?

SOURCES

Appiah, Kwame Anthony. *Cosmopolitanism: Ethics in a World of Strangers.* New York: W.W. Norton, 2010.

Australian Institute of Aboriginal, and Torres Strait Islander Studies. *The Encyclopaedia of Aboriginal Australia: Aboriginal and Torres Strait Islander History, Society and Culture.* David Horton, ed., vol. 2. Aboriginal Studies Press, 1994.

Burke Museum. "The Ancient One, Kennewick Man." February 20, 2017, http://www.burke museum.org/blog/ennewick-man-ancient-one.

Fisher, Max. *Washington Post*, May 16, 2013, https://www.washingtonpost.com/news/world views/wp/2013/05/16/a-revealing-map-of-the-worlds-most-and-least-ethnically-diverse -countries/.

Imhoff, Sarah. "Half Jewish, Just Jewish, and the Oddities of Religious Identification." In *Religion and Identity*, Ronald A. Simkins and Thomas M. Kelly, eds., Supplement 13, 2016, pp. 76–89, https://scholarworks.iu.edu/dspace/handle/2022/21872.

Jensen, Eric, et al. "Measuring Racial and Ethnic Diversity for the 2020 Census." US Census, August 4, 2021, https://www.census.gov/newsroom/blogs/random-samplings/2021/08/ measuring-racial-ethnic-diversity-2020-census.html.

Kant, Immanuel. *Toward Perpetual Peace and Other Writings on Politics, Peace, and History*, with essays by J. Waldron, M. W. Doyle, A. Wood, and P. Kleingeld (ed.), D. L. Colclasure (trans.). New Haven, CT: Yale University Press, 2006.

Lew, Josh. "How the Pineapple Became a Worldwide Symbol of Hospitality." Tree Hugger, April 28, 2020, https://www.treehugger.com/how-pineapple-became-worldwide-symbol -hospitality-4863915.

Mikaelian, Allen J. "'The Call of the Human': The Cosmopolitan Club Movement and Early Twentieth-Century Internationalism." ProQuest Dissertations Publishing, 2017, 1026570, https://www.proquest.com/openview/385f9d433fdeda4773455aa3451b0cad/1 ?pq-origsite=gscholar&cbl=18750.

Minthorn, Armand. "Ancient One—Kennewick Man: Human Remains Should Be Reburied." Confederated Tribes of the Umatilla Indian Reservation. September 1996. Archived from the original. https://web.archive.org/web/20140812090048/http:/ctuir.org/kman1.html.

Roberts, Sam. "Listening to (and Saving) the World's Languages." *New York Times*, April 29, 2010, https://www.nytimes.com/2010/04/29/nyregion/29lost.html#:~:text=While%20 there%20is%20no%20precise,on%20their%202000%20census%20forms.

Sheth, Falguni. "The Racialization of Muslims in the Post-9/11 United States." In *The Oxford Handbook of Philosophy and Race*, Naomi Zack, ed. Oxford, UK: Oxford University Press, 2017, pp. 342–51, https://www.oxfordhandbooks.com/view/10.1093/oxford hb/9780190236953.001.0001/oxfordhb-9780190236953-e-49.

Sollers, Werner, ed. *The Invention of Ethnicity.* Oxford, UK: Oxford University Press, 1991.

Whitman, James Q. "Hitler's American Model: The United States and the Making of Nazi Race Law." Princeton, NJ: Princeton University Press, 2017, https://www.law.nyu.edu/ sites/default/files/upload_documents/Hitler%27s%20American%20Model%20for%20 NYU.pdf.

Williams, Victoria Grieve. "Culture, Not Colour, Is the Heart of Aboriginal Identity." The Conversation, Australian Research Council, University of Sidney, September 17, 2014, http://theconversation.com/culture-not-colour-is-the-heart-of-aboriginal-identity-30102.

Videos

ELI Talks, "Happiness and the Jewish Identity." YouTube, September 20, 2016, https://www
.youtube.com/watch?v=69hcf5dXmd4.

#IwasThere. "What Really Happened at Standing Rock?" YouTube, September 25, 2020,
https://www.youtube.com/watch?v=J1yD2J8vHAk.

McCauley, Michelle, and Myrton Running Wolf. "Native American Identity in the 21st
Century." YouTube, March 25, 2016, https://www.youtube.com/watch?v=Rb6VjzEJQGk.

Rawji, Kiana. "The Risk of a Dying Cosmopolitan Ethic." TEDx Deerfield Academy,
YouTube, June 16, 2016, https://www.youtube.com/watch?v=T_mmKodFZg4.

Record, Ian. "Retiring 'Indian' School Mascots: Informing, Tracking, and Fueling a Growing National Movement," YouTube, November 12, 2020, https://www.youtube.com/
watch?v=1LfF5xysOOA&t=17s.

19

Intersectionality and Gender

Kimberlé Crenshaw speaks onstage at the 3rd Annual One Billion Rising: REVOLUTION at Hammerstein Ballroom on February 7, 2015, in New York City. Getty Images: Paul Zimmerman / Stringer.

As of this writing in October 2021, if you search for "intersectionality" on the internet, there are almost thirty million entries. What is intersectionality? **Intersectionality** is two things. The first is a method of understanding oppression and the second is complicated reality itself. Intersectional understanding works by developing a theory or hypothesis and then applying it to real people, to see how their multiple identities, each of which is a site of oppression, work together. That is, intersectionality is a focus on the effects on people of more than one system of oppression, such as sexism, racism, ableism, xenophobia, and poverty (see figure 19.1). Because oppression is a moral wrong, consideration of intersected identities is a moral project.

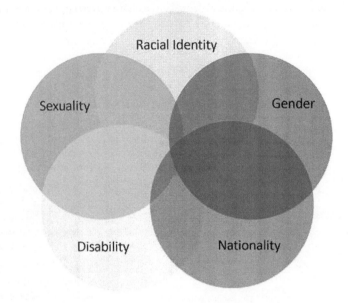

Figure 19.1 What is intersectionality? Adapted from intersectionality 101, What is intersectionality and why is it important? Womankind Worldwide, https://www.womankind.org.uk/intersectionality-101-what-is-it-and-why-is-it-important/.

In the late 1980s, employment lawyer, scholar, and activist, Kimberlé Crenshaw wrote about her black female clients who were hired last, faced discrimination on the job, and were fired first. But they had no legal remedy, so they could not get justice in court. Both blacks and women were **protected classes** in antidiscrimination law, but the courts could not recognize Crenshaw's clients' experiences of job discrimination because there were no patterns of discrimination against either blacks or women where they worked. Even after the civil rights movement legislation, the courts did not have the conceptual tools or legal foundation to recognize that the blacks treated justly were mostly male or that the women treated justly were mostly white. Crenshaw identified the plight of her clients in terms of their real identities as black women who were not recognized as black women in law because the law split up their identities into blacks and women and did not look further into the gender of blacks and the race of women. To do that required what became known as intersectionality, or a recognition that some black people were women and some women were black people. As a result, Crenshaw viewed black women as having an intersected identity—they experienced racism in ways that black men did not and they experienced sexism in ways that white women did not, which was a uniquely combined form of oppression. Crenshaw's insight inaugurated both the study of intersectionality and recognition of it in the lives of real women.

Crenshaw collaborated with other theorists to explore intersectional methodology in 2013, defining this methodology as including three kinds of practices: "applications of an intersectional framework or investigations of intersectional dynamics; debates about the scope and content of intersectionality as a theoretical and methodological paradigm; and political interventions employing an intersectional lens." They did not think all three practices could be unified into one practice but proposed a field of study emphasizing "collaboration and literacy, rather than unity." We can see that Crenshaw's initial insight about black women facing employment discrimination was an application of an intersectionality framework—at the same time that it was invented. Crenshaw's #SayHerName project, which will be discussed in the first section of this chapter, is an instance of intersectional political intervention.

Theoretical debates about intersectionality revolve around obvious questions: How many intersections are there? How do we know what qualifies as an intersection? What is the nature of intersection itself? The answers are simple but may not be satisfactory to theorists who demand more methodological precision: There is no way of knowing how many intersections there are before focusing on specific ones. Intersections are unavoidably ad hoc, and we cannot list them in advance because the urgency of any particular intersection may only be evident at a certain time. Intersectionality is a metaphor, which is vague, but the vast interest in it shows that it resonates broadly. We know that there is an intersection when members of a group experience multiple oppressions and at least one of them has been overlooked in viewing the group as a whole. For instance, much is said about black people but less about black women who experience both racism and sexism.

This chapter will focus on intersectionality in race/ethnicity and gender. We already know that race is intersected because there are the classic five US census racial identities and they intersect with Hispanic/non-Hispanic, as well as combine in many different configurations of mixed race. Gender has traditionally been divided into male and female but today some people also identify themselves as **nonbinary**, neither male nor female or sometimes both. There are also intersections based on sexual preference and transgender. Given the plethora of possibilities—thousands upon thousands considering race/ethnicity and gender—our focus will be narrowed to these three topics in the sections of the chapter: black women's recognition, constructions of black male gender, Latina identities.

BLACK WOMEN'S RECOGNITION

Insights from awareness of intersectionality have inspired new recognition of the historical-cultural contributions of black women. Well-known are Sojourner Truth, Harriet Tubman, Rosa Parks, and Ida B. Wells. Attention may be riveted by black women who have recently been elected to high political office, most notably Vice President Kamala Harris. The achievements of the past were often necessary for achievements in subsequent generations. It is therefore important when studying

black leadership to pay attention to historical intersected figures, such as Isabel de
Olvera, Frances Thompson, and Augusta Savage. All three of these groundbreaking
women lived intersections of black race and female gender with the further intersect-
ing factors of exploration, transgender, and art, which presented additional obstacles
and hardships. Thus:

- Isabel de Olvera was born to an Indian mother, with an African father, in the
  late 1500s in Querétaro, Mexico. She sought permission to join an expedition
  to New Spain, now New Mexico, Arizona, and Florida. She required a statement from the mayor of Querétaro stating that she was a free woman because
  otherwise, she could be claimed as property in the course of traveling. After
  eight months, she was able to go on the 1,400-mile expedition.
- Frances Thompson was born a slave and designated male in 1840. By age
  twenty-six, she was freed and lived as a female in Memphis, Tennessee. She
  and her black female roommate were robbed and gang-raped by white men,
  including police officers, during the Memphis Riot of 1866. She testified before
  Congress that she had not given consent and then experienced a decade of persecution. In 1876, Thompson was jailed for cross-dressing and died soon after.
- Augusta Savage (1892–1962) achieved artistic prominence for her sculpture
  "Realization," which was funded by the Work's Progress Administration's Federal Aid Art Project. The sculpture has been interpreted to depict the realization
  of the horror of being enslaved (see figure 19.2). Savage was born in Green Cove
  Springs, Florida. From an early age, her father, a Methodist minister, destroyed
  her artwork and whipped her for it. After two marriages, she went to New York
  to pursue her career as an artist, experiencing many obstacles of race and gender,
  but she also fought for black voting rights.

Figure 19.2 "Realization," with
the artist, Augusta Savage, 1938.
Alamy Stock Photo. Science
History Images.

We know that transgender is a site for oppression, but while exploration and art are difficult, people choose to pursue them, so they cannot be considered oppressions. However, when combined with another identity that is oppressed, the total result is an oppressed intersection, and even though it may be chosen, the person struggles. Thus, the woman who is an explorer or an artist would struggle anyway, because these are male-dominated fields, even today. And the woman of color who is an explorer or an artist faces additional challenges.

After her initial work on intersectionality, Crenshaw focused on black women as intersected victims of police homicide and brutality in her #SayHerName project. Crenshaw pointed out that not only black men and boys but black women and girls have been killed and brutalized by police officers in the United States. And yet, their names don't make it to the lists of high-profile cases. The audience in Crenshaw's TED Talk signaled that although they recognized the names Trayvon Martin, Eric Garner, Tamir Rice, Michael Stewart, and Michael Brown, the names of the women victimized by police were unknown to most of them. The intersection here is black people who are female and subject to unjust violence by police officers. This group has a long history going back to women who were lynched during Jim Crow, but even with a new awareness of intersectionality, it has remained obscure and overlooked. The legal system and white people often focus on race vaguely, without making gender distinctions. They also focus on women vaguely, without making racial distinctions. And yet, black women, in particular, have worked and suffered in ways that neither black men nor white women have. Black women have created knowledge based on their intersected experience of race and gender, including knowledge of oppression and oppressors that has been ignored and discredited. Crenshaw brings an instance of this kind of knowledge to the visual and auditory life at the end of her TED Talk. (In her TED Talk, Crenshaw gives the neglected names that have not been widely said—see video.)

CONSTRUCTIONS OF BLACK MALE GENDER

In the history of male dominance in society, black men, compared to white men, have not received the same honors and recognition for achievement. Also, black male gender has been **feminized** or constructed as female. Black men are also widely and frequently regarded as dangerous, violent criminals and rapists. The police practice of **racial profiling** or treating black men as suspects without evidence of wrongdoing confirms this criminalization. (See chapter 10.)

The United States has a long history of absent or belated recognition of black men for achievements and honors earned. Black soldiers have fought in every US war since the Revolutionary War but they also had to fight for the privilege of doing that and were placed in separate regiments. It was not until 1948 that President Harry Truman desegregated the US military. And it was not until 2015 that President Barack Obama posthumously bestowed Medals of Honor, the nation's highest award for combat bravery, on two World War I veterans, Henry Johnson and William Shemin. Philosopher Leonard Harris has explained the importance of public honor for recognizing an individual's membership in the moral community. For members of a group excluded from the dominant moral community, public honor to individuals from that group constitutes recognition that the entire excluded group is part of the entire black and white moral community. They are thereby recognized as humanly valuable and worthy of respect.

In his 2017 *The Man-Not: Race, Class, Gender, and the Dilemmas of Black Manhood,* Tommy J. Curry argues for a new, multidisciplinary field of Black Male Studies, because feminism or the study of women's oppression has eclipsed the reality of life for black men in assuming that they have normal privileges as men. Drawing on historical examples, Curry argues that black men and boys cannot be studied as males partially intersected with racial oppression because they have never had the benefit of male privilege, despite feminist claims that they have been dominant over black women. Documenting historical and contemporary examples of sexual abuse that have not been given serious attention, Curry shows how black men and boys have been deprived of masculinity and that they have not striven for or been able to participate in **patriarchy** or men's dominance throughout modern Western society. While Crenshaw's use of the idea and method of intersectionality has been strongly associated with black women, Curry offers a more general method of intersectionality that applies to black men as well.

All constructions of masculinity have been questioned in recent years, especially *toxic* or destructive masculinity, within historical contexts where manhood itself has been valued. Nevertheless, white males continue to have high status and privilege and, in relation to that, the low status and criminalization of black men is a stark contrast. But there is a paradox or apparent contradiction: How can black men be both feminized and thereby made to seem weak and lacking in traits of white manhood and at the same time portrayed as dangerous predators when they are criminalized? The answer is that both feminization and criminalization create myths and stereotypes of black men that are harmful to them, without justification. We can easily see how feminizing males in a society that values strong masculinity is disparaging and humiliating. But how is unjustified criminalization harmful?

Unjustified and unjust criminalization is itself a form of abuse. Unjust criminalization opens the door to further unjust suspicion, surveillance, and official harm. As a form of abuse, or when widespread as oppression, unjust criminalization is a kind of **demonization** or a characterization of people as dangerous and threatening, regardless of whether or not they are. The demonization of black men is therefore in keeping with their feminization as a form of racial oppression. The criminalization of black men is not merely a form of slander, but real, violent unjust aggression, from lynchings during the Jim Crow era to more recent high-profile police shootings of unarmed black men. French psychiatrist Frantz Fanon (1925–1961) and contemporary African American philosophers such as George Yancy have analyzed how this criminalization affects and disrupts ordinary subjective bodily experience, in immediate time and space. Fanon famously related how a child's reaction to his mere appearance with "Look! A Negro!" was itself a racial slur.

LATINA IDENTITIES

Sociologists and others in the sciences and humanities often talk about Hispanic/ Latino people as though they are a homogenous minority group. On the grounds of different national origins alone—United States, Mexico, Central America, Puerto Rico, and South America—there is already diversity in culture. Not everyone who identifies as Hispanic/Latino speaks Spanish. Many Americans of Hispanic/Latino descent speak only English and the language of Brazil is Portuguese. In addition, there are many dialectical variations in how Spanish is spoken. These differences, which may constitute disadvantages and vulnerability to oppression, are further contextualized by gender, not only male or female, but LGBTQ+ identities also. The idea of **Latina identities** of women or female-identified Hispanic/Latino people thus points to multiple intersections.

The national diversity among Latinas is compounded by racial diversity because more black slaves were brought to countries in South America than to the United States, and Latina-Americans have nationalities of origin from those countries. About a quarter of all US Hispanic/Latino people have African ancestry and identify as Afro-Latino. Another quarter identifies as indigenous, with affiliations to Native American tribes. Latinas may begin, when asked about identity, to respond that identity is personal, exactly because of the national, linguistic dialect, and racial diversity. But even multiple intersected identities are not unique to sole individuals and there are commonalities, not only among those who share the same national origins and language but within the larger Hispanic/Latino community. In the United States, the idea of pan-Hispanic/Latino identity has been officially imposed—the US census requires "Hispanic/Latino or not Hispanic/Latino" identification—and must be declared for entitlements, employment where diversity is a goal, and to construct resistance to institutional racism and ethnicism. The results of these official and quasi-official identifications are an essentialization of Hispanic/Latino identities—it is implied that they all share the same important thing or determining factor.

Latinas are aware, as all women are, that there are expectations of how they should look once their national-origin identities are stated. This focus on appearance is supported by stereotypes in the media that favor white Latinas, so that Afro-Latinas, for instance, may be told that they do not look "Hispanic/Latino" or how people from their countries of origins are supposed to look. Also, tall Mexican women may be told they do not "look Mexican"; Peru has a large Chinese population and when Asian people are heard speaking Spanish, there is no simple way for others to categorize them. Personal intrusions, based on "Where are you from?" questions, may be imposed on Latinas born in the United States and are thereby microaggressions (see chapter 14). Media stereotypes may emphasize the stories of recent immigrants, to the neglect of hundreds of years of history as citizens and residents of the United States. In addition, there may be stereotypes and racism within Hispanic/Latino communities, such as **colorism** or preference for lighter-skinned people. Also, indigenous Hispanic/Latinos and LGBTQ+ people may be excluded from full community recognition and membership.

Latinas have also needed to struggle against traditional expectations that they become wives and mothers in their communities of origin. Chicana scholar and cultural writer Gloria E. Anzaldúa wrote:

> The culture expects women to show greater acceptance of, and commitment to, the value system than men. The culture and the Church insist that women are subservient to males. If a woman rebels she is a *mujer mala* (bad woman). If a woman doesn't renounce herself in favor of the male, she is selfish. If a woman remains a virgin until she marries, she is a good woman. For a woman of my culture there used to be only three directions she could turn: to the Church as a nun, to the streets as a prostitute, or to the home as a mother. Today some of us have a fourth choice: entering the world by way of education and career and becoming self-autonomous persons. A very few of us.

Many Latinas, like women from all disadvantaged ethnic groups, have had to work outside of the home. Often this has consisted of isolated jobs cleaning or back-breaking work in factories, in addition to employment as maids, which has carried its own stereotypes affecting all Latinas (see chapter 20). In recent decades, service sector jobs have been widely available, for low pay. Home and hospital medical aid provide occupations that often require **emotional labor** or caring, personal interaction. Domestic service is an ongoing source of income and portrayals of Latina maids in film and television have been an ongoing practice of stereotyping (see chapter 20). During the COVID-19 pandemic, Latinas often lost employment in the service sector. Latina feminists have written about their specific difficulties in academic life, as representatives of difference that is not well understood. More broadly, American Latinas have far-reaching histories as activists for labor rights and immigrant rights.

Some younger Latinas believe that the term **Latinx** as an umbrella idea for all Hispanic/Latino diversities is useful for inclusiveness, especially for LGBTQ+ people and those who do not speak Spanish. Part of the reason for this choice is that many Hispanic/Latino people are unlikely to use the designation of Hispanic/Latino since they prefer identities based on their specific national-origin identities. In those countries of origin, the idea of identity is not easily understood, because everyone has the same nationality. The term Latinx may also relate to members of indigenous communities, who for religious and cultural reasons do not identify as Hispanic/Latino. Thus, people who identify as Latinx may represent a project for unification *after* multiple intersections are recognized.

QUESTIONS FOR THINKING, DISCUSSION, AND WRITING

1. Explain Kimberlé Crenshaw's insight about intersected identities, using her experience with black female employees.
2. What are some problems with intersectionality, as a method or theory?
3. Select one of the examples from the section on black women and explain in detail how that woman's experience is an intersection.

4. How do you think black men could be constructed both as dangerous and as not masculine? Explain how this is not a real contradiction.
5. How is the identity of Latinas intersected in unique ways that do not apply to black men and women in the United States?

SOURCES

Anzaldúa, Gloria E. *Borderlands/La Frontera: The New Mestiza*. Aunt Lute Book Company, 1987, quotation p. 17.

Bowman, Tom. "Obama Awards Posthumous Medals of Honor to Two World War I Veterans." All Things Considered, NPR, WNYC, June 2, 2015, https://www.npr.org/2015/06/02/411533519/obama-awards-posthumous-medals-of-honor-to-two-world-war-i-veterans.

Cho, Sumi, Kimberlé Williams Crenshaw, and Leslie McCall. "Toward a Field of Intersectionality Studies: Theory, Applications, and Praxis." *Signs* 38, no. 4 (2013): 785 810, doi:10.1086/669608.

Crenshaw, Kimberlé. "Demarginalizing the Intersection of Race and Sex: A Black Feminist Critique of Antidiscrimination Doctrine, Feminist Theory and Antiracist Politics." *The University of Chicago Legal Forum* 140 (1989): 139–67.

Crenshaw, Kimberlé. "Mapping the Margins: Intersectionality, Identity Politics, and Violence Against Women of Color." *Stanford Law Review* 43, no. 6 (1991): 1241–99, http://multipleidentitieslgbtq.wiki.westga.edu/file/view/Crenshaw1991.pdf, http://blogs.law.columbia.edu/critique1313/files/2020/02/1229039.pdf.

Curry, Tommy J. "Ethnological Theories of Race/Sex in Nineteenth-Century Black Thought: Implications for the Race/Gender Debate of the Twenty-First Century." In *The Oxford Handbook of Philosophy and Race*, Naomi Zack, ed. New York: Oxford University Press, 2017, pp. 565–75.

Curry, Tommy J. *The Man-Not: Race, Class, Gender, and the Dilemmas of Black Manhood*. Philadelphia, PA: Temple University Press, 2017.

Fanon, Frantz. "The Lived Experience of the Black Man." In *Black Skin, White Masks*, Éditions du Seuil, 1952, quotation p. 91.

Gage, Carolyn. "Realization by Augusta Savage." April 4, 2016, https://carolyngage.weebly.com/blog/realization-by-augusta-savage.

Harris, Leonard. "Honor: Emasculation and Empowerment (1992)." In *A Philosophy of Struggle: The Leonard Harris Reader*, Lee A. Mc Bride, III, ed. Bloomsbury Academic, pp. 113–29.

Mann, Krishna. "These 5 Black Women Made History—and Here's Why You Should Know Their Stories." Ideas.Ted.Com, Feb 25, 2021, https://ideas.ted.com/5-black-women-american-history-and-heres-why-you-should-know-their-stories/.

Nash, Jennifer C. "Re-Thinking Intersectionality." *Feminist Review* 89, no. 1 (June 2008): 1–15.

#SayHerName. 2020, https://www.aapf.org/sayhername.

Segura, Denise A., and Elisa Facio. "Adelante Mujer: Latina Activism, Feminism, and Empowerment." In *Latinas/os in the United States: Changing the Face of América*, H. Rodríguez, R. Sáenz, and C. Menjívar, eds. Boston: Springer, 2008, https://link.springer

.com/chapter/10.1007/978-0-387-71943-6_19#citeas, https://doi.org/10.1007/978-0-387-71943-6_19.

Smiley, Calvin John, and David Fakunle. "From 'Brute' to 'Thug': The Demonization and Criminalization of Unarmed Black Male Victims in America." *Journal of Human Behavior in the Social Environment* 26, no. 3–4 (2016): 350–66, DOI: 10.1080/10911359.2015.1129256.

Villanueva, Margaret. "Ambivalent Sisterhood: Latina Feminism and Women's Studies Latina/o Discourses in Academe." *Discourse* 21, no. 3 (Fall 1999): 49–76.

Yancy, George. "Whiteness and the Return of the Black Body." *Journal of Speculative Philosophy* 19, no. 4 (2005): 215–41, https://www.jstor.org/stable/25670583?seq=1#metadata_info_tab_contents.

Zack, Naomi. *Inclusive Feminism: A Third Wave Theory of Women's Commonality.* Lanham, MD: Rowman & Littlefield, 2005, pp. 1–22.

Videos

BPLvideos. "George Yancy, Keynote Speaker 2018 #NightofPhilosophy at Brooklyn Public Library." YouTube, March 18, 2020, https://www.youtube.com/watch?v=nsTtNM2Jc88.

Crenshaw, Kimberlé. "The Urgency of Intersectionality." TED Women 2016, https://www.ted.com/talks/kimberle_crenshaw_the_urgency_of_intersectionality?language=en#t-1234.

Flores, Ana, Tristen Norman, Francesca Bacarossi, and Patricia Mota. "The Female Quotient, Intersectionality and Latinx Identity." September 29, 2020, YouTube, https://www.youtube.com/watch?v=83P1TXw5_h8.

20

Representation in Media and Society

Surrounded by small mementos and rocks, a battleground memorial plaque marks the site of the Sand Creek Massacre National Historic Site in southeast Colorado. On November 29, 1864, US troops under Colonel Chivington attacked and killed at least 165 friendly Cheyenne and Arapahoe Indians. Those that survived, including Chief Black Kettle, fled north. Getty Images: milehightraveler.

People of color may or may not be represented politically or through government programs that help them. Diversity policies in business and higher education may or may not adequately include people of color so that they are represented in those contexts. Both political and employment representation are part of physical reality that pertains to how people live, how much money they earn, and how much power they have. But there is another kind of representation that occurs in portrayals of reality.

Plato famously distinguished between the experience of reality and illusion in his allegory of the cave in the *Republic*: A group of people are chained to the wall in a dark cave where they see only shadows of the real things in sunlight. One of them makes it outside and reports back, but the account is mocked. Viewing the shadows is preferred to imagining reality. Of course, for Plato, reality itself consisted of **forms**, perfect ideal things that could only be glimpsed after arduous study. But for us, reality consists of physical things, animals, and people, plus thought and language about them that can be checked for truth and accuracy, ultimately through the natural or social sciences. For us, all the accounts of human life in literature, movies, films, news, social media, and public memorials are the "shadows" of the real things. When they are shadows of actual people of color, scholars and cultural critics consider them part of the subject or issue of **representation**.

Representations of people of color can be checked for truth or accuracy in everyday life, as well as science. Cultural critics continually raise fundamental questions about these representations: Who is represented and how are they represented? Sometimes, representations of people of color are simply left out of the context in which they should be represented, or they are not equally represented. Such omission or erasure constitutes inequality in representation if white people are more fully represented. Other times, people of color are represented as negative or demeaning stereotypes and that is another kind of inequality. Both the inequality of omission and stereotypes in representation are morally wrong because they misinform or distort information for white people about people of color. They are also, and perhaps more importantly, morally wrong because they may lead those whose groups are left out to feel unimportant, and those whose groups are stereotyped may feel demeaned or humiliated.

Representation is important because people depend on media and news to enlarge what they know about the social world, which goes beyond their direct experience. Before considering specifics in these problems of representation, we should consider how representation works, apart from how misrepresentation can be harmful to individuals. The source of representation is supposed to be the underlying reality of life in society. But not all, or even any representation is simple realism. Stereotyping and omission may structure both news accounts and documentary films, which present themselves as truthful and accurate. If people of color are left out or distorted in how they are represented in what is presented as true and accurate, then the collective picture of society is incomplete or distorted. That can influence how people vote, who they want to have as neighbors, and how they spend their money. Representation can also be aspirational or idealistic, but when falsely rosy pictures are presented as accurate, the public may be misled about the nature of collective problems.

Media representation and memorials are not parallel examples if media is considered for one group and memorials for others. But such mixed examples can serve to build an overall thesis that minority representation remains inadequate in American society. The first section of this chapter considers stereotypical representations of

Latinas in popular media, followed by representations of Asian Americans in Hollywood movies. The chapter concludes with representation through public memorials for African Americans and Native Americans.

LATINA REPRESENTATION

Either Latinx women are not represented at all throughout various media, or else they are represented through stereotypes. The absence of representation is an erasure of Latinx women's identity and experience that many who are non-Latinx may not notice, although the message to those left out says they are insignificant, not members of the whole collective, or simply do not exist. As a result, that gap in representation is its own pejorative content. In stereotyped representation, two *tropes* or symbols that evoke a whole segment of both representation and reality stand out— *marianismo* and maid. Together they constitute a trapped social location.

As discussed in terms of Gloria Anzaldúa's insight in *Borderlands/La Frontera* in chapter 19, Latinas are expected to devote themselves to their roles as wives and mothers in the home, and outside the home, their work opportunities do not support career development. ***Marianismo*** is a representation of *La Virgen Maria* (the Virgin Mary, mother of Jesus Christ) as a Catholic religious and practical ideal for Latinx women that has been established for centuries. Evelyn Stevens first introduced the concept of *marianismo* as a match for **machismo**, ideals of male leadership and strength, in 1973. Latinx girls are encouraged to be like Maria, as well as look up to her. This means they are expected and strive to be chaste until marriage, to help others, and to obey men. There is no opportunity to develop their own sexuality, ambition, or intellect. Widely viewed *telenovelas*, Spanish language series and soap operas, depict their female heroines as imbued with *marianismo*.

Based on both *marianismo* and under-education, it is not surprising that many young Latinx women who do work outside the home are employed in helping, caring, low-paying service jobs, especially domestic service. Many work as maids, and Latinas have been widely represented in movies and television shows as maids. Indeed, Michelle Herrera Mulligan, editor-in-chief of *Cosmo for Latinas*, refers to a survey in which 60 percent of respondents said that "maid" represented Latinas "well."

Herrera denounced the television show *Devious Maids* that began airing on Lifetime in 2013, calling the representation of Latina maids "a waste" because they could and should have been represented as autonomous working women. She voiced her criticism in a post to Mexican American actress and activist Eva Longoria, who was involved on both sides of the camera in *Devious Maids*. In 2012 Longoria had cochaired President Barack Obama's reelection and spoke out against anti-immigration legislation. And in 2014, Longoria founded the Latino Victory Project to help encourage voting and donations for candidates among Hispanic/Latino-Americans. Herrera called for Longoria to represent her own experience and success as an upwardly mobile and ambitious Latina.

Longoria defended *Devious Maids* as presenting a deeper than superficial stereotyped representation of Latinas as maids. In the first episode, a maid is murdered and the mother of a man who is in prison for murder is hired as a replacement. While the series is not empowering by showing Latina liberation from Anglo money and opinion, it does present the maids as real people with relatable working-class problems. The criticism and defense are interesting because they raise issues of human dignity and uplift in a working-class context with limited opportunity, which has both economic and psychological causes. Are maids morally obligated to aspire to socioeconomic advancement? Is personal empowerment in ways that can overcome ethnicism also a moral obligation?

ASIAN AMERICAN REPRESENTATION

Asian Americans are a numerically small minority in the United States. According to many measurements, their income, wealth, and higher education averages exceed those of all other racial and ethnic groups. There is also official recognition. In 1978 a joint US congressional resolution established Asian/Pacific American Heritage Week. The arrival of the first Japanese immigrants on May 7, 1843, and Chinese worker contributions to the transcontinental railroad that was completed on May 10, 1869, were both to be celebrated. In 1992, this week was expanded to a month. And in 1997, the one joint category was divided into two separate identities—Asian and Native Hawaiian and Other Pacific Islander.

However, economic and educational success has not protected Asian Americans from eruptions of racist hatred and violence during the COVID-19 pandemic. And congressional recognition came late given the internment of Japanese American citizens during World War II and the brutal exploitation of nineteenth-century Chinese railroad workers that was followed by laws prohibiting them to immigrate to the United States. After immigration reform from the 1965 Immigration and Nationality Act, Asian immigration substantially increased. We can now ask how representation in media reflects both Asian American success and oppression at this time. This question is important because it might reveal how the majority of Americans reconcile discrimination against a group with its members' evident skills and determination.

Asian Americans make up 7 percent of the total population, but they are underrepresented in US media, especially television, where they are less than 4 percent of characters. Also, their representation conforms to stereotypes, because they are cast in nerdy, technically proficient roles with little personal charisma or glamor. Part of the reason for this is the widespread belief, with some statistical support, that Asian Americans excel in science, technology, and mathematics. Such stereotyping conforms to the **model minority** designation of Asian Americans, which includes success in the professions. But the racial stereotyping goes beyond this to show preferences for white leading characters. For example, in the 2009 live-action film *Dragon Ball Z*, which was based on a Japanese anime with Japanese characters, the lead was portrayed by a white actor. Also, several female Asian American stars and newscasters have revealed that they have undergone cosmetic surgery to "Westernize" their facial features.

Apparent exceptions to Asian under-representation were the blockbuster success of the popular 2015 sitcom *Fresh Off the Boat* and the 2019 movie *Crazy Rich Asians*. *Fresh Off the Boat* features twelve-year-old, hip-hop-loving Eddie who has moved with his parents to suburban Orlando from DC's Chinatown. Eddie and his immigrant family pursue the American Dream in comedic episodes. The movie *Crazy Rich Asians* is based on a romantic novel by Singapore-American Kevin Kwan. The novel follows twenty-eight-year-old economics professor Rachel Chu who accompanies her long-term boyfriend, Nick Young, to his home in Singapore. Rachel learns that he is the scion of a very rich and powerful family that does not approve of her background. Although, eventually love conquers snobbery.

Fresh Off the Boat has been criticized for performing the model minority status of Asian Americans, against the black-white paradigm, through the use of white American family ideals and sitcom comedy. The show also leaves out the struggles through hard work and poverty of Asian immigrants who are "fresh off the boat." Critics have claimed that the absence of darker-skinned Asians in the *Crazy Rich Asians* cast perpetuates colorism within the Asian American community.

PUBLIC MEMORIALS FOR AFRICAN AMERICANS AND NATIVE AMERICANS

Public memorials represent events and people who are important for everyone to remember if they occurred or lived in the recent past, or to acknowledge if what is represented predates onlookers' lives. They can evoke emotions of sadness, celebration, shame, as well as historical reflection. American communities and nations where minorities have been brutally oppressed in the past are not eager to construct memorials to such events. Their social importance, for both the descendants of victims and perpetrators, has to be argued for.

It is not surprising that members of dominant groups are most likely to be memorialized for achievements and virtues of character. However, memorialization of white Americans has not always had straightforward motives. In the spring of 2020 during the George Floyd protests, 1,700 Confederate statues were estimated to remain in public view throughout the United States. Activists had already argued for their removal because leaders of the Confederacy had defended slavery and defied the government of the United States. Also, many of the statues targeted for removal were not put up right after the Civil War, but later, from the 1890s to 1920, when new voter suppression laws were passed in Southern towns. Other Confederate monuments were rededicated after the US Supreme Court ruled that school segregation was unconstitutional, in 1954. Real bronze statues are expensive, but the Monumental Bronze Company sold zinc statues for under $500. Thus, many of these monuments not only celebrated a defeated and unjust cause but were representations that were intended to tell the public that white dominance over African Americans and racial segregation were still valued in their communities.

However, other, presumably liberatory and progressive monuments, such as the Emancipation Memorial, also became targets for removal in 2020. The Emancipation Memorial, also known as the "Freedman's Memorial" and the "Emancipation Group," has been sited in Lincoln Park, in the Capitol Hill neighborhood of Washington, DC, since 1876. Lincoln's right hand rests on the Emancipation Proclamation that is on a pedestal, and his left arm is extended above a black man who kneels on one knee, naked to the waist, with his broken chain at Lincoln's feet. The statue of this former slave was a portrait of Archer Alexander, an emancipated slave. The memorial was proposed immediately after Lincoln's assassination, and Charlotte Scott, a former slave in Virginia, made the first contribution of $5 from her earnings and additional funding came from more freed slaves. But soon after the monument was dedicated in 1876, Frederick Douglass focused on what the monument failed to record about political citizenship. He wrote:

> While the mere act of breaking the [N]egro's chains was the act of Abraham Lincoln . . . the act by which the negro was made a citizen of the United States and invested with the elective franchise was preeminently the act of President U. S. Grant, and this is nowhere seen in the Lincoln monument. The negro here, though rising, is still on his knees and nude. What I want to see before I die is a monument representing the negro, not couchant on his knees like a four-footed animal, but erect on his feet like a man.

National Guard troops were posted around the Emancipation Memorial in June 2020, to protect it from George Floyd protesters.

In recent years, there have been two noteworthy national memorials to the historic experience of African Americans. The Smithsonian Institution opened the National Museum of African American History and Culture on September 24, 2016. It is the only national museum devoted exclusively to the documentation of African American life, art, history, and culture. The Legacy Museum opened on April 26, 2018, founded by Montgomery, Alabama's Equal Justice Initiative as a counterpart to the National Memorial for Peace and Justice, which is dedicated to the memory of the victims of lynching (see figure 20.1).

Museums and dedicated memorials are not the same as statues and memorials on free public view. While not as prominent or numerous as statues of white leaders and public figures, there are a large number of public statues throughout the United

Figure 20.1 Nkyinkim Sculpture by West African artist Kwame Akoto-Bamfo at the National Memorial for Peace and Justice. Source: Soniakapadia CC BY-SA 4.0.

States that honor African Americans. According to *NewsOne*, an online news site with an African American audience, the top ten are: Martin Luther King Jr. Memorial, Washington, DC; Malcolm X, Harlem, New York; Adam Clayton Powell, Harlem, New York; Joe Louis, Detroit, Michigan; George Washington Carver, Newton County, Missouri; Crispus Attucks, Boston, Massachusetts; Harriet Tubman, Harlem, New York; W. E. B. Du Bois, Nashville, Tennessee; Medgar Evers, Jackson, Mississippi; and Tupac Shakur, Atlanta, Georgia. There are also numerous schools and street names in honor of Martin Luther King Jr. and Abraham Lincoln.

While Native American cultural sites are protected on public lands, there are few commemorative statues or museums throughout the United States. Moreover, the upkeep of these monuments, which is the responsibility of the US federal government since the 1906 Antiquities Act, has not been consistent. The US Wilderness Society includes these top ten: Mesa Verde National Park (Colorado); Casa Grande Ruins National Monument (Arizona); Organ Mountains-Desert Peaks National Monument (New Mexico); Effigy Mounds National Monument (Iowa); Chaco Culture National Historical Park (New Mexico); Hopewell Culture National Historical Park (Ohio); Canyons of the Ancients National Monument (Colorado); Aztec Ruins National and Gila Monument (New Mexico); Ocmulgee Mounds National Historical Park (Georgia); and Gila Cliff Dwellings National Monument (New Mexico).

QUESTIONS FOR THINKING, DISCUSSION, AND WRITING

1. What is media representation and why is it important?
2. Do you agree with Michelle Herrera Mulligan or Eva Longoria about *Devious Maids*? Give reasons either way.
3. How would you evaluate the positive stereotyping of Asian Americans as a model minority at the cost of real-life Asians' immigrant struggles in *Fresh Off the Boat* and under-representation of darker-skinned Asians in *Crazy Rich Asians*?
4. Do you think it's important to memorialize painful experiences of black oppression? Why or why not? Give reasons.
5. Think of another minority or disadvantaged group in the United States who are under-represented in media. Explain why they should be better represented.

SOURCES

Bailey, Isaac J. "America's New Lynching Memorial Is Gut-Wrenching, Gruesome, and Beautiful." Vice, April 27, 2018, www.vice.com/en_us/article/kzxvgm/americas-newlynching-memorial-is-gut-wrenching-gruesome-and-beautiful.

Blossom, Priscilla. "We Need to Talk about Marianismo." Family, HipLatina.com, March 13, 2018, https://hiplatina.com/marianismo/.

Budiman, Abby, and Neil G. Ruiz. "Key Facts about Asian Americans, a Diverse and Growing Population." Pew Research Center, April 29, 2021, https://www.pewresearch.org/fact-tank/2021/04/29/key-facts-about-asian-americans/.

Gandbhir, Geeta, and Michèle Stephenson. "A Conversation with Asian-Americans on Race." *New York Times*, April 5, 2016, https://www.nytimes.com/video/opinion/100000004308529/a-conversation-with-asians-on-race.html.

Hang, Truong Minh, and Phung Ha Thanh. "Fresh Off the Boat and the Modern Minority Stereotype: A Foucauldian Discourse Analysis." *VNU Journal of Foreign Studies*, October 2, 2018, https://js.vnu.edu.vn/FS/article/view/4304.

Hernandez, Clarissa. "Why Asians Are Under-Represented in Modern Media." May 4, 2015, The Lexington Line, http://info.limcollege.edu/lexington-line/where-the-asians-at-why-we-need-greater-media-diversity.

Kavi, Aishvarya. "Activists Push for Removal of Statue of Freed Slave Kneeling before Lincoln." *New York Times*, June 27, 2020, https://www.nytimes.com/2020/06/27/us/politics/lincoln-slave-statue-emancipation.html.

Lee, Grace. "The Big Sick, and Crazy Rich Asians: Nuances of Representation." Dialogues @RU, pp. 280–91, https://dialogues.rutgers.edu/images/Journals_PDF/dialogues-issue15-web.pdf#page=286.

Legacy Museum from Enslavement to Mass Incarceration. National Memorial for Peace and Justice, https://museumandmemorial.eji.org/museum.

Mulligan, Michelle Herrera. "Devious Maids Misrepresents Latinas." https://unlimitedwebsitetraffic1.blogspot.com/2013/10/michelle-herrera-mulligan-devious-maids.html.

National Museum of African American History, Art and Culture, https://nmaahc.si.edu/about/museum.

PBS Learning Media. "Asian Americans." 5-part series, https://ny.pbslearningmedia.org/resource/asian-americans-full-film-video-gallery/asian-americans/.

Plato. *The Republic* (514a–520a).

Ristau, Reece. "Eva Longoria Talks 'Devious Maids' Backlash, Latino Perceptions at Produced by Conference." *Variety*, May 31, 2015, https://variety.com/2015/tv/news/eva-longoria-devious-maids-latino-1201509025/.

Scully, Rachel, and James Bikales. "A List of the Statues across the US Toppled, Vandalized or Officially Removed amid Protests." *The Hill*, June 12, 2020, https://thehill.com/home news/state-watch/502492-list-statues-toppled-vandalized-removed-protests.

Stevens, Evelyn. "Marianismo: The Other Face of Machismo." In *Female and Male in Latin America*, Ann Pescatello, ed., 89–101. Pittsburgh, PA: Pittsburgh University Press, 1973.

Timmerman, Travis. "A Case for Removing Confederate Monuments." In *Ethics, Left and Right: The Moral Issues That Divide Us*, Bob Fischer, ed. New York: Oxford University Press, 2020, 513–22, and https://philpapers.org/rec/TIMACF.

"Top 10 Monuments to Black Americans." NewsOne, October 14, 2011, https://newsone.com/1458145/top-10-monuments-to-black-americans/.

US Census Bureau. "Asian-American and Pacific Islander Heritage Month: May 2018." Release Number CB18-FF.04, https://www.census.gov/newsroom/facts-for-features/2018/asian-american.html.

White, Jonathan W., and Scott Sandage. "What Frederick Douglass Had to Say about Monuments," Smithsonian, June 30, 2020, https://www.smithsonianmag.com/history/what-frederick-douglass-had-say-about-monuments-180975225/.

Wilderness Society. "10 Extraordinary Native American Cultural Sites Protected on Public Lands." https://www.wilderness.org/articles/article/10-extraordinary-native-american-cul tural-sites-protected-public-lands.

Young, Rodney A. "Great Emancipator, Supplicant Slave: The Freed-man's Memorial to Abraham Lincoln," Slaves, Soldiers, and Stone: An Introduction to Slavery in American Memory (Washington, DC: American University), December 6, 2003, https://web.archive.org/web/20120229192309/https://www.american.edu/bgriff/dighistprojects/wym/rodney_3.htm (retrieved July 2020).

Videos

"Devious Maids." 4 seasons, YouTube, https://www.youtube.com/show/SC0XS0y3Pp_VN6V R24IYvqAw?season=1&sbp=CgEx.

Movie Fanatic. "Wedding Scene from Crazy Rich Asians." YouTube, February 14, 2019, https://www.youtube.com/watch?v=ipgt1MnQni4.

sgctellandshow. "First Impression: Fresh Off the Boat Season 1 Episode 1." YouTube, February 19, 2015, https://www.youtube.com/watch?v=_kDQC3AyCMw.

Wise, Justin. "Troops Guard Steps of Lincoln Memorial Amid Protest." *The Hill*, June 2, 2020, https://thehill.com/homenews/administration/500824-troops-guard-steps-of-lincoln-memorial-amid-protest.

21

Sport

USA's Simone Biles in the women's balance beam final at Ariake Gymnastic Centre on the eleventh day of the Tokyo 2020 Olympic Games in Japan on August 3, 2021. Alamy Stock Photo. Giuliano Bevilacqu, Abaca Press.

Sport has an exalted history in Western society and top athletes have always been honored and admired. The ancient Greek Olympic Games, competitions among city-state representatives, were held in honor of Zeus from 776 BC to AD 393, and perhaps later. Only freeborn males could compete in the events, which included boxing, chariot racing, running, long jump, discus throwing, and pentathlon. The elite nature of such athletic displays has persisted over history, and certain sports have always required money and leisure to participate. At present, sports such as sailing, tennis, golf, polo and dressage, skiing, hiking, falconry and bird-watching, as well as big-game hunting, have an aura of wealth and privilege. Except for traditional cultural practices in rural areas and indigenous communities, much of contemporary leisure sport is dominated by members of dominant groups in society. Members of racial and ethnic minorities do not usually practice or follow them as adult spare-time activities. But since the late nineteenth and early twentieth century, some sports have stood out as opportunities for members of minority groups to excel and rise socioeconomically—jockeying, boxing, basketball, baseball, and football, to name a few.

At different times, members of specific minority groups have led in particular sports, leading many to associate their physical traits or distinctive styles arising from same-group participation with excellence in these sports. For example, for many decades over the twentieth and early twenty-first century, Americans have assumed that basketball is a "black game." But the history of basketball tells a different story. The origins of basketball are white, followed by Jewish and black.

In 1891, James Naismith, a physical education teacher, invented basketball as an indoor winter sport, at the request of officials at the International Young Men's Christian Training School (now Springfield College) in Massachusetts. The goal was to keep students fit during the winter, without raucous behavior. The first basketball players were white college students but the sport soon became popular in inner cities, where it was taken up by the sons of European Jewish immigrants. Basketball first became popular in Brooklyn, New York, because there was no room for baseball or football. Basketball then spread to the Lower East Side of Manhattan, and Philadelphia had a Hebrew all-stars team. The Jewish basketball players had a distinctive style: "A lot of passing, a lot of ball-handling, a lot of working off the top of the circle, off the pick, going back door, weaving, using the ball, every man working together." The earliest players of the National Basketball Association (NBA) were Jewish and on November 1, 1946, the first NBA basket was scored by Ossie Schectman of the New York Knicks. However, by the 1960s, many Jewish families had moved to the suburbs and the urban centers closed down. Enthusiasm for the game was not exported by Jews who left the cities.

During the first half of the twentieth century, basketball became popular among urban African American youth in the Northeast, especially in YMCAs and YWCAs. Edwin B. Henderson, head of physical education for what was then called the Colored School Division in Washington, DC, promoted basketball as an amateur sport. The Smart Set Club was created in about 1905 to introduce basketball as a competitive sport for men and women, although women were later blocked from admission to some of its teams. Basketball did not spread among African Americans in the largely rural South. Still, by 1909, students at Howard University, Hampton Institute, Virginia Union University, and several other black colleges began playing basketball. Some black players competed in the Northeast and Midwest, where segregationists created obstacles until the 1950s—black teams did not play against white teams. However, black professional teams arose in 1923, because owning them could be profitable. The famous Harlem Rens were very successful against both black and white teams. The Harlem Globetrotters, who originated in Chicago and incorporated comedy into their playing, became world famous.

Much of the black basketball style originated from urban street games that were up-tempo, expressive, and creative and they also introduced the dunk shot. But the famous "jitterbug dribble" was invented by Marques Haynes, who was the star of Langston University's basketball team in 1942. Basketball became integrated after the 1964 Civil Rights Act. Title IX of the Education Amendments Act of 1972 stipulated that colleges and universities that received federal funds had to provide sports programs for women and that brought women securely into the game.

The focus of this chapter is minority equality within sport and how race relations within society are evident in sport. The first part of this chapter is a brief history of how racism in society has been mirrored by racism in sport. The second part is about the vulnerabilities of athletes. The third part is about star athletes speaking out about social justice.

HOW RACISM IN SPORT HAS MIRRORED SOCIETY

At present, African Americans such as Serena Williams, Venus Williams, Tiger Woods, LeBron James, Naomi Osaka, Simone Biles, as well Colin Kaepernick, are so well known as to be household names. The same was true of athletes from the recent past, such as Muhammad Ali, Mike Tyson, Michael Jordan, and Magic Johnson. Sports gear associated with famous black athletes is a billion-dollar industry with profits for Nike, Under Armour, and Adidas, to name a few, from goods, especially shoes, manufactured abroad by low-paid workers of color, including children. Broadcast events featuring black athletes represent a hefty investment by the NBA, the NCAA March Madness, and the NFL Super Bowl. However, black athletes were not always as prominent as they are now, and even now, their power remains limited by white coaches, white dominant athletic associations, and white sports team owners. While contemporary black athletes are more outspoken than in the past, their decisions and comportment receive special scrutiny. These strictures over work and life are both a legacy of overt racism in the past and a reflection of ongoing racism in the present.

Philosopher John McClendon surveys the history of African Americans in sport in terms of institutional racism, or social structures that have been oppressive. For instance, slave owners profited from male boxers who won fights against other slaves. Sylvia Dubois (1788–1888), a female slave boxer, was entered in fights with white men because owners did not want to risk a black male slave winning against a white opponent. But male or female, such slave boxers, while rewarded when they won, remained property.

Black jockeys were allowed to compete against white opponents, both before and after the Civil War. On May 17, 1875, Oliver Lewis won the first Kentucky Derby, and the trainer of his horse was also a former slave. But by the end of the nineteenth century, black jockeys were forced out of horse racing because of racism and the cost of maintaining training stables. Nevertheless, black excellence in sport continued throughout the twentieth century: Jack Johnson, the "Galveston Giant," became the first African American heavyweight boxing champion in 1910; Jesse Owens won four gold medals at the 1936 Berlin Olympics; Joe Louis won the heavyweight championship in 1937; the Harlem Rens, black owned and with a black coach, won the basketball world championship in 1939; in 1947, Jackie Robinson became the first African American admitted to Major League Baseball. Also well known had been local black baseball leagues such as the Colored Texas League founded in 1916 and the Texas Negro League of 1920.

However, McClendon, writing in 2017, notes that meritocracy in sport is still racially incomplete. For instance, black women are still not visibly present in the Ladies Professional Golf Association (LPGA), even after the legendary exploits of Althea Gibson (1927–2003), the first African American to win the Grand Slam in tennis, who had turned to golf at age thirty-seven. McClendon argues that individual accomplishments, while they may bring fame and honor to elite individuals, do not change the overall economic and power structures of sport that continue to disadvantage athletes of color. Moreover, individual excellence in racially oppressive athletic and social frameworks is accompanied by individual vulnerabilities, as we will see in the next section.

The racism associated with US sport is not blatantly evident among fans. However, in Europe, antiblack racism against African and African American athletes has been blatant in recent years, particularly against soccer and tennis stars. Taunts have taken the form of throwing bananas onto fields, in addition to caricaturing black male players as monkeys and exaggerating the sexual traits of female tennis stars such as Serena Williams. One reason for this difference may be that in a European context, black players are foreign to dominant white populations, whereas in the United States, they are already recognized as American. But in addition to xenophobia, there may be less restraints on overt white antiblack racism in some European cultures.

VULNERABILITIES OF ATHLETES

African American male athletes have been especially vulnerable to injuries related to contact sports such as boxing and football. Female athletes of color in all US sports, despite Title IX, have been vulnerable to inadequate material resources, sexual abuse, and pressures of media exposure that have threatened their psychological well-being. These injuries also have white sufferers, but nonwhite race compounds them. For instance, college athletes, despite the money their sponsoring institutions make from exhibitions and broadcasts, have only recently been cleared by the NCAA to receive payment, although not directly for playing. Instead, college athletes are permitted to earn money from autographs, endorsements, and other individual activities on social media. This new policy will be especially beneficial for athletes of color who may not have financial resources comparable to those of white athletes.

A retrospective study of white and black athletes, ages twelve to twenty-three, who were treated for sport-related concussion (SRC) between 2012 and 2015 was published in 2021. Days to symptom resolution, return to school, and changes in daily activities were compared by race. The result was that black athletes recovered faster, returned to school faster, and reported less disruption in daily life. Sports performance was the same for both groups. The authors conclude that insofar as race has not been previously studied in SRC, their results suggest that faster black recovery times may be the result of socioeconomic factors associated with race following SRC. Black athletes often receive diagnosis and treatment from emergency rooms instead of their own doctors and may not have access to ongoing care. This concern is supported and should be extended, given information on how SRC has been compensated, years after original injuries.

Also in 2021, fifty thousand petitions from retired black professional football players and their families and supporters demanded an end to the use of "race norming" for NFL payouts to black players in settlements of brain injury claims. The "race norming" algorithm used for accessing dementia assumed that black men had lower cognitive skills to begin with and therefore suffered less damage from football injuries than their white counterparts. This raises the question of how it is medically determined, as recorded in the retrospective SRC study, that black players, compared to white, have recovered from athletic injuries.

Sexual abuse of elite female athletes made national headlines during the trial of Larry Nassar. On January 24, 2018, Nassar was sentenced to 40 to 175 years for his sexual abuse of more than 150 young female athletes during his tenure at USA Gymnastics and the US Olympic Committee. Social critics have pointed to trends after Title IX, when males were appointed as women's coaches and athletic directors, to shore up competition with the Soviet Union and "feminize" the women who participated in sport. In women's college sports, again, despite Title IX, facilities are often unequal to those made available to male athletes. This was brought to embarrassing public attention during the NCAA-sponsored March Madness in 2021. While there is no evidence that sexual abuse or material inequality specifically involves race, it compounds experiences of racism for women of color.

The intense personal media focus on elite female athletes of color became a topic of discussion after it was obvious that Serena Williams was a lightning rod for racist and sexist abuse. For example, after winning the French Open in June 2015, Williams was compared to an animal and a man, and said to be "ugly." One Twitter user wrote that Williams "looks like a gorilla and sounds like a gorilla when she grunts while hitting the ball. In conclusion, she is a gorilla." Observers have commented that the trend of such abuse has led Williams's fans to brace themselves whenever she wins. Naomi Osaka defeated Williams in the 2018 US Open, in which Williams claimed sexist bias in penalties imposed on her by the umpire. Osaka, who is Japanese and Haitian, was depicted as white in cartoons, which erased her biracial identity. Because the penalties against Williams may not have been fair, Osaka was said to be denied a win on her merits.

Even in the absence of overt racist personal abuse, the pressures on black female athletes threaten their psychological well-being. Naomi Osaka won the Australian Open in February 2021, but did not participate in the French Open's news conferences, for what she said were reasons involving her mental health. Osaka went on to light the Opening Ceremony of the Olympics but did not win a medal. In gymnastics at the same Olympics in Japan, Simone Biles withdrew from individual balance beam routines, citing "the twisties," or spatial disorientation while aloft. It was not clear why Biles suffered from that syndrome then, but she was well regarded for not risking her life with routines in which she was ten feet in the air.

STAR ATHLETES SPEAKING OUT
ABOUT SOCIAL JUSTICE

Star athletes of color obviously have influence beyond their playing success. That is why they are sought after to endorse athletic gear, as well as other goods and services, which everyone now expects. However, controversy has been sparked when they have spoken out politically on social justice issues involving race. Also, there is a difference between raising voices for social justice while off the playing field and doing so in the course of games. The first question is whether such protest, on or off the field, is effective. That is, when athletes endorse commercial products and services, their fans buy them, so what is the payoff when they endorse social justice causes?

After a grand jury did not charge Louisville police officers with killing Breonna Taylor, Los Angeles Lakers' LeBron James, spoke out about the news in a postgame interview: "We lost a beautiful woman in Breonna that has no say in what's going on right now. We want justice no matter how long it takes." Earlier, there had been an NBA strike after police shot Jacob Blake in Kenosha, Wisconsin, which spread to the WNBA, MLS, MLB, and professional tennis. Before the 2020 presidential election, James founded a group to protect black voting rights and encourage people to vote. *Politico* asked the question of whether such activism was effective. The majority of African Americans who responded to *Politico*'s survey said that Colin Kaepernick (discussed shortly) had inspired them to vote. Overall, both Kaepernick and James had higher approval ratings than the Democratic presidential candidate, Joe Biden. So there is little question about the political effectiveness, at this time, of black athletes speaking out.

However, there are moral questions and issues of integrity raised by such political activism when it becomes part of athletic activity itself. Sport in the United States and throughout the world is an impassioned form of recreation for both players and audience. (Although it is a serious career for players, despite its recreational origins.) Like poetry or philosophy, it occupies its own sphere in social life. Spectators can relax when involved in sports and disputes have traditionally revolved around the merits of particular teams and players. But if sport overall becomes politicized, its refuge and recreational role changes. Sport becomes partly an extension of politics, with new attention paid to racial identities insofar as nonwhites align with progressive politics and candidates, that is with the Democratic Party, and whites align with conservatives and reactionaries—that is, with the Republican Party. Does political involvement by athletes in that context compromise the integrity of sport?

What about the integrity of individual players? Many objected to Colin Kaepernick first "taking the knee." Kaepernick played six seasons for the San Francisco 49ers in the NFL. In 2016, in protest of police brutality and racial inequality in the United States, he knelt during the national anthem at the start of NFL games. He said, "I am not going to stand up to show pride in a flag for a country that oppresses Black people and people of color. . . . To me, this is bigger than football and it would be selfish on my part to look the other way." He added that he would continue to "take the knee" during the national anthem until seeing "significant change" for minorities. After the 2016 season, Kaepernick became a free agent. In 2017, he filed a grievance against NFL owners for colluding to deny him employment. He later reached a confidential settlement with the NFL but has not since played for a team. In 2018, Kaepernick became the face of Nike's thirty-year commemorative campaign with the slogan, "Just Do It." Below his face were the words, "Believe in something. Even if it means sacrificing everything." After this aired, there were media images of some consumers burning their Nike gear.

Kaepernick has not compromised his own integrity, but it has likely cost him his football career—although he has continually claimed that he is waiting for one of the "thirty-two teams and thirty-two owners" in the NFL to sign him. Also there is little question about the justice of the cause Kaepernick supports. On the one hand, his public declarations are protected free speech. But on the other hand, he would not have gotten attention for them had he not already been a famous athlete. There is also some irony in Nike's support of Kaepernick, which is probably based on market research about black consumer behavior. Has Kaepernick traded his athletic career for another form of commercial success? Are there moral issues of integrity involved in that exchange? Does the NFL have a moral obligation to protect football from becoming political during games?

QUESTIONS FOR THINKING, DISCUSSION, AND WRITING

1. Explain how social conditions and not physical traits influenced who played basketball in its early years.
2. Provide examples of how racism in sport has historically mirrored racism in society.
3. How are athletes of color individually vulnerable to racism and sport injuries?
4. Discuss recent issues of psychological well-being among star athletes as intersections of the pressures of fame, gender, race, and specific sports.
5. What is your position on the moral questions brought up by what we know about Colin Kaepernick?

SOURCES

Abad-Santos, Alex. "Serena Williams's US Open Fight with Umpire Carlos Ramos, Explained." Vox, September 10, 2018, https://www.vox.com/2018/9/10/17837598/serena-williams-us-open-umpire-carlos-ramos.

Blaschke, Anne. "Nassar's Abuse Reflects More Than 50 Years of Men's Power over Female Athletes." The Conversation, January 30, 2018, https://theconversation.com/nassars-abuse-reflects-more-than-50-years-of-mens-power-over-female-athletes-90722.

Dale, Maryclaire, and Michelle R. Smith. "Retired Black Players Say NFL Brain-Injury Payouts Show Bias." AP, May 14, 2021, https://apnews.com/article/health-nfl-race-and-ethnicity-sports-066d9fd6bd85f5b5023207467701fde4.

Desmond-Harris, Jenée. "Serena Williams Is Constantly the Target of Disgusting Racist and Sexist Attacks." Vox, September 7, 2016, https://www.vox.com/2015/3/11/8189679/serena-williams-indian-wells-racism.

"Colin Kaepernick, 1987– ." https://www.biography.com/athlete/colin-kaepernick.

Hamilton, Tom. "Olympics 2021: Naomi Osaka's Legacy Still Filled with Hope Despite Tennis Loss." ESPN, July 27, 2021, https://www.espn.com/olympics/story/_/id/31893632/olympics-2021-naomi-osaka-legacy-filled-hope-loss.

International Olympic Committee. "Welcome to the Ancient Olympic Games." https://olympics.com/ioc/ancient-olympic-games.

Landler, Mark. "After Defeat, England's Black Soccer Players Face a Racist Outburst." New York Times, July 12, 1921, https://www.nytimes.com/2021/07/12/world/europe/england-european-championships-racism.html.

Lever, Katie. "What Is Going on in Women's NCAA Sports Right Now?" The Huddle, LRT Sports, March 22, 2021, https://www.lrt-sports.com/blog/what-is-going-on-in-womens-ncaa-sports-right-now/.

Presswood, Mark. "The Negro Leagues in Texas." Texas Almanac, 2008–9, https://www.texasalmanac.com/articles/the-negro-leagues-in-texas.

Roe, Donald. "Basketball." Oxford African American Studies Center, February 9, 2009, https://oxfordaasc.com/view/10.1093/acref/9780195301731.001.0001/acref-9780195301731-e-45253.

Yengo-Kahn, Aaron M., Jessica Wallace, Viviana Jimenez, Douglas J. Totten, Christopher M. Bonfield, and Scott L. Zuckerman. "Exploring the Outcomes and Experiences of Black and White Athletes Following a Sport-Related Concussion: A Retrospective Cohort Study." Journal of Neurosurgery, August 24, 2021, https://thejns.org/pediatrics/view/journals/j-neurosurg-pediatr/aop/article-10.3171-2021.2.PEDS2130/article-10.3171-2021.2.PEDS2130.xml DOI link: https://doi.org/10.3171/2021.2.PEDS2130.

Videos

KTVU FOX 2, San Francisco. "Colin Kaepernick Explains Why He Won't Stand during National Anthem." YouTube, August 29, 2016, https://www.youtube.com/watch?v=ka0446tibig.

Molski, Max, and Kelley Ekert. "16 College Athletes Already Getting Paid under New NCAA Rule." NBC Sports, July 2, 2021, https://www.nbcsports.com/chicago/15-college-athletes-already-getting-paid-under-new-ncaa-rule.

NBC Sports. "Simone Biles Opens Up about 'Twisties,' Making Best Decision for Team." Tokyo Olympics, NBC Sports, YouTube, August 4, 2021, https://www.youtube.com/watch?v=t-4eJ2TZytY.

Secret Base. "Candace Parker's Historic Dunk Deserves a Deep Rewind." 2006 NCAA Tournament. YouTube, March 19, 2020, https://www.youtube.com/watch?v=E086XpwpcgM.

Towler, Christopher C., Nyron N. Crawford, and Robert A. Bennett III. "Why Black Athletes Political Activism Matters." Politico, October 4, 2020, https://www.politico.com/news/magazine/2020/10/04/why-black-athletes-political-activism-matters-425473.

VI

THE NATURAL AND
INTERNATIONAL WORLD

The natural world, especially concerning weather, is the international world, particularly concerning climate change. However, even within the United States, there are racial and ethnic divisions concerning the effects of disaster and resilience after it. But even within the United States, an international moral lens could offer solutions to current impasses.

Chapter 22 examines the socially constructed nature of natural disasters and the importance of preparation. The effects of Hurricane Harvey in Texas and Hurricane Maria in Puerto Rico are compared in terms of ethnicity and preexisting infrastructure. In chapter 23, the socially constructed effects of disaster in terms of race and ethnicity are considered through the COVID-19 pandemic in its different impacts on African Americans, Hispanic/Latinx Americans, and Native Americans, differences that are all related to prepandemic disadvantages.

Chapter 24 draws on global ideas of humanitarianism, an approach toward equality that is more general than race and racial differences. The capabilities approach is related to US ideas of equity, as is the human security paradigm. Finally, climate change is considered in terms of humanity, as a general identity that requires universal recognition as well as international cooperation to protect. At the same time, world differences in wealth will raise new moral questions for those better off.

22

Natural Disasters

Seaside scene in Rincon, Puerto Rico, after Hurricane Marie showing damage to businesses. Getty Images: cestes001.

Natural disasters and pandemics have both purely physical and socially constructed aspects. The physical aspects are obvious, such as the extreme weather of hurricanes and the SARS-CoV-2 virus in the case of COVID-19. **Resilience** or the ability to recover from such external environmental disasters requires both material resources and moral virtues for preparation and response. Preparation consists of getting things and skills ready before a disaster occurs; response is how people react to disaster during and after it occurs. Present natural disasters and those to come through climate change require the virtue of prudence. **Prudence** is a disposition or character trait in individuals and groups that involves a stance toward risk. **Risk** is either present or future danger that has a measurable probability of occurring. For instance, although the weather forecasts sunshine for today, there is still a risk that it will rain. Or, the conditions for a major earthquake may be present, but the risk of it happening on any given day may be very low. People go about their business in situations of low risk, especially if the risk is uncertain. However, a certain risk of great danger requires a prudent stance. For floods, earthquakes, and cyclones, although the risk may be low on any given day, it is nevertheless prudent to prepare for them, in practical ways that do not interfere with daily life too much, although there may be an initial cost. For example, after the Fukushima earthquake and tsunami hit Japan in March 2011, some buildings were spared because their foundations were on springs that could absorb shock. That resulted in an ambitious program to build new skyscrapers on shock-absorbing materials in preparation for future earthquakes.

Ongoing pandemics require not only practical preparation in accord with prudence, but intellectual virtues such as rationality and critical thinking. Racial and ethnic minorities suffer most in all kinds of disaster, not because they lack such virtues, but because their social circumstances, which are socially constructed, entail that majorities beyond their communities have not developed group virtues of equality that extend to disadvantaged groups given the risks of disaster. In this chapter and chapter 23, we will consider disaster and minority inequality from a moral point of view, with an emphasis on the relevant virtues. The first section of this chapter is about the social construction of natural disaster. The second section focuses on preparation. The third section consists of comparative case studies in light of the analyses of the first two sections: Hurricane Harvey in Houston, Texas, and Hurricane Maria in Puerto Rico during the 2017 storm season.

DISASTER AND RACIAL SOCIAL CONSTRUCTION

To say that disaster is socially constructed requires some historical background. At 9:30 a.m. on November 1, 1755, an earthquake struck Lisbon, Portugal, the fourth-largest city in Europe at that time. Many residents were at mass. The earthquake hit the center of the city, destroying houses of the nobility and the Royal Palace. Low-lying areas were devasted and a major fire destroyed wooden buildings. As many as 70,000 were said to have died and only 3,000 of 20,000 dwellings were unscathed. Because Lisbon was a European cultural center, intellectuals of the day debated the significance of this disaster. Among them, Jean-Jacques Rousseau (1712–1778) probably had the most modern interpretation because he introduced the idea of the social construction of disaster.

Rousseau observed that earthquakes in nature, without human habitation, did not represent the same kind of problems as the Lisbon earthquake. As a free thinker, Rousseau rejected the idea that the earthquake was a punishment from God. Instead, he asked why so many had died and so much had been destroyed. He answered that people were overly attached to their possessions and had reentered collapsing or burning buildings to retrieve them. He also noted that the seven-story buildings in Lisbon were a human invention that created vulnerability. It could have been said that God punished the residents of Lisbon for their graspingness and architectural pride. However, that was not Rousseau's point. His point was that the natural, physical event of the Lisbon earthquake was a disaster because of how it intersected with human society. That was Rousseau's insight about the social construction of disaster: **Disaster** = natural event + human culture at a certain time, in a particular place.

Rousseau's insight has influenced contemporary disaster theory. A **natural disaster** is an unwanted and destructive natural event, usually occurring over a short period, which overwhelms existing human capabilities to avoid or respond to it, so that normal functioning is disrupted. Sociologist E. L. Quarantelli (1924–2017) provided this definition:

> Disasters are ad hoc, irregular occasions that involve a crisis; there is relative consensus that things have to be done, but the wherewithal is not enough to meet the demand. In a disaster, there is considerable variation in how the everyday capability/resource and demand/need balance gets unbalanced.

Quarantelli goes on to analyze how the effects of disaster on individuals and society should be considered part of the disaster itself. For example, if some individuals become depressed or have other mental health disruptions, that is part of the disaster. A further insight from Quarantelli, which we will consider in chapter 23, is that disasters tend to bring people together as help rushes in, whereas destruction in situations of violent conflict drives people apart because the site of trouble is avoided.

Racial differences and divisions are also social constructions. Not only is there no biological foundation for different human races in science, as discussed in chapter 4, but within society, social racial divisions have their own constructions. That is, the social construction of race was invented and goes on, in the absence of real biological foundations. Races are not only real in society, but they are not simply varieties. Races are related to differences in society concerning possession and opportunities for human goods, such as food, housing, education, and medical care. For all these goods, nonwhites are generally less well off than whites, even when members of both groups are in the same socioeconomic class or have equal opportunities to acquire them.

The intersection of natural disasters with racial differences in society has resulted in greater vulnerabilities among people of color compared to white people. Surviving and thriving after a disaster require both physical and individual resources—money, equipment, secure employment, stable housing, and access to medical care. People of color are more vulnerable in natural disasters than white people because their resources are not as adequate before the disaster. In addition, efforts to help may be impaired by preexisting racism or discrimination. For instance, the *Washington Post* identified these impediments as *racial cues* in media reports of Hurricane Katrina:

> Not only did Katrina raise questions about the government's ability to deal with large-scale flooding, it also rekindled longstanding issues concerning the standing of African-Americans. The people who remained left behind in New Orleans to suffer the brunt of the hurricane's consequences were disproportionately black. Post-hurricane publicity, although sympathetic to victims, was criticized as seeming to be racially biased at times. The media publicized instances of looting by blacks while characterizing similar activity on the part of whites as "looking for food." Other reports alleged that gangs of armed blacks had attempted to shoot down rescue helicopters. Quite unexpectedly, Katrina became a metaphor for the state of race relations in America.

Drawing on Quarantelli's insight that the effects of a disaster are part of the disaster, we could conclude that heightened antiblack racism in representations of Katrina victims was part of that disaster.

DISASTER PREPARATION

According to data collected by the US Federal Reserve in 2019, when unemployment was at a nearly half-century low, 40 percent of Americans reported that they would struggle to meet a $400 emergency expense, and some said they could not meet it at all. The 40 percent are therefore individually unprepared for emergencies in their normal lives, without even considering disaster. But if they have medical, home, or car insurance, that degree of normal-life preparation already exists. Also, disaster preparation is not generally left up to individuals but is usually considered a matter of public well-being in the US federal system, where it is the responsibility of state governments, with federal assistance if state governors request it. (The Stafford Act of 1988 provides for the mechanics of federal aid.)

Individuals should be as well prepared for likely national disasters as they are able, and they should have a plan for how they will respond, for example, a place to meet up if all household members are not in the same place when a disaster occurs. Indeed, there have been numerous public service announcements in recent years advising citizens that they will be on their own immediately after a disaster occurs and should therefore have stored food, medication, battery power, and other supplies on hand. One could plausibly claim that such private preparation is an individual moral responsibility because it involves human survival. However, in complex societies, large-scale disaster response, as well as preparation, can be coordinated only by government entities. It, therefore, makes sense to consider disaster preparation in terms of public policy. Government planners and emergency departments need to be prudent.

Prudence is a cardinal virtue involving knowledge and action about danger. **Disaster preparation** is action about danger, which follows from the virtue of prudence. However, disaster preparation is not only a virtue, but for the ethics or morality of public policy, it also includes both deontological and utilitarian considerations. That is, prudent disaster preparation is an obligation of government and the ethics of disaster preparation are both utilitarian and deontological. Disaster response or the immediate reaction to disaster is almost always utilitarian, following the principle of Save the Greatest Number (SGN). But, how large that number is will depend on the preparation made beforehand. Those who are not saved, such as the black residents left behind in the response to Hurricane Katrina, and their relatives and friends will always have cause for moral complaint because every human life is intrinsically valuable.

Saving those who would not be saved with normal preparation and response to save a majority is a deontological consideration that ensures fairness. Adequate preparation will enlarge the number making up SGN because more personnel and supplies will be on hand to respond when disaster occurs. It is well known that racial and ethnic minorities, who have fewer resources and may experience greater government distrust, are worse affected by natural disasters. Therefore, SGN, with its deontological augmentation, now requires extra efforts to reach minority populations before disaster occurs. For instance, after disasters, the Federal Emergency Management Agency (FEMA) often gives more aid to white households than those to people of color, for reasons related to racial bias in property values, and this is a government policy requiring equitable reform. Policies based on **equity** correct for racial and ethnic inequalities in outcomes when people appear to be treated equally but are unable to benefit equally from such treatment because of minority racial or ethnic status.

COMPARING HARVEY AND MARIA

The comparison between Hurricanes Maria and Harvey shows how preexisting circumstances associated with ethnicity and the economic environment affect losses from natural disaster. Hurricane Harvey was the first hurricane to hit the Texas coast since 2008. Here is the official description from the National Weather Service:

> Hurricane Harvey started as a tropical wave off the African coast on Sunday, August 13th [2017]. . . . Harvey made landfall along the Texas coast near Port Aransas around 10:00 p.m. on August 25th as a cat 4 and brought devastating impacts. As Harvey moved inland, its forward motion slowed to near 5 mph after landfall and then meandered just north of Victoria, TX by the 26th. Rain bands on the eastern side of the circulation of Harvey moved into southeast Texas on the morning of the 25th and continued through much of the night and into the 26th. A strong rain band developed over Fort Bend and Brazoria Counties during the evening hours of the 26th and spread into Harris County and slowed while training from south to north. This resulted in a rapid development of flash flooding between 10:00 p.m. and 1:00 a.m. as tremendous

rainfall rates occurred across much of Harris County. The morning of the 27th saw additional rain bands continued to develop and produced additional excessive rainfall amounts. As the center of Harvey slowly moved east-southeast and back offshore heavy rainfall continued to spread through much of the 29th and the 30th exacerbating the ongoing widespread and devastating flooding. All of this rainfall caused catastrophic drainage issues and made rivers rise greatly. Only around 10 percent of the river forecast points in southeast Texas remained below flood stage due to the event, and approximately 46 percent of the river forecast points reached new record levels. Harvey maintained tropical storm intensity the entire time while inland over the Texas coastal bend and southeast Texas.

Houston, with a population close to 7 million, is vulnerable to floods, because urban sprawl has favored road construction over preservation of marshlands and prairies that would otherwise absorb floodwaters, and canals that would redirect them. During Harvey, roads, houses, and municipal buildings were unusable for a while. Houston's mayor had told people the storm was coming and that they should not retreat to their attics unless they took an ax with them. The initial death toll was seventy, later raised to eighty-eight. Compared to over 1,800 deaths from Katrina, in the same region sixteen years earlier, these figures occasioned self-congratulation about preparation and immediate response. About 24,000 residents were initially displaced but most or all found housing within months.

Harvey was estimated to cost $121 billion, although the federal government initially provided only $5 billion. Nevertheless, the economic analysis of Harvey's impact was upbeat from the beginning. On August 28, Ellen Zentner, chief US economist at Morgan Stanley, said that although Hurricane Harvey's impact on national gross domestic product in the third quarter might be fairly neutral, "the lagged effects of rebuilding homes and replacing motor vehicles can last longer, providing a lift to gross domestic product in the fourth quarter and beyond." Thus, for Houston, Hurricane Harvey was an opportunity for further growth in an already booming local economy, with little appetite for preparation for the next big storm. This almost celebratory response to Harvey not only overlooked the finality of those lives that were lost, but it absorbed the storm into ongoing business profitability in an already booming economy. On that model of disaster response (which is not prudent), natural disaster is no more than an opportunity for further growth.

Hurricane Maria hit Puerto Rico on September 20, 2017, as part of an extended storm system. Here is the National Weather Service's description:

Maria formed from an African easterly wave that moved across the tropical Atlantic Ocean during the week of September 10th to September 17th, 2017. It was not until 200 PM AST (1800 UTC) on September 16th, that its convective organization improved that the NHC classified the system as a tropical depression about 700 miles east-southeast of the Lesser Antilles. At the 500 PM AST (2100 UTC) advisory, just three hours later, the depression was upgraded to Tropical Storm Maria with maximum sustained winds of 50 mph. Thereafter, Maria gradually intensified and became the

8th hurricane of the 2017 Atlantic hurricane season with 75 mph maximum sustained winds at 500 PM AST (2100 UTC) on September 17th. . . . Within an 18 hour period, Maria underwent rapid intensification, strengthening from a category 1 to an extremely dangerous category 5 hurricane. At approximately 615 AM AST (1015 UTC), Maria made landfall in Yabucoa, Puerto Rico as a strong category 4 hurricane with maximum sustained winds of 155 mph. As the center of the storm moved west-northwestward over southeastern PR into the interior and northwestern PR, widespread hurricane force winds spread all over mainland PR along with extremely heavy rainfall that produced major to catastrophic flooding and flash flooding, especially across the northern half of Puerto Rico. Maria's center moved over the coastal waters off northwestern Puerto Rico early that afternoon. Even though hurricane force winds started to diminish once the system moved offshore, tropical storm force winds continued well into the evening and overnight hours across mainland Puerto Rico.

Hurricane Maria was a Category 4 storm when it hit Puerto Rico, affecting its 3.5 million residents. Damages were officially estimated at $90 billion. The death toll was first tallied at sixty-four but more comprehensive analyses placed it first over 1,000 and later at 3,000, given hurricane-related disruptions to transportation and medical treatment, especially for those in rural areas. Cell phone towers fell and the whole island lost power. Federal aid was slow and inadequate. Given prior infrastructure problems, it was estimated that full recovery, if possible, would take years. Four years later, it was estimated that Puerto Rico's power grid would not survive a Category 1 hurricane.

Despite urban expansion without adequate flood relief structures, Houston did alright through Harvey, because it was a booming area, with excellent infrastructure and response lessons learned from Katrina. But although Puerto Rico's recovery has been related to poor prior infrastructure, as well as an inadequate response from Washington, it is not fully comparable to Houston. A Category 4 hurricane hit Puerto Rico, but Houston sustained (only) a tropical storm. Insofar as the population and leadership of Houston are white dominant and that of Puerto Rico Latinx, the ongoing racial/ethnic comparison of disaster vulnerabilities still holds. Dynamic, rich, urban white areas are far less vulnerable to natural disasters than poor, minority, largely rural areas. While Puerto Rico is not a state, those born there are nonetheless US citizens.

People of color are more vulnerable to environmental stresses in disasters, but before disasters occur, their environments are already more stressed, less beautiful, and more dangerous than places occupied by white people. Robert Bullard, often called "the father of contemporary environmental justice," has repeatedly emphasized such racial disparities. That is, contrasts in disaster resilience such as Puerto Rico and Houston can be found in many aspects of predisaster life. Environments in minority communities are often slow-moving disasters that are accepted as part of ordinary life in the United States. Indeed, as discussed throughout this book, all of the physical racial disparities in where people live and go to school, as well as differences in health and recreation, show that public and private facilities, services, and conditions are not as good for people of color as they are for white residents.

QUESTIONS FOR THINKING, DISCUSSION, AND WRITING

1. Explain what makes the effects of a disaster part of the disaster.
2. Explain how constructions of race intersect with the social construction of disaster.
3. Why is disaster preparation a moral issue, generally?
4. What do you think individuals should do for disaster preparation? What have you done?
5. How is comparing Hurricane Harvey in Houston and Hurricane Maria in Puerto Rico not apt comparison?

SOURCES

Acevedo, Nicole. "Puerto Rico's Progress Still Stalled Four Years after Maria." NBC News, September 19, 2021, https://www.nbcnews.com/news/latino/puerto-rico-four-years-hurricane-maria-far-recovery-rcna2073.

Afiune, Giulia. "State Says Harvey's Death Toll Has Reached 88." *The Texas Tribune*, October 13, 2017, https://www.texastribune.org/2017/10/13/harveys-death-toll-reaches-93-people/.

Berke, Philip R. "Why Is Houston So Vulnerable to Devastating Floods?" BBC News, August 31, 2017, http://www.bbc.com/news/world-us-canada-41107049.

Bullard, R. D., and B. H. Wright. *The Wrong Complexion for Protection: Environmental Health and Racial Equity in the United States: Building Environmentally Just, Sustainable, and Livable Communities*. Washington, DC: American Public Health Association, 2011.

Dougherty, Conor, and Nelson D. Schwartz. "Hurricane to Cost Tens of Billions, but a Quick Recovery Is Expected." *New York Times*, August 28, 2017, https://www.nytimes.com/2017/08/28/business/economy/texas-hurricane-harvey-economic-impact.html.

Dynes, Russell R. "The Dialogue between Voltaire and Rousseau on the Lisbon Earthquake: The Emergence of a Social Science View." Disaster Research Center, 1999, http://udspace.udel.edu/handle/19716/435.

FEMA. Stafford Act, https://www.fema.gov/disaster/stafford-act.

Flavelle, Christopher. "Why Does Disaster Aid Often Favor White People?" *New York Times*, June 7, 1921, https://www.nytimes.com/2021/06/07/climate/FEMA-race-climate.html.

Henriques, Martha. "How Japan's Skyscrapers Are Built to Survive Earthquakes." Future, BBC, January 16, 2019, https://www.bbc.com/future/article/20190114-how-japans-skyscrapers-are-built-to-survive-earthquakes.

Isaacson, Walter. "Robert Bullard: How Environmental Racism Shapes the US." Interview. Anapour & Co., PBS, March 3, 2020, https://www.pbs.org/wnet/amanpour-and-company/video/robert-bullard-how-environmental-racism-shapes-the-us/.

Iyengar, Shanto, and Richard Mor. "Natural Disasters in Black and White: How Racial Cues Influenced Public Response to Hurricane Katrina." *Washington Post*, June 8, 2006, https://pcl.stanford.edu/press/2006/wp-naturaldisasters.pdf.

Mullin, John R. "The Reconstruction of Lisbon Following the Earthquake of 1755: A Study in Despotic Planning." *Journal of the International History of City Planning Association* (1992): 45, https://scholarworks.umass.edu/larp_faculty_pubs/45/.

National Weather Service. Houston, Galveston, TX. "Hurricane Harvey and Its Impacts on Southeast Texas from August 25th to 29th, 2017." US Dept of Commerce, National Oceanic and Atmospheric Administration, US Dept of Commerce, April 2018, https://www.weather.gov/hgx/hurricaneharvey.

National Weather Service. San Juan, PR. "Major Hurricane Maria—September 20, 2017." https://www.weather.gov/sju/maria2017.

NOLA. "Relatively Low Harvey Death Toll Is 'Astounding' to Experts." September 6, 2017, http://www.nola.com/hurricane/index.ssf/2017/09/harvey_death_toll_relatively_l.html.

Quarantelli, E. L. "What Is Disaster? The Need for Clarification in Definition and Conceptualization in Research." Disaster Research Center, University of Delaware, Research, Series Report, Article 177 (1985): 41–73, citable URI, quotation p.13, http://udspace.udel.edu/handle/19716/1119.

Sherter, Alain. "Nearly 40% of Americans Can't Cover a Surprise $400 Expense." MONEYWATCH, CBS News, May 23, 2019, https://www.cbsnews.com/news/nearly-40-of-americans-cant-cover-a-surprise-400-expense/.

Zack, Naomi. "Ethics of Disaster Planning." *Philosophy of Management*, Special Issue, *Ethics of Crisis*, Per Sandin, ed., 8, no 2 (2009): 53–64.

Videos

AccuWeather. "Puerto Rican Resilience after Maria." Oct. 14, 2021, https://video.search.yahoo.com/search/video;_ylt=AwrJ7JRaCXNhEekAnttXNyoA;_ylu=Y29sbwNiZjEEcG9zAzEEdnRpZAMEc2VjA3BpdnM-?p=hurricane+maria+puerto+rico&fr2=piv-web&type=E211US105G0&fr=mcafee#id=2&vid=efb137dc82a024246bec43cba4f84d81&action=view.

Houston Mayor's Office. "Mayor Turner Provides Update on Four-Year Anniversary of Hurricane Harvey." Press Release, 2021, https://www.houstontx.gov/mayor/press/2021/four-year-harvey-report.html.

Teichner, Martha. "New Orleans after Katrina: A Tale of Two Cities." CBS Sunday Morning, August 30, 2015, YouTube, https://www.youtube.com/watch?v=602rez0ZA60.

Vance, Bryan M. "Impending Cascadia Subduction Zone Quake Back in the News." OPB, March 6, 2016, https://www.opb.org/news/series/unprepared/northwest-earthquake-cascadia-subduction-zone-unprepared/.

23

COVID-19

Demonstrators protesting on the street against racism. Getty Images: Xavier Lorenzo.

Invisible to the naked eye, but detectable through chemistry and genetic sequencing, the SARS-CoV-2 virus has been the catalyst for the COVID-19 pandemic. On October 23, 2021, the Coronavirus Resource Center of the Johns Hopkins School of Medicine reported 4,941,710 worldwide deaths from COVID-19 and 243,242,313 cases of infection. The United States, premier international mecca for medical research and scientific technology, outpaced the rest of the world with 735,507 deaths and 45,414,523 cases of infection. Anyone who spent January 2020 through October 2021 on a desert island, or in a coma, would be astounded by these figures!

The main cause was inadequate preparation. E. L. Quarantelli thought that the next big disaster, which he called X, would be a viral pandemic. COVID-19 has turned out to be X. Billionaire philanthropist and Microsoft cofounder Bill Gates warned that the world was not ready for a pandemic in a 2015 Ted Talk, and in 2021 he advised that preparation for the next pandemic would save money in the long run. Others in government and research have sounded similar alarms but when the COVID-19 pandemic began in the United States, the national stockpile had been exhausted, an Obama administration playbook about a pandemic response was not consulted, and there was not enough personal protective equipment (PPE) for over-worked medical personnel in over-crowded hospitals in the Northeast.

A second contributing cause to the high number of US pandemic casualties was the politicization of pandemic-related mitigation, from the beginning. An issue becomes politicized when differences of opinion are aligned with political party politics. From the beginning of the COVID-19 pandemic in the United States, with some exceptions and crosscurrents, as well as independent voters, acceptance or de-nial of the reality of COVID-19 and reactions to **mitigation** or measures to address it, such as mask wearing, social distancing, lockdowns, and vaccination, were lined up with Democratic or Republican political affiliation. At the same time, conspiracy theories about the origin of the virus, its transmission, and the dangers and profits from vaccination proliferated, especially on social media. This misinformation and falsehood was closely tied to mistrust, or a lack of understanding of the nature of modern science, among those who rejected the reports of experts.

A communication crisis resulted because the now-politicized factions do not share a common standard for knowledge or justified belief—there has been no **epis-temology** or theory of knowledge umpire to apply standards. Mistrust of the civil service administrative part of the US government was led by Donald Trump while he was president. The politicization and conspiracy circulation and mistrust, as well as inadequate preparation, can be viewed together as the social construction of the COVID-19 disaster. Inadequate preparation was a preexisting cause but the polariza-tion and conspiracy circulation were both effects of COVID-19 that became part of the disaster. Overall, the American experience of COVID-19 has been a tragedy. A **tragedy** in Aristotle's classic sense is a downfall resulting from errors of judgment.

All has not been tragic, however. The COVID-19 pandemic has had beneficial consequences, such as great progress in digital communication and broad public and political agreement that it has been the obligation of the federal government to provide compensation for those most damaged by the pandemic. Federal compensa-tion under both the Trump and Biden presidential administrations has amounted to trillions of dollars in payouts to individuals, businesses, and state and local gov-ernments. There has also been a renewed focus and reflection on racial and ethnic inequality, throughout media and institutions within US society. The greater impact of the COVID-19 pandemic on US racial and ethnic minorities and collateral social damage and violence is morally wrong, exactly because of its association with minor-ity racial and ethnic status.

In chapter 13, we considered the comparative health of racial and ethnic mi-norities in the United States before COVID-19. So-called preexisting **comorbidities** were the foundation for 2019 statistics for COVID-19 infection and death among US minorities compared to whites. Returning to those statistics from the CDC table (see table 23.1), it was evident that African Americans and Hispanic Americans had almost three times the hospitalization rates as white non-Hispanic Americans and twice the death rates. The highest rates of hospitalization and death occurred among Native Americans.

The September 2021 CDC update is the same as the race-related statistics in 2019 (see table 23.2). Either the impact of COVID-19 on racial and ethnic minorities has been very consistent throughout the US COVID-19 pandemic, or else the CDC has not had time to collect and fully update its data.

Statistics can relate only to numerical bottom lines. In this chapter, we provide further real-life perspective on the disproportionate illness and deaths as well as violent attacks against minority groups in the context of COVID-19. Overt racism has become more intense, illness and death among minority groups have been related to comparatively lower rates of vaccination, and employment and environmental factors have had different impacts. The first section of this chapter focuses on increasingly violent racism against Asian Americans and Jewish Americans. Further consideration of the effects of COVID-19 on African Americans, Latinx Americans, and Native Americans follows.

Table 23.1 CDC, Risk for COVID-19 Infection, Hospitalization, and Death by Race/Ethnicity.

Rate ratios compared to White, Non-Hispanic persons	American Indian or Alaska Native, Non-Hispanic persons	Asian, Non-Hispanic persons	Black or African American, Non-Hispanic persons	Hispanic or Latino persons
Cases	1.7x	0.7x	1.1x	1.9x
Hospitalization	3.5x	1.0x	2.8x	2.8x
Death	2.4x	1.0x	2.0x	2.3x

Race and ethnicity are risk markers for other underlying conditions that impact health. Source: CDC, https://www.cdc.gov/coronavirus/2019-ncov/covid-data/investigations-discovery/hospitalization-death-by-race-ethnicity.html.

Table 23.2 CDC, Risk for COVID-19 Infection, Hospitalization, and Death by Race/Ethnicity, Updated September 9, 2021.

Rate ratios compared to White, Non-Hispanic persons	American Indian or Alaska Native, Non-Hispanic persons	Asian, Non-Hispanic persons	Black or African American, Non-Hispanic persons	Hispanic or Latino persons
Cases	1.7x	0.7x	1.1x	1.9x
Hospitalization	3.5x	1.0x	2.8x	2.8x
Death	2.4x	1.0x	2.0x	2.3x

Race and ethnicity are risk markers for other underlying conditions that affect health, including socioeconomic status, access to health care, and exposure to the virus related to occupation, e.g., frontline, essential, and critical infrastructure workers. Source: CDC, https://www.cdc.gov/coronavirus/2019-ncov/covid-data/investigations-discovery/hospitalization-death-by-race-ethnicity.html.

INCREASINGLY VIOLENT RACISM AGAINST
ASIAN AMERICANS AND JEWISH AMERICANS

There is an important difference between the effects of a pandemic on those with preexisting vulnerabilities in health and inadequate resources and more intense ideological racism that is expressed in violent physical attacks. It is the difference between illness and hate crimes. The US COVID-19 pandemic has seen a rise in anti-Asian racism and anti-Semitism, as well as the ongoing black racism related to police shootings of unarmed black men (see chapters 9, 10, and 15). Hate crimes overall increased during 2020, and the 31 percent increase in California was led by antiblack bias. Still, while individual cases of anti-Asian and anti-Semitic hate crimes receive instant media attention, these attacks are often not fully recognized as part of well-established conspiracy theories and **ideologies** or systems of belief that present false views of reality to further the interests of some at the expense of others.

Conspiracy theories posit powerful actors behind the scenes who secretly plan to harm others for their own gain. The conspiracy theories that have targeted Asian Americans during the COVID-19 pandemic identify the virus with its first outbreaks in China in late 2019 and early 2020. There are varying claims that Dr. Anthony Fauci, director of the National Institute of Allergy and Infectious Diseases and the chief medical advisor to the president, was involved in funding research at a Wuhan laboratory, which increased the virulence and transmissibility of the SARS-CoV-2 virus, and then released it. This research is believed to have been undertaken so that profits could be made from vaccines. There were also conspiracy theories in China that the virus had originated in the United States and was exported as a bioweapon. Neither the American nor the Chinese conspiracies have direct evidence. The US conspiracies have motivated hate crimes against Asian Americans.

Over the COVID-19 pandemic, there have been close to three thousand reported hate crimes against Asian Americans. Between March and May 2020, over 1,700 anti-Asian incidents in forty-five states were reported, including stabbing, beating, shunning, workplace discrimination, business vandalization, and verbal abuse of individuals. These violent incidents create an atmosphere of fear among Asian Americans, especially among elderly people who have been reported to be afraid to leave their homes unaccompanied. There was also constant blame and suspicion from Republicans who referred to the "Chinese" or "Wuhan" virus. Asian enclaves in urban areas throughout the United States also suffered severe economic loss from the closure of restaurants and other services, leisure, and personal care businesses. High unemployment and an uncertain business future loom as the general economy reopens.

In May 2021, after support from both chambers of Congress, President Biden signed the COVID-19 Hate Crimes Act, legislation addressing hate crimes, with emphasis on violence against Asian Americans. Following overwhelming support from both chambers of Congress, reporting of hate crimes will be made more accessible at the local and state levels through increased public outreach in multiple languages. Also, the Department of Justice is directed to designate a point person to expedite the review of hate crimes related to COVID-19 and grants will be available for state and local governments to conduct crime-reduction programs to prevent and respond to hate crimes. Many Asian Americans, including Vice President Kamala Harris, are optimistic that these measures will reduce hate crime violence. But at the same time, activists and scholars knowledgeable about Asian American history are aware that such hate and violence against members of their communities is not new at grassroots levels. The difference now, at least under the Biden administration, is that the government does not support anti-Asian policies as it did during Japanese internment during World War II and immigration strictures before 1965.

Anti-Semitic attacks were on the rise in the United States before COVID-19, as part of growing extremist white supremacy, some of whose followers were politically aligned with President Trump. A white supremacist neo-Nazi rally in Charlottesville, Virginia, in August 2017 resulted in the death of a peaceful counter-protester (see chapter 16). That perpetrator was arrested, tried, and convicted of murder. However, in the absence of further legal action against the organizers and leaders of that rally, a group of fourteen peaceful demonstrators who were physically injured and traumatized have begun a civil lawsuit against twelve leaders and organizers. The defendants are claiming that they were exercising their right to free speech and that any violence they were involved in was self-defense against violent protestors.

On October 17, 2018, a man shouting anti-Semitic slurs and armed with an AR-15-type assault rifle and handguns had opened fire inside the Pittsburgh Tree of Life synagogue. Services were in process. Eleven worshippers were killed and four police officers and two others wounded. Following years of cemetery desecrations and attacks on individuals, this was among the deadliest violent incidents against American Jews in US history.

PANDEMIC EFFECTS ON AFRICAN AMERICANS, HISPANIC AMERICANS, LATINX AMERICANS, AND NATIVE AMERICANS

The disproportionate illness and deaths of African Americans during COVID-19 are the effects of centuries-old inequalities in life that have resulted in the cumulative stress of so-called preexisting comorbidities or diseases that magnify the effects of SARS-CoV-2. However, hypertension, diabetes, asthma, obesity, and heart disease are not simply medical ills but conditions of everyday life and their quality that everyone has come to accept and take for granted as "normal." Goods of life are not now and never have been equally available to African Americans in American society. Disparities in income, family wealth, education, and life expectancy, as well as health and safety from law enforcement predators, are not abstract quantities but constant qualities of existence. These differences are the result of ongoing racism and discrimination, so overall, they are part of the social construction of race.

According to the *Journal of the American Medical Association* on June 29, 2020, although black people account for 13 percent of the population, they have had 24 percent of COVID-19 deaths. The disparity is more intense in some places. A description of the pandemic in Chicago captured this disparity:

> In Chicago, more than 50% of COVID-19 cases and nearly 70% of COVID-19 deaths involve black individuals, although blacks make up only 30% of the population. Moreover, these deaths are concentrated mostly in just 5 neighborhoods on the city's South Side. In Louisiana, 70.5% of deaths have occurred among black persons, who represent 32.2% of the state's population. In Michigan, 33% of COVID-19 cases and 40% of deaths have occurred among black individuals, who represent 14% of the population. If New York City has become the epicenter, this disproportionate burden is validated again in underrepresented minorities, especially blacks and now Hispanics, who have accounted for 28% and 34% of deaths, respectively (population representation: 22% and 29%, respectively).

Both Latinx Americans and Native Americans have been disproportionately affected by the COVID-19 pandemic, although for different reasons. Latinx Americans have been affected largely because of their specific occupations in the US economic system. Native Americans, by contrast, have been affected as a result of their nonparticipation in the US economic system and their residence in relatively isolated rural areas. Both sets of circumstances show how impossible it has been for vulnerable groups to avoid the direct ravages of the pandemic, as well as reactions to it.

In recent years, Latinx Americans have increased their educational participation in K–12 and college, and with that income has risen. The Latinx high school dropout rate has decreased from 32 percent in 2000 to 12 percent in 2014. College enrollment has also increased but mostly for two-year degrees. The Hispanic/Latinx percentage of the US workforce increased from 8.5 percent in 1990 to 18 in 2020. The Bureau of Labor Statistics projects that Hispanic/Latinx workers will be about 20 percent of the total workforce by 2030. Farming, fishing, and forestry have the highest percentage of Latinx workers at 43 percent, followed by building and grounds cleaning and maintenance at about 40 percent. Food preparation and service and transportation and moving are 27 and 24 percent Latinx. Latinx are over 10 percent of management employment, double the 2000 rate.

However, despite the upward trends within a population that is relatively younger than the US population overall, Hispanic/Latinx people have not done proportionately well during the COVID-19 pandemic. Reasons include extensive work in service jobs as frontline workers, multigenerational households with vulnerable elders, and preexisting poverty. By April 2020, the Pew Research Center reported that half of Latinx had experienced a pay cut or lost a job, in contrast to a third of all American adults. (Pay cuts and layoffs were not significantly different among foreign and US born.) Eight million Latinx were employed in restaurants, hotels, other jobs in the service sector, and food-related processing, work which either shut down or continued under dangerous conditions. Many, especially recent immigrants employed in slaughterhouses, faced the choice of quitting their jobs and losing family income or risking COVID-19, in workplace conditions that were already dangerous before the pandemic.

Native Americans have high rates of comorbidities for COVID-19, which cause extreme reactions. At first, some tribes did well because they were aware of their vulnerabilities and followed CDC advisory guidelines. They knew that the effects of COVID-19 would be devastating within reservations, where medical resources were low and preexisting comorbidities high. Prevention of such disproportionate effects of the disease was resolutely undertaken by tribal lockdowns, although at the cost of being able to self-fund vital services. Forty percent of the 574 US tribes have relied on taxes from casinos to finance law enforcement, health care, and education, revenue that dried up when casinos were closed as part of lockdowns. Some tribes chose prevention so that extensive treatment capabilities for an outbreak would not be necessary.

In May 2020, the Oglala Lakota people of the Pine Ridge Reservation in South Dakota put up six checkpoints blocking tourists from entering their reservation. The governor gave them forty-eight hours to remove these barriers before sending in the National Guard. The tribe held firm, and the governor did not follow through. In Eagle Butte, on the Cheyenne River Reservation, similar checkpoints were installed. Several state legislators supported the tribal action. These actions were preventative given high rates of susceptibility due to preexisting diabetes, obesity, lung disease, and heart disease, and low medical care capacity. In May 2020, COVID-19 was not rampant in South Dakota, but with over eight thousand cases and 123 deaths two months later, the preventative actions paid off.

However, as the COVID-19 pandemic progressed, medical services for many tribes in rural areas were overwhelmed and facilities in nearby urban centers could not admit new patients. Although it came after the fact, federal relief promised improvements in structural vulnerabilities, as well as the immediate impact of the disease. The Indian Health Service (IHS), the federal health program for American Indians and Alaska Natives, has coordinated an ongoing COVID-19 response with local and state public health officials as American Indians and Alaska Natives had infection rates over 3.5 times higher than non-Hispanic whites with four times the rate of hospitalization and higher deaths for young people compared to non-Hispanic whites. IHS received $9 billion from the federal government to address preexisting health disparities, and speed in the implementation of these resources is considered a priority.

QUESTIONS FOR THINKING, DISCUSSION, AND WRITING

1. Explain how violence against Asians has been related to false information about the origin of the COVID-19 pandemic. Do you think this is a simple case of misinformation? Explain.

2. Why do you think the COVID-19 pandemic has made US anti-Semitic attacks more violent and intense?
3. What socially constructed factors have made African Americans more vulnerable to COVID-19?
4. Explain how the nature of their employment has been a liability for Latinx Americans during COVID-19.
5. Explain how and why Native Americans have suffered disproportionately during the COVID-19 pandemic.

SOURCES

Abourezk, Kevin. "Tribal Citizens Defend Coronavirus Checkpoints amid Threat from State." *Lakota Times*, May 13, 2020, https://www.lakotatimes.com/articles/tribal-citizens-defend -coronavirus-checkpoints-amid-threat-from-state/.

Cheung, Helier, Zhaoyin Feng, and Boer Deng. "Coronavirus: What Attacks on Asians Reveal about American Identity." BBC News, May 27, 2020, https://www.bbc.com/news/world -us-canada-52714804.

De La Cruz-Viesca, Melany. "Report Shows Major Effects of COVID-19 on Asian American Labor Force." Phys.org, July 23, 2020, https://phys.org/news/2020-07-major-effects-covid -asian-american.html.

Dubina, Kevin. "Hispanics in the Labor Force: 5 Facts." US Department of Labor Blog, September 15, 2021, https://blog.dol.gov/2021/09/15/hispanics-in-the-labor-force-5-facts.

Greenblatt, Jonathan A. "Covid Quarantine Didn't Stop Antisemitic Attacks from Rising to Near-Historic Highs." THINK, NBC News, https://www.nbcnews.com/think/opinion/ covid-quarantine-didn-t-stop-antisemitic-attacks-rising-near-historic-ncna1265425.

Indian Health Service (IHS). "Coronavirus (COVID-19)." https://www.ihs.gov/coronavirus/.

Johns Hopkins University of Medicine. Corona Virus Resource Center. Retrieved October 23, 2021, excellent ongoing information on the COVID-19 pandemic, https://coronavirus .jhu.edu/map.html.

Kellman, Laurie. "Report: Pandemic Amped Up Anti-Semitism, Forced It Online." APA News, April 7, 2021, https://apnews.com/article/race-and-ethnicity-conspiracy-theories -israel-coronavirus-pandemic-financial-markets-32bc8c63d8759ded9c1f2cb8ca7301e0.

Krogstad, Jens Manuel. "5 Facts about Latinos and Education." Pew Research Center, July 28, 2016, https://www.pewresearch.org/fact-tank/2016/07/28/5-facts-about-latinos-and -education/.

Krogstad, Jens Manuel, Ana Gonzalez-Barrera, and Luis Noe-Bustamante. "U.S. Latinos among Hardest Hit by Pay Cuts, Job Losses due to Coronavirus." Pew Research Center, April 3, 2020, https://www.pewresearch.org/fact-tank/2020/04/03/u-s-latinos-among -hardest-hit-by-pay-cuts-job-losses-due-to-coronavirus/.

MacFarquhar, Neil. "The Charlottesville Rally Civil Trial, Explained." *New York Times*, October 25, 2021, https://www.nytimes.com/live/2021/charlottesville-rally-trial-explained.

Mineo, Liz. "For Native Americans, COVID-19 Is 'the Worst of Both Worlds at the Same Time.'" *Harvard Gazette*, May 8, 2020, https://news.harvard.edu/gazette/story/2020/05/ the-impact-of-covid-19-on-native-american-communities/.

Puente, Michael. "Meatpacking Workers' Dilemma: Quit Job or Face COVID-19 Risks." NPR, WNYC, May 14, 2020, https://www.npr.org/local/309/2020/05/14/856162183/meatpacking-workers-dilemma-quit-job-or-face-c-o-v-i-d-19-risks.

Quarantelli, E. L., P. Lagadec, and A. Boin. "A Heuristic Approach to Future Disasters and Crises: New, Old, and In-Between Types." In *Handbook of Disaster Research, Handbooks of Sociology and Social Research*, E. L. Quarantelli, ed. New York: Springer, 2007.

Robertson, Campbell, Christopher Mele, and Sabrina Tavernise. "11 Killed in Synagogue Massacre; Suspect Charged with 29 Counts." *New York Times*, October 27, 2018, https://www.nytimes.com/2018/10/27/us/active-shooter-pittsburgh-synagogue-shooting.html.

Sardarizadeh, Shayan, and Olga Robinson. "Coronavirus: US and China Trade Conspiracy Theories." BBC Monitoring, April 26, 2020, https://www.bbc.com/news/world-52224331.

Smith, Timothy M. "Why COVID-19 Is Decimating Some Native American Communities." American Medical Association (AMA), May 13, 2020, https://www.ama-assn.org/delivering-care/population-care/why-covid-19-decimating-some-native-american-communities.

Sprunt, Barbara. "Here's What the New Hate Crimes Law Aims to Do as Attacks on Asian Americans Rise." NPR NY, May 21, 2021, https://www.npr.org/2021/05/20/998599775/biden-to-sign-the-covid-19-hate-crimes-bill-as-anti-asian-american-attacks-rise.

University Neighborhood Housing Program. "Bronx Reality before Covid Is Manifesting Devastating and Deadly Consequences." June 2, 2020, https://unhp.org/blog/bronx-reality-before-covid-is-manifesting-devastating-and-deadly-consequenc.

Yancy, Clyde W., MD. "COVID-19 and African Americans." JAMA Network, March 19, 2020, https://jamanetwork.com/journals/jama/fullarticle/2764789.

Zack, Naomi. *The American Tragedy of COVID-19: Social and Political Crises of 2020*. Lanham, MD: Rowman & Littlefield, 2021.

Zhou, Li, Anne Anlin Cheng, and Manju Kulkarni. "The Rise in Anti-Asian Attacks during the COVID-19 Pandemic." NPR, WNYC, March 10, 2021, https://www.npr.org/2021/03/10/975722882/the-rise-of-anti-asian-attacks-during-the-covid-19-pandemic?t=1636996214792.

Videos

Callahan, Chrissy. "Hispanic Food Processing and Farm Workers More Likely to Be Diagnosed with COVID-19." Today, October 21, 2020, https://www.today.com/food/hispanic-food-processing-farm-workers-more-likely-be-diagnosed-covid-t195497.

MSNBC. #BillGates #Covid #MSNBC. "Bill Gates Warns the "Next Pandemic" Is Coming after Covid-19—And How to Stop It." January 28, 2021, YouTube, https://www.youtube.com/watch?v=tDjQ8ivwbCU.

Yensi, Amy. "Bronx Zip Codes Hardest Hit by Coronavirus." *Spectrum News* 1 NY, May 17, 2020, https://www.ny1.com/nyc/bronx/news/2020/05/20/here-are-some-of-the-bronx-zip-codes-hardest-hit-by-coronavirus.

24

Global Issues and Humanitarianism

Palace of Nations, seat of the United Nations in Geneva, Switzerland. Getty Images: Aliaksandr Antanovich.

The United Nations has projected that by 2021, eight out of ten people in the world will live in Asia or Africa (see figure 24.1). This figure in itself establishes that the majority of the world's population is nonwhite, although world populations are not usually described by race, but by nationality and region. And because world populations are described by nationality and regions, the intersection of ethics and race that has seemed so relevant from a US perspective does not have much traction globally. Still, colonialism and the modern idea of race did divide the world into whites and nonwhites in persistent ways that now divide the world into rich and poor, or

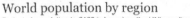

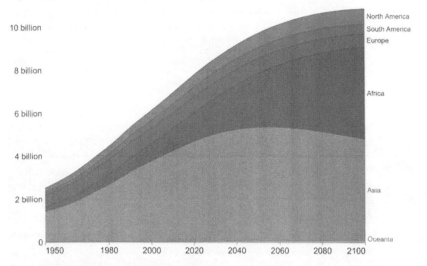

Figure 24.1 World Population by Region. Source: Our World in Data, https://ourworld indata.org/region-population-2100.

developed and developing, or "underdeveloped." The world language of inequality that corresponds to the discussion of racial inequality that has occupied this book respects sovereign national boundaries and the fact that racial difference is not deeply understood in most countries of the world that are racially homogenous—although they may suffer from ethnic divisions to the point of civil war.

What might be called "racial equality" or "social justice" in the United States is taken up worldwide in a more universal language of human equality or humanism. This could be interpreted as a euphemism, for surely the old colonial ideas about race that set off the modern period persist, but it is something more than that, and fundamentally more elevating and aspirational. The main principle of humanism or humanitarianism is that all human beings share a common humanity, regardless of race, as well as regardless of nationality. Shared humanity is understood to be more than a shared biological *homo sapiens* species identity because it includes the value of life and subjectivity to each human, as well as something like a spiritual dimension that need not rely on specific religious affiliation or church membership. Discussion of human justice not only sets forth ideas of racial justice but goes beyond those ideas to unite members of different races who might be politically or culturally opposed. For example, when Derek Chauvin was convicted of murder, jurors of his trial revealed that they did not discuss race or racism in coming to their verdict. Instead, they considered the moral wrong of Chauvin's knee on

Floyd's neck and the omission of care that police officers were obligated to provide (see video). These two considerations about what humans are not permitted to do to other humans, and that they are morally responsible for what they fail to do when they are obligated to act, are the two major principles behind global humanism or humanitarianism.

There is no world government, although there are many international agreements and non-government organizations (NGOs) as well as international charities and aid organizations. However, the United Nations has functioned as a source of world moral guidance. Its military and judicial enforcement capabilities are meager and it depends on funding from its members, the most powerful of which have veto powers over humanitarian resolutions. Nevertheless, the language and goals of the UN are **humanitarian** or for the good of humanity, encompassing both the good of the greatest number in utilitarian terms and concern for small group and individual rights in a deontological sense. Humanitarian views are more fundamental than cosmopolitan ideas. Cosmopolitanism urges people to choose to empathize with and reach out to others beyond their cultures (see chapter 18). But humanitarianism posits a universal similarity that does not require such choice and is more fundamental than it, requiring only recognition.

For this chapter, we should keep in mind how humanitarianism applies to racial and ethnic minorities, such as those identified in the United States, and how it applies to all human beings on the planet, as a moral doctrine. The first section is about Amartya Sen's capabilities approach, followed by the United Nations Human Security Paradigm. The last section addresses climate change to raise questions about human loss and suffering in the underdeveloped world that rich and developed countries could alleviate and what their moral responsibility is.

THE CAPABILITIES APPROACH

Nobel Prize–winning Indian economist Amartya Sen (1933–) introduced the capabilities approach for addressing world poverty in the late 1980s. Sen's **capabilities approach** proposed that aid and support to poor populations should be based on what they were able to take advantage of, given their existing capabilities, instead of aiming for ideal conditions for those populations.

In his 1981 *Poverty and Famines: An Essay on Entitlement and Deprivation*, Sen had shown how famine is often not the result of food shortages but of inequalities in how food is distributed within poor populations. For instance, during the Bengal famine of 1943, which Sen had experienced as a child, rural workers could not afford to buy food because their incomes had not kept up with rising food prices. Sen argued that the death of three million from starvation had been unnecessary based on available food at the time. Sen applied the same reasoning to the Ethiopian famines of 1973 and 1974, the Bangladesh famine of 1974, and the famines in the African Sahel during the 1970s.

According to Sen, a person's capability is their real ability to do something, rather than their freedom from interference with their action. Thus, Sen did not focus on negative rights or freedoms from imposed limits—those who died during the Bengal famine were not prevented from buying food. The question was what they were actually free to do, and they were not free to buy food if they could not afford it. Positive freedom would have meant that they were entitled to participate in the rules for food distribution. In theoretical terms, the capabilities approach is based on the claim that attaining human well-being is morally important and should take into account people's capabilities and functionings. **Capabilities** are how people can be, and what they are, if they choose or act on their preferences. **Functionings** are the culmination of capabilities, such as becoming educated or well nourished.

The capabilities approach has been widely applied in fields such as development and health. Although it seems to focus on individuals, this does not preclude taking into account the importance of group belonging as both capabilities and functionings. For example, a study of women in Afghanistan has found that community and same-gender support has been an important supplement to efforts that focus solely on better education and more societal freedom.

The capabilities approach also translates into what, given the rejection of affirmative action policies for US minorities, is now considered **equity** (see chapter 7). Policies promoting equity fill in racial and ethnic gaps in achievement in contexts of equal opportunity by focusing on access or the actual ability to use opportunities. Black and brown, as well as white middle-class, high school students have the same opportunities to apply for college admission. But if parents cannot afford preparation courses for standardized tests or if under-resourced schools have not prepared students academically, there is unequal capability. Equity may have the same goal as affirmative action, but its methods, like those of augmenting capabilities, are more "granular" and less likely to appear to be racial or ethnic preferences that the white majority considers unfair. For example, since 2015, the New York City Department of Education has instituted a program called "Excellence and Equity for ALL," which includes: K–3 and Pre-K in ALL initiatives, literacy programs in elementary, middle, and high school, and Computer Science for ALL, Algebra for ALL, AP for ALL, and College Access for ALL. The functioning at stake here is college admission and before that the capability is the qualification for college admission.

THE HUMAN SECURITY PARADIGM

The civilian residents of underdeveloped nations are often subject to internal conflict, without protection from their own governments or external peace-making intervention. Their poverty itself makes it unlikely that they would benefit from military security alone, or that their problems could be solved by the imposition of democratic political structures. Their greatest needs are for human security, a focus on the needs of actual human beings, which locates security with people instead of territories and substitutes development for military armament. According to the United Nations *1994 Human Development Report*, which was influenced by Amartya Sen, the idea of human security, posits physical safety, as well as freedom from want or extreme poverty, as more useful for progress than either national or military security. Needed are many of the goods declared as rights in 1948 in the United Nations Universal Declaration of Human Rights (UDHR), which included both rights against limits on individual freedom and rights to the necessities of life. The development report specifically posited the following: "Investing in human development, not in arms; Engaging policymakers to address the emerging peace dividend; Giving the United Nations a clear mandate to promote and sustain development; Enlarging the concept of development cooperation so that it includes all flows, not just aid; Agreeing that 20 percent of national budgets and 20 percent of foreign aid be used for human development; and Establishing an Economic Security Council."

The democratic rights of indigenous peoples throughout the world have been neglected, in terms of both the UDHR and their legally stated treaty rights in relation to those governments in which they are **dependent sovereignties** or independent countries subject to the authority of larger independent countries within which they may be contained. However, the broad scope of human security may have enabled a renewed focus on indigenous rights. The United Nations issued its Declaration on the Rights of Indigenous Peoples (UNDRIP) that was adopted by the General Assembly on September 13, 2007, with 144 votes in favor of its adoption by the General Assembly, 11 abstentions, and 4 against. Those who voted against the UNDRIP were Australia, Canada, New Zealand, and the United States, which all had long, oppressive histories, without substantial reparation, concerning their indigenous populations. Work on the UNDRIP had begun in 1982 but was delayed due to concerns from some nations with existing indigenous claims to resources and self-determination. The UN recognized global discrimination against indigenous peoples and asserted their human and political rights. It also specified that their treaty rights within nations were international issues. That specification amounts to an assertion that humanitarian rights override the absence of specific rights within nations and it suggests that human security could be used as a test for whether humanitarian rights are respected.

The idea of human security as guidance for development brings real human needs into focus in ways that match Amartya Sen's capabilities approach, because the focus in both cases is on the world as we find it, not as it ideally should be. In recent years, goals of sustainable development have been added to the human security paradigm (see video). A striking example has been building and distributing cooking stoves that do not impair respiration and eyesight or contribute to global warming (see video).

CLIMATE CHANGE AND HUMANITY

There is now near-universal scientific consensus about the destructive potential of **climate change** and how it works is not difficult to understand. Planet Earth gets light and heat from the sun and also radiates heat (infrared radiation). Some gases in the earth's atmosphere, such as oxygen, are transparent, so light and heat can pass through them. Other gases—greenhouse gases (GHG)—retain heat that is radiated from the Earth, and they reflect that heat back to Earth. GHG include carbon dioxide (CO_2), methane (CH_4), nitrous oxide (N_2O), and fluorinated gases. Increasing amounts of these gases are the cause of what is called "global warming," a rise in average Earth temperatures that is higher than preindustrial levels. About 80 percent of global warming is believed to be caused by CO_2 from fossil fuel use, and about 17 percent is from animal agriculture fertilizers (N_2O) and gases (CH_4). Both fossil fuel use and animal agriculture are distinctively human activities. Similar to the effects of the SARS-CoV-2 virus (see chapter 23), climate change is not a matter of numbers but of how those numbers represent changes that affect human life and well-being.

As with the COVID-19 pandemic, those who are already relatively worse off will suffer more from climate change than those better off, because they have fewer resources. Globally, poor and underdeveloped countries will be hit hardest as sea levels rise and land areas dry out from rising temperatures. Europe and the United States will experience more flooding and forest fires will continue to ravage the US West. Drought will cause farmland to turn into desert as heat waves increase in the Middle East, and Australia will also experience extreme drought. Some island nations in the Pacific will become submerged. Food shortages will affect much of Africa. The overall effect is that nations that have done the least to accelerate climate change will suffer the most and many of their inhabitants will become climate refugees.

The situation of climate change requires international government action, which wealthy nations have been reluctant to take because of disruptions to their economies. There is little individuals can do except pressure their elected officials in democracies. On the one hand, policies are needed to mitigate internal effects of climate change in rich countries, but on the other hand, there is a growing sense of the need for international cooperation and special attention to what will happen to the inhabitants of underdeveloped countries. Historically, many underdeveloped areas of the world are former Euro-American colonies and their poverty is the result of resource extraction, environmental depredation, and societal disruption by more technologically advanced and aggressive invasions from the North and West.

Preparing for climate change includes both planning to reduce fossil fuel consumption and planning how to address the extreme weather effects of climate change, including the plight of those who suffer directly from it. The **precautionary principle** (PP) holds that we should prepare for known risks and also prepare if we do not know the effects of not preparing. Not knowing the effects of not preparing is in many cases the present situation, when hurricanes and floods occur as surprising events, even though it was known beforehand that weather would get worse, as a result of missed opportunities to reduce fossil fuel consumption. The PP has been adopted as an international moral principle, subject to a large range of policy and legal interpretations. The World Commission on the Ethics of Scientific Knowledge and Technology (COMEST) offers this definition:

Over the past decades, the PP has become an underlying rationale for a large and increasing number of international treaties and declarations in the fields of sustainable development, environmental protection, health, trade and food safety. In its most basic form, the PP is a strategy to cope with scientific uncertainties in the assessment and management of risks. It is about the wisdom of action under uncertainty: "Look before you leap," "better safe than sorry," and many other folkloristic idioms capture some aspect of this wisdom. Precaution means taking action to protect human health and the environment against possible danger of severe damage.

Finally, if we are thinking morally or ethically about humanity, including the problems of race and ethnicity as part of that, the suffering and likely death of individuals from the underdeveloped world and underdeveloped parts of the developed world raise compelling questions. For example, Human Rights Watch, an international humanitarian organization, has tracked how black and brown prisoners were treated during Hurricane Katrina, observing that many were left to drown in 2005, and in 2020 the same populations remained vulnerable to unjust incarceration, as well as future storms. Broad issues concern future risks, from new pandemics as well as the effects of climate change. We know in advance that those already worse off will fare worse. So the first question is what do we, collectively and as individuals, who are already better off, owe those worse off? Should the United States open its borders to climate refugees? Should a greater part of the wealth in developed nations be dedicated to alleviating dispossession, illness, and famine in other parts of the world? As moral questions, without the force of world government to compel answers or place avoidance of answering in stark relief, such questions can in fact be ignored. But does shared humanity compel attention to them? Does humanitarianism require new sacrifice and inconvenience? And what does it say about those who are already advantaged if they are unwilling to meet such requirements?

QUESTIONS FOR THINKING, DISCUSSION, AND WRITING

1. Explain what the language of humanitarianism leaves out in terms of ethics and race and what it contributes.
2. How does the idea of human security bring humanitarianism to actual individual levels?
3. Why is the capabilities approach important for foreign aid?
4. Discuss the historical and contemporary background of those populations likely to suffer most from climate change.
5. Which of the questions raised in the last paragraph of this book do you find most compelling? How do you answer it?

SOURCES

BBC News, Science. "What Is Climate Change? A Really Simple Guide." October 13, 2021, https://www.bbc.com/news/science-environment-24021772.

Climatenexus. "Animal Agriculture's Impact on Climate Change." https://climatenexus.org/
    climate-issues/food/animal-agricultures-impact-on-climate-change/.
Gollier, C., and N. Treich. "The Precautionary Principle." In *Encyclopedia of Energy, Natural
    Resource, and Environmental Economics*, 2013, Science Direct, https://www.sciencedirect
    .com/topics/earth-and-planetary-sciences/precautionary-principle.
Hansen, James. "Climate Change in a Nutshell: The Gathering Storm." Columbia.com,
    December 18, 2018, http://www.columbia.edu/~jeh1/mailings/2018/20181206_Nutshell
    .pdf.
Jacobsen, Jeremiah. "'It Was Based on the Evidence': Chauvin Jurors Sit Down for CNN
    Interview." KARE 11, October 28, 2021, https://www.kare11.com/article/news/local/
    george-floyd/chauvin-jurors-sit-down-for-cnn-interview/89-54fc2920-d337-49e8-8053
    -9a65437bc768.
NYC Department of Education. "Equity and Excellence for All." https://www.schools.nyc
    .gov/about-us/vision-and-mission/equity-and-excellence.
Root, Brian. "Hurricane Katrina in the US: 15 Years Later, Poverty, Racial Inequality
    Still Afflict Louisiana." Human Rights Watch, August 29, 2020, https://www.hrw.org/
    news/2020/08/29/hurricane-katrina-us-15-years-later#.
Sen, Amartya. "Capability and Well-Being." In *The Quality of Life*, Martha Nussbaum and
    Sen Amartya, eds. Oxford: Clarendon Press, pp. 30–53.
Sen, Amartya. *Poverty and Famines: An Essay on Entitlement and Deprivation*. Oxford, UK:
    Oxford University Press, 1981.
Trani, Jean-Francois, Parul Bakhshi, and Cécile Rolland, "Capabilities, Perception of Well-
    Being and Development Effort: Some Evidence from Afghanistan." *Oxford Development
    Studies* 39, no. 4 (2011): 403–26, https://openscholarship.wustl.edu/cgi/viewcontent
    .cgi?article=1034&context=brown_facpubs.
United Nations Development Project (UNDP), "Human Development Report 1994:
    New Dimensions of Human Security." http://www.hdr.undp.org/en/content/human
    -development-report-1994.
US Environmental Protection Agency (EPA). "Overview of Greenhouse Gases." Greenhouse
    Gas Emissions, https://www.epa.gov/ghgemissions/overview-greenhouse-gases.
World Commission on the Ethics of Scientific Knowledge and Technology (COMEST). "The
    Precautionary Principle." 2005, https://unesdoc.unesco.org/ark:/48223/pf0000139578.

Videos

Lasky, Natasha. "Kiribati: Battling for Survival (Rising Sea Levels)." In "Rising Sea Level
    Threatens Very Existence of Island Nations." Worldwarzero.com, August 14, 2021,
    https://worldwarzero.com/magazine/2021/08/rising-sea-level-threatens-existence-of-island
    -nations/.
PBS, NewsHour. "Designing Cleaner Stoves for the Developing World." February 26, 2014,
    YouTube, https://www.youtube.com/watch?v=Z0XrARfLfuk.
Sen, Amartya. "Creating Capabilities: Sources and Consequences for Law and Social Policy."
    University of Chicago Law School, July 12, 2013, YouTube, https://www.youtube.com/
    watch?v=PDgmVbWtkIc.
Tavanti, Marco. "The Basics of Sustainable Human Security." World Engagement Institute
    (WEI), 2013, http://www.weinstitute.org/human-security.html.

Glossary

accommodationist nineteenth-century black leadership position of accepting white dominance.

affirmative action policy to increase employment and admission of people of color and women; sometimes included **quotas** or preset number of women and minorities.

altruism goal or action to improve the well-being of others.

amour de soi according to Jean-Jacques Rousseau, direct self-love.

amour propre according to Jean-Jacques Rousseau, self-love based on the views of others.

apartheid in South Africa, from 1948 to 1991, segregation of the majority African population, without civil rights, with surveillance and control.

argument set of sentences that follow a **pattern of logical reasoning: sound argument** if premises are true and no logical mistake is made in getting to the conclusion; **valid argument** if no logical mistake is made in getting to the conclusion; **epistemic argument–** about what is true or what a person should believe; **moral argument** conclusion is normative/moral; **practical argument** conclusion is an action/doing something.

autonomy self-rule in life and lifestyle choices.

aversion tendancy to avoid or reject others.

binary an either/or but not both system, such as male or female, or racially black or racially white.

capabilities how people can be, and what they are, if they choose or act on their preferences.

capabilities approach proposal that aid and support to poor populations should be based on what they are able to take advantage of, given their existing capabilities, instead of aiming for ideal conditions for those populations.

capital punishment the death penalty.

categorical imperative absolute moral command that one can will everyone should obey.

certification official record of a course of study, a degree.

character disposition or tendency to act virtuously, or not.

civil disobedience refusal to obey law for a cause believed to be just.

civil rights rights of citizens in societies under government to participate in government and public life, including the political rights of citizens to participate in government, particularly the right to vote.

climate change rise in average planetary temperatures as the result of human fossil fuel use and animal farming.

clines biological physical traits that vary gradually and continuously over distance.

cognitive theory of emotions view that emotions evoked at a given time depend on what people believe.

colorism preference, usually for lighter skin tones.

commons, the cultural, humanmade, and natural resources that are available to all members of a society.

comorbidities preexisting diseases or disabilities that increase vulnerability to new health threats.

compensation direct help or funds to help offset loss or harm.

consequentialism moral view that actions and rules should be judged according to the goodness or badness of their consequences.

cosmopolitanism an ideal that locates individuals into a diverse totality of humanity.

critical race theory (CRT) view that racism today is the result of racism required by law in the past.

critical reasoning skills mental abilities to think logically in favor of and against assertions and beliefs.

deductive reasoning true premises lead to conclusions that are logically certain.

dehumanization treatment of a human being as less than human.

demonization characterization of people as dangerous and threatening, regardless of whether or not they are.

dependent sovereignties independent countries subject to the authority of larger independent countries.

dignity absolute worth of human beings that makes them valuable and irreplaceable to themselves and others.

disaster intersection of destructive natural event with human culture at a certain time and place.

disaster preparation prior action or supplies to better react to a disaster; action about danger that follows from the virtue of prudence.

disaster response how people react to disaster during and after it occurs.

discrimination unjust treatment based on race or ethnicity.

diversity inclusion of minorities in contexts dominated by whites.

duty ethics or **deontology** moral system, developed by Immanuel Kant, based on universal obligation that is categorical or absolute and not instrumental.

economic dignity being able to afford the necessities of life in a given society.

emotional aversion non-cognitive feelings to avoid or simple dislike.

emotional labor work that requires caring, personal interaction.

emotivism view that moral judgments express emotions.

entitlements government-supported policies that help those whose material circumstances, as measured in prices such as their income and wealth, injure their dignity without such help.

environmental racism conditions in minority neighborhoods that have less access to coastlines, fresh air, and areas free of industrial pollution.

epistemic arguments arguments about how knowledge is acquired and what constitutes knowledge.

epistemology theory of knowledge, standards for true belief or knowledge.

Equal Protection Clause of the Fourteenth Amendment, specifying that race could not be used as a factor for unequal protection under the law.

equity filling in racial and ethnic gaps in achievement in contexts of equal opportunity by focusing on **access** or the actual ability to use opportunities.

essential frontline workers those necessary to keep infrastructure functioning, includes **frontline workers** whose jobs concern interacting with the public.

essentialism the belief that there is one all-important trait that all members of a race share.

ethical matter human well-being or life is at stake.

ethics general human thought process and standard for action for which philosophers have identified at least three specific systems: **virtue ethics**, **deontology**, and **utilitarianism** or consequentialism.

ethnic pertaining to minority culture, in ways not explicitly racial, which may be racial.

eugenicist pertaining to selective breeding and eugenics.

eugenics movement early twentieth-century policy to control breeding and immigration toward preserving a white racial majority.

everyday racism patterns of racism that people take for granted.

exclusionary rule requirement that criminal evidence be obtained lawfully, before police make an arrest.

factorials mathematical result when a number is multiplied by each of its lower numbers leading up to it.

feminized constructed as female, as a form of oppression.

food deserts residential areas without access to fresh food or supermarkets within one mile.

forms according to Plato, perfect ideal things that could only be glimpsed after arduous study.

functionings the culmination of capabilities, such as becoming educated or well nourished.

genealogical pertaining to inheritance from parents, grandparents, great grandparents, and so on.

genocide the aim to wipe out an entire people.

genome complete DNA data for an individual or species.

gentrification process in which white middle-class buyers bid up the cost of homes in minority neighborhoods, driving out their initial occupants who are poor and often nonwhite.

guaranteed income fixed amount of money that either everyone or some preselected income group receives.

halakha Jewish law.

hate crime a traditional offense like murder, arson, or vandalism with an added element of racial, gender, or other bias.

hate speech written or spoken language that expresses hatred for a specific group, usually a group that is already vulnerable in some way.

homeless without one's own dwelling for sleep and privacy.

homicide killing of one person by another.

human right what everyone deserves to have, or not have their freedom restricted.

human security focus on safety and freedom from want of individuals.

humanitarian for the good of humanity, encompassing both the good of the greatest number in utilitarian terms and concern for small group and individual rights in a deontological sense; has virtue of humanitarian recognition.

ideologies systems of belief that present false views of reality to further the interests of some at the expense of others.

incitement dangerous form of speech because it explicitly and deliberately aims at triggering discrimination, hostility, and violence, which may also lead to or include terrorism or atrocity crimes.

income amount of money a person regularly earns or is paid from other sources.

inductive argument premise and conclusion are not certain but probably true.

institutional racism racism in an institution or structural racism in society that does not require individual racist intent.

institutionalized when membership or participation in an institution deeply changes people, so that they carry out the institution's rules and practices within the institution and when they leave it.

intent in law, an intention to do an action so that the action is deliberate.

intersectionality a method of understanding oppression or the complicated reality of multiple forms of oppression affecting the same person or group.

intuitionism view that people make moral judgements based on their intuitions.

Jim Crow term for legalized discrimination that followed the US Civil War.

Latina identities identities of Hispanic/Latino women.

Latinx term for an umbrella idea that includes all Hispanic/Latino diversities, especially LGBTQ+ people and those who do not speak Spanish.

Law what's written down and enforced by government.

law of retribution *lex talionis*, that the punishment should fit the crime.

legacies anything that is inherited; also refers to descendants of college alumni who have easier access to admission.

leisure in the ancient world, pursuits by those who did not have to do manual labor.

literal institution voluntary or compulsory to join, with set rules and behavior, and an actual location or physical center.

logical contradictory two things cannot both be true, or cannot both be false if one is the logical contradictory of the other.

machismo style or behavior attending a preferred masculine norm.

manifest destiny doctrine justifying settler expansion of the United States "from sea to shining sea."

marianismo representation of *La Virgen Maria* (the Virgin Mary, mother of Jesus Christ) as a Catholic religious and practical ideal for Latinx women.

mass incarceration imprisonment of large numbers.

mens rea the "guilty mind" according to criminal law.

microaggressions everyday acts and patterns of behavior that are harmful to people of color in small ways, regardless of the perpetrator's intentions.

mitigation measures to address disaster, such as wearing masks during a viral pandemic.

model minority term used to discuss Asian Americans as successful.

moral argument argument that something is morally right or morally wrong; not the same as legal arguments based on standing law.

morally relative view belief that culture is all powerful and determines what is good and right.

natural disaster an unwanted and destructive natural event, usually occurring over a short period.

natural rights rights human beings are supposed to have, either before the existence of government or morally, independently of government.

naturalized citizenship citizenship granted to immigrants who were not born in the United States.

negative rights freedoms from certain harms as legally specified.

net worth total value an individual, household, or organization has in monetary times, consisting of assets minus debts.

nonbinary neither male nor female in gender, or sometimes both.

one-drop rule mythical idea that one drop of "black blood" determines a person's race to be black.

over-criminalization treatment and attitude toward an individual or group as criminal, which goes beyond evidence.

patriarchy men's dominance over women throughout modern Western society; "rule by fathers."

phenotypes visible physical traits of individuals often associated with racial identities, although not limited to race.

phenotypic variation different inherited traits of individuals such as skin color.

police reform policies to change police practices toward more justice for minorities and less use of force.

policy social rules and practices that may apply law or create egalitarian progress that is not prohibited by law.

political rights part of civil rights pertaining to political participation, such as voting rights.

politicization turning a nonpolitical issue into a matter of party politics.

populations groups in the same geographic area who breed within themselves.

positive rights claims for greater well-being.

poverty a relative lack of income and wealth.

practical argument argument in favor of what people should do, based on what they are able to do.

practical wisdom *phronesis*, knowing how to act and doing it.

precautionary principle (PP) holds that we should prepare for known risks and also prepare if we do not know the effects of not preparing.

prejudice unwarranted judgement based on race.

progressive furthering progress toward legal and social equality of minority groups

protected class minority group protected in law or entitled to special treatment.

prudence a cardinal virtue involving knowledge and action about danger.

public defenders defense attorneys provided by a court.

public memorials representations of events and people who are important for everyone to remember or acknowledge.

quota system relating to affirmative action, a fixed number of minorities to be hired or admitted.

"race" believed to refer to human group differences and there is broad belief that racial differences rest on natural or biological differences.

racial achievement gap difference in scores on standardized tests between white and black test-takers.

racial conservationism advocacy for the retention of ideas of race.

racial eliminativism advocacy for the removal of ideas of biological race throughout society, particularly in education.

racial eliminativists those who argue for the elimination of racial categories in society.

racial essence unconfirmed posit of some unchanging and fundamental thing or quality associated with specific racial identity or identities.

racial integration practice or policy that is inclusive of nonwhites along with whites.

racial profiling practice of suspecting people of color of wrongdoing by police without any evidence.

racialized made into a race or treated as nonwhite in the course of oppression or discrimination.

racially diverse quality of a unit or whole group that contains individuals of different races.

racism attitudes and behavior from whites that disadvantage, harm, or unjustly punish or limit the life opportunities of nonwhites.

reconciliation policy enabling both sides of past injustice to move on.

rectification addressing past unjust harm with acceptance of moral blame and responsibility, including punishment.

redlining discriminatory practice by lenders of making mortgages more difficult and costly for people of color, especially African Americans.

regressive trait of those who want to go back to periods of history they view as more favorable to their racial and ethnic groups.

reparations official recognition of past harm, with apology, and some monetary benefit.

representation depictions of people and things in public media; special subject in humanities regarding presence of minorities in public media.

resilience ability to recover from disasters.

restorative justice efforts to move past harms inflicted, involving both victims and perpetrators; may involve reconciliation as a goal for moving ahead.

reverse discrimination accusation that dominant groups, usually whites, are being discriminated against.

social construction system or idea created in society and not natural apart from that.

sound argument an argument with true premises and a conclusion that logically follows from them.

spectacle public show or display, put on for a cause.

status stable trait or position that guarantees a certain social rank.

stereotype threat the negative performance effect on test-takers of prior reminders that members of the group to which they belong do not perform as well as others on such tests.

stop and frisk police practice of stopping people and searching them over their clothing.

subject of affirmative action person who benefits from affirmative action.

subject of diversity group or unit that benefits from diversity.

syllogisms standard form of logical argument.

taxonomy system of categorization in biology, or typology.

terra nullius doctrine during Age of Discovery that lands inhabited by indigenous peoples had no inhabitants.

tragedy in Aristotle's classic sense, a downfall resulting from errors of judgment.

transitional justice aim to make it possible for a society in which some groups have been treated unjustly by other groups to resolve both anger and guilt in order to move on with greater harmony.

ubuntu "I am because we are"; African idea that community support is necessary for individual personhood.

utilitarianism moral system developed by Jeremy Bentham and John Stuart Mill advocating the greatest good (happiness or pleasure) for the greatest number.

valid quality of an argument in which the conclusion follows logically from its premises (but not **sound** if premises are false.)

virtue epistemology a morally good approach to the workings of the mind.

virtue ethics moral system based on Aristotle's writing that human excellence consists in individual virtues.

wealth total monetary value of what a person owns, made up of cash, savings, investments, and material possessions, especially equity in real estate.

white privilege advantages based on being white that white people can take for granted.

white racial status highest-ranked racial status.

white supremacists those who implicitly believe or act or benefit from system in which white people have advantages due to their race.

Index

care ethics, 6
Castile, Philando, 89
categorical imperative, 5–6
CDC. *See* Centers for Disease Control and Prevention
Celera Genomics, 32
Census, US, 7, 101, 162
Census Bureau, 100
Centers for Disease Control and Prevention (CDC), 104, 118, 120, 222–23
certification, 108
Challenging Multiracial Identity (Spencer), 166
Charlottesville, Virginia rally (2017), 21, 153, 225
Chatters, James, 173
Chauvin, Derek, 89, 232–33
Cheyenne River Reservation, 227
Chicago, Illinois, 226
children, antiracist coping strategies of, 135–36
Chinese Americans, 192
Chinese Exclusion Act (1882), 51
Chinese immigrants, 51–52
Chomsky, Noam, 155
Cicero, Marcus Tullius, 53, 175
civil disobedience, 150
civil rights, 37, 39; legislation, 129; minority, 41–43; movement, 3, 40, 41–43, 59, 151, 180; VRA (Voting Rights Act), and, 42, 43–44, 152
Civil Rights Act (1957), 42
Civil Rights Act (1964), *39*, 42, 61, 62, 143, 201
Civil Rights Act (1968), 43
Civil War, US, 41, 43, 72, 153, 194, 201
Clemens, Samuel Langhorne (Mark Twain), 24
climate change, 209, 235–37
clines, 32, 161
Coates, Ta-Nehisi, 71
cocaine, 88
Code of Justinian, 22
Cohen Veterans Network, 122

Coles, Robert, 9
Colored School Division, 200
colorism, 185
Columbia University, 123, 132
COMEST. *See* World Commission on the Ethics of Scientific Knowledge and Technology
Committee on Equal Employment Opportunity, 61
common good, 15–17, 24, 68
the commons, 4, 14–15; cultural commons, 12
comorbidities, 118, 222, 225
compensation, 67, 68, 69
Confederacy (of US Civil War), 153, 193
Confederate statues, 193–94
Congress, US, 72
consequentialism (and utilitarianism), 5, 6, 13, 81
"The Conservation of Races" (Du Bois), 33
conspiracy theories, 224
Constitution, US, 113; First Amendment, 141; Fourth Amendment, 90, 91–92; Sixth Amendment, 83; Eighth Amendment, 81, 82; Thirteenth Amendment, 43; Fourteenth Amendment, 90; Fifteenth Amendment, 43
controversial content, 112–14
Conway, Andrew, 31
Conyers, John, Jr., 72
Cooper, Anna J., 112
Cooper, Christian, 131
coping strategies, antiracist, 135–36
COPS. *See* Office of Community Oriented Policing Services
Coronavirus Resource Center, 221
Cosmo for Latinas, 191
cosmopolitanism, 53, 171, 174–76
COVID-19, 39, 100–104, 112, 118–19, 186, 209, 211; African, Hispanic/Latinx, and Native Americans and, 225–27; Asian Americans and, 146, 192, 224–25; environmental racism

About the Author

Naomi Zack, PhD, Columbia University, has been Professor of Philosophy at Lehman College, CUNY, since 2019. She earlier taught at SUNY, Albany and the University of Oregon. Her most recent book is *The American Tragedy of COVID-19: Social and Political Crises of 2020* (March 2021). Also recent is *Progressive Anonymity: From Identity Politics to Evidence-Based Government* (December 2020). Additional books include *Reviving the Social Compact: Inclusive Citizenship in an Age of Extreme Politics* (2018). She edited the *Oxford Handbook on Philosophy and Race* (2017) and *Philosophy of Race: An Introduction* (2018). Earlier books include *The Theory of Applicative Justice: An Empirical Pragmatic Approach to Correcting Racial Injustice* (2016), *White Privilege and Black Rights: The Injustice of US Police Racial Profiling and Homicide* (April 2015), *The Ethics and Mores of Race: Equality after the History of Philosophy* (2011/2015), *Ethics for Disaster* (2009, 2010–2011), *Inclusive Feminism: A Third Wave Theory of Women's Commonality* (2005), *Philosophy of Science and Race* (2002), and *Race and Mixed Race* (1992).

Naomi Zack was awarded the Phi Beta Kappa-Romanell Professorship, 2019–2020, with three lectures on intersectionality to be given on the Lehman campus, which were delayed until March 2022 due to COVID-19 lockdowns in New York City. She gave the John Dewey Lecture at the Pacific Division Meeting of the American Philosophical Society in April 2021. Zack has been teaching a new course, "Disaster and Corona," at Lehman College, in addition to courses in modern philosophy, ethics, democracy, and race and ethnicity and ethics and race.